THE INSTITUTES OF JOHN CASSIAN

THE TWELVE BOOKS OF JOHN CASSIAN ON THE
INSTITUTES OF THE COENOBIA, AND THE REMEDIES
FOR THE EIGHT PRINCIPAL FAULTS

ST SHENOUDA MONASTERY

SYDNEY, AUSTRALIA

The Institutes of St John Cassian

From a Select Library of Nicene and Post-Nicene Fathers of the Christian Church New York, 1894.

Chapter 6 translated from Institutions De Cassien Paris, 1872.

Published by:
St. Shenouda Monastery
8419 Putty Rd, Putty
NSW 2330 Australia

February 2021

ISBN: 978-0-6481234-5-3

Special thanks to all the youth who helped to put this together, God reward you all.

Front cover: Fr Theodore St Shenouda

ST SHENOUDA THE ARCHIMANDRITE

Contents

PROLEGOMENA 9

BOOK 1
    OF THE DRESS OF THE MONKS 35

BOOK 2
    OF THE CANONICAL SYSTEM OF THE NOCTURNAL PRAYERS AND PSALMS 45

BOOK 3
    OF THE CANONICAL SYSTEM OF THE DAILY PRAYERS AND PSALMS 65

BOOK 4
    OF THE INSTITUTES OF THE RENUNCIANTS 81

BOOK 5
    OF THE SPIRIT OF GLUTTONY 119

BOOK 6
    ON THE SPIRIT OF FORNICATION 159

BOOK 7
    OF THE SPIRIT OF COVETOUSNESS 175

BOOK 8
    OF THE SPIRIT OF ANGER 201

BOOK 9
    OF THE SPIRIT OF DEJECTION 219

BOOK 10
    OF THE SPIRIT OF ACCIDIE 227

BOOK 11
    OF THE SPIRIT OF VAINGLORY 251

BOOK 12
    THE SPIRIT OF PRIDE 265

PROLEGOMENA (INTRODUCTION)

CHAPTER 1
THE LIFE OF CASSIAN

"Cassianus natione Scytha" is the description given by Gennadius of the writer whose works are now for the first time translated into English. In spite, however, of the precision of this statement, considerable doubt hangs over Cassian's nationality, and it is hard to believe that he was in reality a Scythian. Not only is his language and style free from all trace of barbarism, but as a boy he certainly received a liberal education; for in his Conferences he laments that the exertions of his tutor and his own attention to continual study had so weakened him that his mind was so filled with songs of the poets that even at the hour of prayer it was thinking of those trifling fables and stories of battles with which it had from earliest infancy been stored; "and," he adds, "when singing Psalms or asking forgiveness of sins, some wanton recollection of the poems intrudes itself or the image of heroes fighting presents itself before the eyes; and an imagination of such phantoms is always haunting me." Further evidence of the character of his education is also supplied by the fact that in his work on the Incarnation against Nestorius he manifests an acquaintance not only with the works of earlier Christian Fathers, but also with those of such writers as Cicero and Persius, These considerations are sufficient to make us hesitate before accepting the statement of Gennadius in what would at first sight be its natural meaning; although from the fact of his connection with Marseilles, where so much of Cassian's life was spent, as well as the early date at which he wrote (A.D. 495), it is dangerous to reject his authority altogether. It is, however, possible that the term "Scytha" is not really intended to denote a Scythian, but to refer to the desert of Scete, or Scitis, in Egypt, where Cassian passed many years of his life, and with which his fame was closely associated; and, therefore, without going to the length of rejecting the authority of Gennadius altogether, we are free to look for some other country as the birthplace of our author. But little light is thrown on this subject by the statements of other writers. Photius (A.D. 800) calls him ρωμαϊκός, which need mean no more than born within the Roman Empire; while Honorius of Autun (A. D. 1130) speaks of him as Afer. The last-mentioned writer is, however, of too late a date to be of any authority; and it is just possible that the term "Afer," like the "Scytha" of Gennadius, may be owing to his lengthy residence in Egypt. In the writings of Cassian himself there is nothing to enable us to identify the country of his birth with certainty; but, in describing the situation of his ancestral home, he speaks of the delightful pleasantness of the neighborhood, and the recesses of the woods, which would not only delight the heart of a monk but would also furnish him with a plentiful supply of food; while in a later passage he says that in his own country it was impossible to find anyone who had adopted the monastic life. From these notices, compared with a passage in the Preface to the Institutes, where the diocese of Apta Julia in Gallia Narbonensis is spoken of as still without monasteries, some ground is given for the conjecture that Cassian was really a native of Gaul, whither he returned in mature age after his wanderings were ended, and where most of his friends of whom we have any knowledge were settled. On the whole, then, it appears to the present writer to be the most probable view that Cassian was of Western origin, and, perhaps, a native of Provence, although it must be freely acknowledged that it is impossible to speak with certainty on this subject.

Once more: not only is there this doubt about his nationality, but questions have also been raised concerning his original name. Gennadius and Cassiodorus speak of him simply as Cassianus. In his own writings he represents himself as addressed by the monks in Egypt more than once by the name of John. Prosper of Aquitaine (his contemporary and antagonist) combines both names, and speaks of him as "Joannes cognomento Cassianus." In the titles of the majority of the MSS. of his own writing he is merely "Cassianus," though in one case the work is entitled "Beatissimi Joannis quiet Cassiani." Are we, then, with the writer of the last-mentioned MS., to suppose that the names John and Cassian are alternatives; or, with Prosper, that John was his nomen and Cassianus his cognomen, or, more strictly, agnomen? The former view is, perhaps, the more probable, as he may well have taken the name of John at his baptism or at his admission to the monastic life. The theory which has sometimes been advocated — that he received it at his ordination by S. John Chrysostom — fails to the ground when we notice that he represents himself as called John during his residence in Egypt, several years before his ordination and intercourse with S. Chrysostom.

To pass now from the question of his name and nationality to the narrative of Cassian's life. Various considerations point to the date of his birth as about the year 360. Of his family we know nothing, except that in one passage of his writings he incidentally makes mention of a sister; while the language which he uses of his parents would imply that they were well-to-do and pious. As we have already seen, he received a liberal education as a boy, but while still young forsook the world, and was received, together with his friend Germanus, into a monastery at Bethlehem, where he spent several years and became thoroughly familiar with the customs and traditions of the monasteries of Syria. Eager, however, to make further progress in the perfect life, the two friends finally determined to visit Egypt, where, as it was the country in which the monastic life originated, the most famous monasteries existed, and the most illustrious Anchorites were to be found. Permission to undertake the journey was sought and obtained from their superiors, a pledge being required of a speedy return when the object of their visit was gained. Sailing from some port of Syria, perhaps Joppa, the friends arrived at Thennesus, a town at the mouth of the Tanitic branch of the Nile, near Lake Menzaleh. Here they fell in with a celebrated Anchorite named Archebius, bishop of the neighboring town of Panephysis, who had come to Thennesus on business connected with the election of a bishop. He, on hearing the object of their visit to Egypt, at once offered them an introduction to some celebrated Anchorites in his own neighborhood. The offer was gladly accepted, and under his guidance they made their way through a dreary district of salt marshes, many of the villages being in ruins and deserted by their inhabitants owing to the floods which had inundated the country and turned the rising grounds into islands, "and thus afforded the desired solitudes to the holy Anchorites, among whom three old men — Chaeremon, Nesteros, and Joseph — were famed as the Anchorites of the longest standing." Archebius brought them first to Chaeremon, who had already passed his hundredth year, and was so far bent with age and constant prayer that he could no longer walk upright, but crawled upon his hands and knees. The saint's hesitation at allowing himself to be thus interviewed by strangers was soon overcome, and he finally gratified their curiosity by delivering three discourses, on the subjects of Perfection, Chastity, and the Protection of God. From the cell of Chaeremon Cassian and his companion proceeded to that of Abbot Nesteros, who honored them with two discourses, on Spiritual Knowledge, and Divine Gifts; and from him they repaired to Joseph, who belonged to a noble family, and before his renunciation of the world had been "primarius" of his native city, Thmuis. He was naturally better educated than the others, and was able to converse with them in Greek instead of being obliged to have recourse to the help of an interpreter, as had been the case with Chaeremon and Nesteros.

His first question referred to the relationship between Cassian and Germanus: were they brothers? And their reply — that the brotherhood was spiritual and not carnal — furnished the old man with a text for his first discourse, which was on Friendship, and which was followed up on the next day by one on the Obligation of Promises, called forth by the perplexity in which the travelers found themselves owing to their promise to return to Bethlehem, a promise which they were both to break, and which yet they could not fulfill without losing a grand opportunity of making progress in the spiritual life. In their difficulty they consulted Joseph; and, fortified by his authority and advice, they determined to break the letter of their promise and make a longer stay in Egypt, where they accordingly remained for seven years in spite of their brethren at Bethlehem, whose displeasure at their conduct, Cassian tells us, was not removed by their frequent letters home.

It was while Cassian and his fellow-traveler were still in the neighborhood of Panephysis that these energetic precursors of the modern "interviewers" paid a visit to Abbot Pinufius, a priest who presided over a large monastery. This man was an old friend of theirs, whose acquaintance they had previously made at Bethlehem, whither (after an ineffectual attempt to conceal himself in a monastery in the island of Tabenna) he had fled in order to escape the responsibilities of his office. There he had been received as a novice, and had been assigned by the abbot as an inmate of Cassian's cell, until he was recognized by a visitor from Egypt and brought back in triumph to his own monastery. To him, therefore, Cassian and Germanus made their way; and by him they were warmly welcomed; the old man repaying their former hospitality by giving them quarters in his own cell. While staying in this monastery they were so fortunate as to be present at the admission of a novice, and heard the charge which Pinufius made to the new-comer on the occasion; and afterwards the abbot favored them with a discourse "on the end of penitence and the marks of satisfaction." After this, resisting his pressing invitation to remain with him in the monastery, they proceeded once more on their travels, and, crossing the river, came to Diolcos, a town hard by the Sebennytic mouth of the Nile. Here was a barren tract of land between the river and the sea, rendered unfit for cultivation by the saltness of the soil and the dryness of the sand. It was, therefore, eagerly seized upon by the monks, who congregated here in great numbers in spite of the absence of water; the river from which it had to be fetched being some three miles distant. In this neighborhood they made the acquaintance of Abbot Piamun, a most celebrated Anchorite, who explained to them with great care the characteristics of the three kinds of monks; viz., the Coenobites, the Anchorites, and the Sarabaites. This discourse had the effect of exciting their desire more keenly than ever for the Anchorites' life in preference to that of the Coenobite, — a desire which was afterwards confirmed by what they saw and heard in the desert of Scete. They next visited a large monastery in the same neighborhood, which was governed by the Abbot Paul, and which ordinarily accommodated two hundred monks, but was at that moment filled with a much larger number, who had come from the surrounding monasteries to celebrate the "depositio" of the late abbot. Here they met a certain Abbot John, whose humility had led him to give up the life of an Anchorite for that of a Coenobite, in order that he might have the opportunity of practicing the virtues of obedience and subjection, which seemed out of the reach of the solitary.

He was accordingly well qualified to speak of the subject which he selected for his discourse; viz., the aims of the Anchorite and Coenobite life. Another well-known abbot, whose acquaintance they now made, was Theonus, who, when quite a young man, had been married by his parents, and later on, on failing to obtain the consent of his wife to a separation, in order that they might devote themselves to the monastic life, had deserted her and fled away into a monastery, where after a time he had been promoted to the office of almoner. From him they heard a discourse on the relaxation of the fast during Easter-tide and Pentecost, and, later on, one concerning Nocturnal Illusions, and another on Sinlessness. By these various discourses the two friends were rendered more desirous than ever of adopting the Anchorite life, and less inclined than before to return to the subjection of the monastery at Bethlehem. A far better course seemed to them to return to their own home, probably (as we have seen) in Gaul, where they would be free to practice what austerities they pleased without let or hindrance. In their perplexity they consulted Abbot Abraham, who threw cold water on their plan in a discourse on Mortification, which was entirely successful in persuading them to relinquish their half-formed intention. They, therefore, remained in Egypt for some years longer; and it is to the time of their stay in the neighborhood of Diolcos that their acquaintance with Abbot Archebius must be assigned. This man, so Cassian tells us, having discovered their desire to make some stay in the place, offered them the use of his cell, pretending that he was about to go off on a journey. They gladly accepted his offer. He went away for a few days, collected materials, and then returned and proceeded to build a new cell for himself. Shortly afterwards some more brethren came. He at once gave up to them his newly built cell, and once more set to work to build another for himself.

It is difficult to determine whether a stay in the desert of Scete was comprised in the seven years which the two friends now spent in Egypt, or whether they visited it for the first time during their second tour, after their return from Bethlehem. On the one hand, the language used in Conference XVIII. cc. i. and xvi. would almost suggest that they made their way into this remote district during their first sojourn in Egypt; and, on the other hand, that employed in Conference I. c. i. might imply a distinct journey to Egypt for the sake of visiting this region: and in XVII. xxx. Cassian distinctly asserts that they did visit Scete after their return to Bethlehem in fulfillment of their promise. On the whole, it appears the more natural view to suppose that their first tour was not extended beyond the Delta, more distant expeditions being reserved for a future occasion. Adopting, then, this view, we follow the travelers, after a seven years' absence, back to the monastery at Bethlehem, where they managed to pacify the irate brethren, and, strange to say, obtained leave to return to Egypt a second time. On this occasion they penetrated farther into the country than they had previously done. The region which they now visited was the desert of Scete, or Scitis; that is, the southern part of the famous Nitrian Valley, a name which is well known to all students from the rich treasure of Syrian MSS. brought home from thence by the Hon. Robert Curzon and Archdeacon Tattam now more than forty years ago. The district lies "to the northwest of Cairo, three days' journey in the Libyan desert," and gains its name of Nitria from the salt lakes which still furnish abundance of niter, which has been worked for fully two thousand years.

The valley has some claims to be considered the original home of monasticism. Some have thought that a colony of Therapeutae was settled here in the earliest days; and hither S. Frontonius is said to have retired with seventy brethren, to lead the life of ascetics, about the middle of the second century. Less doubtful is the fact that S. Ammon, a contemporary and friend of S. Antony, organized the monastic system here in the fourth century, and "filled the same place in lower Egypt as Antony in the Thebaid." Towards the close of the fourth century the valley was crowded with cells and monasteries. Rufinus, who visited it about 372, mentions fifty monasteries; and the same number is given by Sozomen, who says that "some were inhabited by monks who live together in society, others by monks who have adopted a solitary mode of existence." About twenty years later Palladius passed a considerable time here, and reckons the total number of monks and ascetics at five thousand. They were also visited by S. Jerome about the same time, and various details of the life of the monks are given by him in his Epistles. Some few monks still linger on to the present day to keep up the traditions of nearly eighteen centuries. They were visited (among others) by the Hon. Robert Curzon in 1833; and an interesting account of them is given by him in his volume on "the monasteries of the Levant:" but the latest and best account of them is that given by Mr. A. J. Butler, who succeeded in gaining permission to visit them in 1883, and has described his journey in his excellent work on "the ancient Coptic Churches of Egypt." Four monasteries alone remain; known as Dair Abu Makar, Dair Anba Bishoi, Dair es Suriani, and Dair al Baramus; but the ruins of many others may still be traced in the desert tracts on the west side of the Natron lakes, and the valley of the waterless river which at some very remote period is supposed to have formed the bed of one of the branches of the Nile." The monasteries are all built on the same general plan, so that, as Mr. Butler tells us, a description of one will more or less accurately describe the others. Dair Abu Makar (the monastery of S. Macarius), the first which he visited, which lies strictly within the desert of Scete, is spoken of as "a veritable fortress, standing about one-hundred and fifty yards square, with blind, lofty walls rising sheer out of the sand." "Each monastery has also, either detached or not, a large keep, or tower, standing four-square, and approached only by a draw-bridge. The tower contains the library, store-rooms for the vestments and sacred vessels, cellars for oil and corn, and many strange holes and hiding-places of the monks in the last resort, if their citadel should be taken by the enemy. Within the monastery in enclosed one principal and one or two smaller court-yards, around which stand the cells of the monks, domestic buildings, such as the mill-room, the oven, the refectory, and the like, and the churches." The outward aspect can have changed but little since the fourth century. The buildings are perhaps stronger and more adapted to resist hostile attacks, but the general plan is probably identical with that adopted in the earliest monasteries erected in this remote region. Such, then, was the district to which Cassian and Germanus now made their way. Here they first sought and obtained an interview with Abbot Moses, who had formerly dwelt in the Thebaid near S. Antony, and was now living at a spot in the desert of Scete known as Calamus, and was famous not only for practical goodness but also for contemplative excellence. After much persuasion he yielded to their entreaties and discoursed to them "on the goal or aim of a monk," and, on the following day, on Discretion. They next visited Abbot Paphnutius, or "the Buffalo," as he was named, from his love of solitude. He was an aged priest who had lived for years the life of an Anchorite, only leaving his cell for the purpose of going to the church, which was five miles off, on Saturday and Sunday, and returning with a large bucket of water on his shoulders to last him for the week. From him they heard of the "three kinds of renunciation" necessary for a monk. They also visited his disciple Daniel, who had been ordained priest through the instrumentality of Paphnutius, but was so humble that he would never perform priestly functions in the presence of his master. The subject of his discourse in answer to the inquiry of the two friends was "the lust of the flesh and the spirit." The next ascetic interviewed was Serapion, who spoke of the "eight principal faults" to which a monk was exposed; viz., gluttony, fornication, covetousness, anger, dejection, "accidie," vain glory, and pride. After this they proceeded on a journey of some eighty miles to Cellae, a place that lay between the desert of Scete (properly so called) and the Nitrian Valley, in order to consult Abbot Theodore on a difficulty which the recent massacre of a number of monks in Palestine by the Saracens had brought forcibly before them; viz., why was it that men of such illustrious merits and so great virtues should be slain by robbers, and why should God permit so great a crime to be committed? The difficulty was solved by Abbot Theodore in a discourse on "the death of the saints;" and thus the journey was not taken in vain.

Two other celebrated monks were also visited by the friends, whose discourses are recorded by Cassian: viz., Abbot Serenus, who spoke of "Inconstancy of mind, and Spiritual wickedness," n as well as of the nature of evil spirits, in a Conference on "Principalities;" and Abbot Isaac, who delivered two discourses on the subject of Prayer. A few days after the first of these was delivered there arrived in the desert the "festal letters" of Theophilus, Bishop of Alexandria, in which he denounced the heresy of the Anthropomorphites. This caused a great commotion among the monks of Scete; and Abbot Paphnutius, who presided over the monastery where Cassian was staying, was the only one who would allow the letters to be publicly read in the congregation. Finally, however, owing to the conciliatory firmness of Paphnutius, the great body of the monks was won over to a sounder and less materialistic view of the nature of the Godhead than had hitherto been prevalent among them. These are all the details that can be gathered from Cassian's writings of his stay in Scete, further than which he does not appear to have penetrated, as, when he speaks of the Thebaid and the monasteries there, it is only from hearsay and not from personal knowledge, although his original intention had certainly been to visit this district among others.

In considering the date of Cassian's visit to Egypt there are various indications to guide us. In Conference XVIII. c. xiv., S. Athanasius is spoken of by Abbot Piamun as "of blessed memory;" and the language used of the Emperor Valens in c. vii. is such as to imply that he was already dead. The former died in 373, and the latter in 378. Again, in Conference XXIV. c. xxvi. Abbot Abraham is made to speak of John of Lycopolis as so famous that he was consulted by the very lords of creation, who sought his advice, and entrusted to his prayers and merits the crown of their empire and the fortunes of war. These expressions evidently allude to John's announcement to Theodosius of his victory over Maxentius in 388, and his success against Eugenius in 395. If they stood alone, we could scarcely rely on these indications of date with any great confidence because the Conferences were not written till many years later, and it is impossible to determine with certainty how far they really represent the discourses actually spoken by the Egyptian Fathers, or how far they are the ideal compositions of Cassian himself. But, as we have seen, it is certain that Cassian was actually in Egypt at the time of the Anthropomorphite controversy raised by the letters of Theophilus in 399; and, as the other notices of events previously mentioned coincide very fairly with this, we cannot be far wrong in placing the two visits to Egypt between 380 and 400. About the last-named date Cassian must have finally left the country; and we next hear of him in Constantinople, where he was ordained deacon by S. Chrysostom, and, together with his friend Germanus, put in charge of the treasury, the only part of the Cathedral which escaped the flames in the terrible conflagration of 404. Thus Cassian was a witness of all the troublous scenes which attended the persecution of S. Chrysostom, whose side he warmly espoused in the controversy which rent the East asunder. And when the Saint was violently deposed and removed from Constantinople, the two friends — Germanus, who was by this time raised to the priesthood, and Cassian, who was still in deacon's orders — were chosen as the bearers of a letter to Pope Innocent I. from the clergy who adhered to Chrysostom, detailing the scandalous scenes that had taken place, and the trials to Which they had been exposed

Of the length of Cassian's stay in Rome we have no information, but it is likely that it was of some considerable duration; and it may have been at this time that he was ordained priest by Innocent. Possibly, also, it was now that he made the acquaintance of one who was then quite young, but was destined afterwards to become famous as Pope Leo the Great; for some years afterwards (A. D. 430) it was at the request of Leo, then Archdeacon of Rome, that Cassian wrote his work on the Incarnation against Nestorius. Leaving Rome, Cassian is next found in Gaul, which (if we are right in the supposition that it was his birthplace) he must have quitted when scarcely more than a child.

East a few monasteries had been founded in the district of the Loire by S. Martin and S. Hilary of Poictiers. Liguge was founded shortly after 360, and Marmoutier rather later, after 371; and about the time of his return similar institutions were beginning to spring up in Provence. In 410 S. Honoratus founded the monastery which will ever be associated with his name, in the island of Lerins, and, in the eloquent words of the historian of the monks of the West, "opened the arms of his love to the sons of all countries who desired to love Christ. A multitude of disciples of all nations joined him. The West could no longer envy the East; and shortly that retreat, destined in the intentions of its founder to renew upon the coasts of Provence the austerities of the Thebaid, became a celebrated school of theology and Christian philosophy, a citadel inaccessible to the waves of barbarian invasion, an asylum for literature and science, which had fled from Italy invaded by the Goths; — in short, a nursery of bishops and saints, who were destined to spread over the whole of Gaul the knowledge of the gospel and the glory of Lerins."

It must have been about the same time — a little earlier or a little later — that Cassian settled at Marseilles; and there, "in the midst of those great forests which had supplied the Phoenician navy, which in the time of Caesar reached as far as the sea-coast, and the mysterious obscurity of which had so terrified the Roman soldiers that the conqueror, to embolden them, had himself taken an axe and struck down an old oak," two monasteries were now established, — one for men, built it is said over the tomb of S. Victor, a martyr in the persecution of Diocletian, and the other for women. Cassian's long residence in the East and his intimate knowledge of the monastic system in vogue in Egypt made him at once looked up to as an authority, and practically as the head of the movement which was so rapidly taking root in Provence; and, although his fame has been overshadowed by that of the greatest of Western monks, S. Benedict of Nursia, yet his is really the credit of being, not indeed the actual founder, but the first organizer and systematizer, of Western monachism: and it is hoped that the copious illustrations from the Benedictine rule given in the notes to the first four books of the Institutes will serve to show how much the founder of the greatest order in the West was really indebted to his less-known predecessor. "He brought to bear upon the organization of Gallic monasteries lessons learnt in the East.

Martin and others were before him, yet his life must be regarded as a new departure for monasticism in the land. The religious communities of S. Martin and S. Victricius in the center of France were doubtless rudimentary and half-developed in discipline when compared with that established by Cassian at Marseilles, and with the many others which speedily arose modeled upon his elaborate rules." The high estimation in which his work was held throughout the Middle Ages is shown not only by the immense number of MSS. of the Institutes and Conferences which still remain scattered throughout the libraries of Europe, but also by the recommendation of them by Cassiodorus, and by S. Benedict himself, who enjoins that the Conferences should be read daily by the monks of his order.

At Marseilles, then, Cassian settled; and here it was that he wrote his three great works, — the Institutes, the

Conferences, and On the Incarnation against Nestorius; the two former being written for the express purpose of encouraging and developing the monastic life. Of these the Institutes was the earliest, being composed in "twelve books on the institutes of the monasteries and the remedies for the eight principal faults," at the request of Castor, Bishop of Apta Julia, some forty miles due north of Marseilles, who was desirous of introducing the monastic life into his diocese, where it was still a thing unknown. As Castor died in 426, and the work is dedicated to him, it must have been written some time between the years 419 and 426. When it was first undertaken Cassian's design already was to follow it up by a second treatise containing the Conferences of the Fathers, to which he several times alludes in the Institutes as a forthcoming work, and which, like the companion volume, was undertaken at Castor's instigation. But, before even the first part of it was ready for publication, the Bishop of Apta was dead; and thus, to Cassian's sorrow, he was unable to dedicate it to him, as he had hoped to do. He therefore dedicated Conferences I.-X. (the first portion of the work) to Leontius, Bishop (probably) of Frejus, and Helladius, who is termed "frater" in the Preface to this work, though, as we see from the Preface 19 Conference XVIII., he was afterwards raised to the episcopate.

This portion of Cassian's work must have been completed shortly after the death of Castor in 426. It was speedily followed by Part II., containing Conferences XI. to XVII. This is dedicated to Honoratus and Eucherius, who are styled "fratres." Eucherius did not become Bishop of Lyons till 434; but, as Honoratus was raised to the see of Arles in 426, the volume must have been published not later than that year, or he would have been termed "Episcopus," as he is in the Preface to Conference XVIII., instead of "frater The third and last part of the work, containing

Conferences XVIII. to XXIV., is dedicated to Jovinian, Minervius, Leontius, and Theodore, who are collectively styled "fratres." Leontius must, therefore, be a different person from the bishop to whom Conferences I.-X. were dedicated; and nothing further is known of him, or of Minervius and Jovinian. Theodore was afterwards raised to the Episcopate, and succeeded Leontius in the see of Frejus in 432. This third part of Cassian's work was ready before the death of Honoratus, Bishop of Arles, who is spoken of in the Preface as if still living; and, therefore, its publication cannot be later than 428, as Honoratus died in January, 429 Thus the whole work was completed between the years 426 and 428; and now Cassian, who was growing old, was desirous of rest, feeling as if his life's work was nearly over. But the repose which he sought was not to be granted to him, for the remaining years of his life were troubled by two controversies, — the Nestorian, and the Pelagian, — or, rather, its offshoot, the Semi-Pelagian. Into the history of the former of these there is no need to enter here in detail. It broke out at Constantinople, where Nestorius had become bishop in succession to Sisinnius, in 428. The immediate occasion which gave rise to the controversy was a sermon by Anastasius, the Bishop's chaplain, in which he inveighed against the title Theotocos, as given to the Blessed Virgin Mary. This at once created a great sensation, as Nestorius warmly supported his chaplain, and proceeded to develop the heresy connected with his name, in a course of sermons. News of the controversy was brought to Egypt, and Cyril of Alexandria at once entered into the fray. After some correspondence between the two bishops, both parties endeavored to gain the adherence of the Church of Rome early in the year 430; and now it was that Cassian became mixed up with the dispute. Greek learning was evidently at a low ebb in the Roman Church at this time; and it was, perhaps, partly owing to Cassian's familiar acquaintance with this language, as well as owing to his connection with Constantinople, where the trouble had now arisen, that Celestine's Archdeacon Leo turned to him at this crisis for help. Anyhow, whatever was the reason, an earnest appeal from Rome reached him, begging him to write a refutation of the new heresy. After some hesitation he consented, and the result of his labors is seen in the seven books on the Incarnation against Nestorius. The work was evidently done in haste, and published in 430, before the Council of Ephesus (for Cassian speaks of Nestorius throughout as still Bishop of Constantinople), and, judging from the way in which Augustine is spoken of in VII. xxvii., before the death of that Father, which took place in August, 430. A great part of the work is occupied with Scripture proof of our Lord's Divinity and unity of Person; but, taken as a whole, the treatise is distinctly of less value than Cassian's earlier writings, and betrays the haste in which it was composed by the occasional use of inaccurate language on the subject of the Incarnation, and of terms and phrases which the mature judgment of the Church has rejected. But the writer's keen penetration is seen by the quickness with which he connects the new heresy with the teaching of Pelagius, the connecting link between the two being found in the errors of Leporius of Treves, who, in propagating Pelagian views of man's sufficiency and strength, had applied them to the case of our Lord, not shrinking from the conclusion that He was a mere man who had used his free will so well as to have lived without sin, and had only been made Christ in virtue of His baptism, whereby the Divine and human were associated in such manner that virtually there were two Christs. The connection between Nestorianism and Pelagianism has often been noticed by later writers, but to Cassian belongs the credit of having been the first to point it out. Of the impression produced by his book we have no record. He appears to have taken no further part in the controversy, which, indeed, must have been to him an episode, coming in the midst of that other controversy with which his name is inseparably associated; viz., that on Semi-Pelagianism, on which something must now be said. The controversy arose in the following way. During the struggle with Pelagianism between the years 410 and 420, Augustine's views on the absolute need of grace were gradually hardening into a theory that grace was irresistible and therefore indefectible. "Intent above all things on magnifying the Divine Sovereignty, he practically forgot the complexity of the problem in hand and failed to do justice to the human element in the mysterious process of man's salvation." The view of an absolute predestination irrespective of foreseen character, and of the irresistible and indefectible character of grace, was put forward by him, in a letter to a Roman priest, Sixtus, in the year 418. Some years afterwards this letter fell into the hands of the monks of Adrumetum, some of whom were puzzled by its teaching; and, in order to allay the disputes among them, the matter was referred to Augustine himself. Thinking that the monks had misunderstood his teaching, he not only explained the letter but also wrote afresh treatise, — "De Gratia et Libero Arbitrio" (426); and, when that failed to satisfy the malcontents, he followed it up with his work "De Correptione et Gratia" (426), which, so far as the monks of Adrumetum were concerned, seems to have ended the controversy.

Elsewhere, however, hesitation was felt in going the full length of Augustine's teaching; and, in the South of Gaul especially, many were seriously disturbed at the turn which the controversy had lately taken, and were prepared to reject Augustine's teaching, as not merely novel, but also practically dangerous. "They said, in effect," to quote Canon Bright's lucid summary of their position, "to treat predestination as irrespective of foreseen conduct, and to limit the Divine good-will to a fixed number of persons thus selected, who, as such, are assured of perseverance, is not only to depart from the older theology, and from the earlier teaching of the Bishop of Hippo himself, but to cut at the root of religious effort, and to encourage either negligence or despair. They insisted that whatever theories might be devised concerning this mystery, which was not a fit subject for popular discussion, the door of salvation should be regarded as open to all, because the Savior 'died for all.' To explain away the Scriptural assurance was, they maintained, to falsify the Divine promise and to nullify human responsibility. They believed in the doctrine of the Fall; they acknowledged the necessity of real grace in order to man's restoration; they even admitted that this grace must be 'prevenient' to such acts of will as resulted in Christian good works: but some of them thought — and herein consisted the error called Semi-Pelagian — that nature, unaided, could take the first step towards its recovery, by desiring to be healed through faith in Christ. If it could not, — if the very beginning of all good were strictly a Divine act, — exhortations seemed to them to be idle, and censure unjust, in regard to those on whom no such act had been wrought, and who, therefore, until it should be wrought, were helpless, and so far guiltless, in the matter." Of the party which took up this position Cassian was the recognized head. True, he did not directly enter into the controversy himself, nor is he the author of any polemical works upon the subject; but it is impossible to doubt that the thirteenth Conference, containing the teaching of Abbot Chaeremon on the Protection of God, was intended to meet what he evidently regarded as a serious error; viz., the implicit denial by the Augustinians of the need of effort on man's part.

Augustine was informed of the teaching of the School of Marseilles, as it was called, by one Hilary (a layman, not to be confounded with his namesake, the Bishop of Arles), who wrote to him two letters, of which the former is lost. The latter is still existing, and contains a careful account of what was maintained at Marseilles. Towards the close of it Hilary says that, as he was pressed for time, he had prevailed upon a friend to write as well, and would attach his letter to his own. This friend was Prosper of Aquitaine, also a layman and an ardent Augustinian, whose epistle has been preserved as well as Hilary's. From these letters, and from the works which Augustine wrote in reply, we learn that the "Massilians" had been first disturbed by some of Augustine's earlier writings, as the Epistle to Paulinus; and that their distrust of his teaching on the subjects of Grace, Predestination, and Freewill had been increased by the receipt of his work "De Correptione et Gratia," although in other matters they agreed with him entirely, and were great admirers of his. Personally, they are spoken of with great respect as men of no common virtue, and of wide influence; and, though Cassian's name is never mentioned in the correspondence, yet it is easy to read between the lines and see that he is referred to.

Augustine replied to his correspondents by writing what proved to be almost his latest works, — the treatises "De Praedestinatione Sanctorum" and "De dono Perseverantiae." In these volumes Augustine, while freely acknowledging the great difference between his opponents and the Pelagians, yet maintained as strongly as ever his own position, and "did not abate an iota of the contention that election and rejection were arbitrary, and that salvation was not really within the reach of all Christians." Thus the books naturally failed to satisfy the recalcitrant party, or to convince those who thought that the denial of the freedom of the will tended to destroy man's responsibility. Prosper, however delighted with the treatises, and proceeded to follow them up with a work of his own, a poem of a thousand lines, "De Ingratis," by which he designates the Pelagians and Semi-Pelagians, whose opinions he speaks of as spreading with alarming rapidity. The date of this publication was probably the early part of 430. It was certainly written before the death of Augustine, which took place on August 28 of the same year. The removal from this life of the great champion of Grace did not bring to an end the controversy to which his writings had given birth. The school of Marseilles continued to propagate its views with unabated vigor, in spite of the protests of Prosper and Hilary, who finally took the important step of appealing to Pope Celestine, from whom they succeeded in obtaining a letter addressed to the Gallican Bishops, Venerius of Marseilles, Leontius of Frejus, Marinus, Auxonius, Arcadius, Filtanius, and the rest., was Celestine speaks strongly of their negligence in not having suppressed what he regarded as a public scandal, and says that "priests ought not to teach so as to invade the episcopal prerogative," an expression in which we may well see an allusion to Cassian, the leading presbyter, of the diocese of Marseilles, whose Bishop is named first in the opening salutation; and the letter concludes with some words of eulogium on Augustine "of holy memory." Never, perhaps, was Gallican independence shown in a more striking manner than in the sturdy way in which the Massilians clung to their views in spite of the authority of the Pope now brought to bear upon them. Prosper and Hilary on their return found the obnoxious teaching daily spreading, so that the former of them finally determined to put down, if possible, the upholders of the objectionable tenets by a direct criticism of Cassian's Conferences. This was the origin of Prosper's work "Contra Collatorem," against the author of the Conferences, a treatise of considerable power and force, although not scrupulously fair. The respect in which Cassian was held is strikingly shown by the fact that his antagonist never once names him directly, but merely speaks of him as a man of priestly rank who surpassed all his companions in power of arguing. The work consists of an examination of the thirteenth Conference, that of Abbot Chaeremon, on the Protection of God, from which Prosper extracts twelve propositions, the first of which he says is orthodox while all the others are erroneous . He concludes by warning his antagonist of the danger of Pelagianism, and expresses a hope that his doctrine may be condemned by Pope Sixtus as it had been by Celestine and his predecessors. The last statement fixes the date of the book as not earlier than 432; for Celestine only died in April in that year.

Cassian was evidently still living when this attack upon him was made; but, so far as we know, he made no reply to it. Its publication is the last event in his life of which we have any knowledge. He probably died shortly afterwards, as the expression used by Gennadius in speaking of his work against Nestorius would seem to imply that it preceded his death by no long interval; for he says that with this he brought to a close his literary labors and his life in the reign of Theodosius and Valentinian. The controversy on Grace and Freewill lingered on for nearly a century longer, and was only finally disposed of by the wise moderation shown by Caesarius of Aries and those who acted with him at the Council of Orange (Arausio), in the year 529.

While it cannot be denied that the teaching of Cassian and his school in denying the necessity of initial and prevenient grace is erroneous and opens a door at which Pelagianism may easily creep in, yet it was an honest attempt to vindicate human responsibility; and it must be frankly admitted that the teaching of Augustine was one-sided and required to be balanced: nor would the question have ever been brought into prominence had it not been for the hard and rigorous way in which the doctrine of Predestination was taught, and the denial that the possibility of salvation lay within the reach of all men. While, then, it is granted that a verdict of guilty must be returned on the charge of Semi-Pelagianism in Cassian's case, we are surely justified in claiming that a recommendation to mercy be attached to it on the plea of extenuating circumstances. Since his death Cassian has ever occupied a somewhat ambiguous position in the mind of the Church. Never formally canonized, his name is not found in the Calendars of the West; nor is he honored with the title of "Saint." He is, however, generally spoken of as "the blessed Cassian," holding in this respect the same position as Theodoret, of whom Dr. Newman says that, though he "has the responsibility of acts which have forfeited to him that oecumenical dignity," yet he is "not without honorary title in the Church's hagiology; for he has ever been known as the 'blessed Theodoret.'" In the East Cassian's position is somewhat better. He is there regarded as a saint, and may possibly be intended by the Cassian who is commemorated on February 29. It is only natural that this difference should be made, for the Eastern Church has always held a milder view of the effect of the Fall than that which has been current in the West since the days of Augustine; and, indeed, Cassian, in making his protest against the rising tide of Augustinianism, was in the main only handing on the teaching which he had received from his Eastern instructors.

CHAPTER 2
THE HISTORY OF CASSIAN'S WRITINGS, MSS., AND EDITIONS

THE LITERARY HISTORY OF CASSIAN'S WORKS IS NOT without an interest of its own. We have already seen the estimation in which they were held in spite of their Semi-Pelagian doctrines. These were naturally accounted a blemish, and it is not surprising that those who most admired their excellences were anxious to avoid propagating their errors. Hence they were often "expurgated," and in many MSS. the text has suffered considerably from the changes made by copyists in the interests of orthodoxy. As early as the fifth century we find two revised versions of portions of his works existing. His friend Eucherius, Bishop of Lyons, was the author of an epitome of the Institutes, which still exists; and although this was compiled for convenience' sake because of the length of the original work, rather than from any suspicion of his teaching, the case is different with a recension made for use in Africa by Victor, Bishop of Martyrites. This is no longer extant, but Cassiodorus distinctly tells us that it was made in the interests of orthodoxy by means of expurgation as well as addition of what was wanting. Yet another epitome of three of the Conferences (I., II., VII.) was made at some time before the tenth century. It was translated into Greek, and known to Photius, who speaks of three works of Cassian as translated into Greek: viz., an Epitome of the Institutes, Books I.-IV.; Epitome of the Institutes, Books V.-XII.

BOOK 1

OF THE DRESS OF THE MONKS

CHAPTER 1
OF THE MONK'S GIRDLE

AS WE ARE GOING TO SPEAK OF THE CUSTOMS AND RULES OF the monasteries, how by God's grace can we better begin than with the actual dress of the monks, for we shall then be able to expound in due course their interior life when we have set their outward man before your eyes. A monk, then, as a soldier of Christ ever ready for battle, ought always to walk with his loins girded. For in this fashion, too, the authority of Holy Scripture shows that they walked who in the Old Testament started the original of this life, — I mean Elijah and Elisha; and, moreover, we know that the leaders and authors of the New Testament, viz., John, Peter, and Paul, and the others of the same rank, walked in the same manner. And of these the first-mentioned, who even in the Old Testament displayed the flowers of a virgin life and an example of chastity and continence, when he had been sent by the Lord to rebuke the messengers of Ahaziah, the wicked king of Israel, because when confined by sickness he had intended to consult Beelzebub, the God of Ekron, on the state of his health, and thereupon the said prophet had met them and said that he should not come down from the bed on which he lay, — this man was made known to the bed-ridden king by the description of the character of his clothing

For when the messengers returned to him and brought back the prophet's message, he asked what the man who had met them and spoken such words was like and how he was dressed. "An hairy man," they said, "and girt with a girdle of leather about his loins;" and by this dress the king at once saw that it was the man of God, and said: "It is Elijah the Tishbite:" i.e., by the evidence of the girdle and the look of the hairy and unkempt body he recognized without the slightest doubt the man of God, because this was always attached to him as he dwelt among so many thousands of Israelites, as if it were impressed as some special sign of his own particular style. Of John also, who came as a sort of sacred boundary between the Old and New Testament, being both a beginning and an ending, we know by the testimony of the Evangelist that "the same John had his raiment of camel's hair and a girdle of skin about his loins." When Peter also had been Jut in prison by Herod and was to be brought forth to be slain on the next day, when the angel stood by him he was charged: "Gird thyself and put on thy shoes." And the angel of the Lord would certainly not have charged him to do this had he not seen that for the sake of his night's rest he had for a while freed his wearied limbs from the girdle usually tied round them. Paul also, going up to Jerusalem and soon to be put in chains by the Jews, was met at Caesarea by the prophet Agabus, who took his girdle and bound his hands and feet to show by his bodily actions the injuries which he was to suffer, and said: "So shall the Jews in Jerusalem bind the man whose girdle this is, and deliver him into the hands of the Gentiles." And surely the prophet would never have brought this forward, or have said "the man whose girdle this is," unless Paul had always been accustomed to fasten it round his loins.

CHAPTER 2
OF THE MONK'S ROBE

LET THE ROBE ALSO OF THE MONK BE SUCH AS MAY MERELY cover the body and prevent the disgrace of nudity, and keep off harm from cold, not such as may foster the seeds of vanity and pride; for the same apostle tells us: "Having food and covering, with these let us be content." "Covering," he says, not "raiment," as is wrongly found in some Latin copies: that is, what may merely cover the body, not what may please the fancy by the splendor of the attire; commonplace, so that it may not be thought remarkable for novelty of color or fashion among other men of the same profession; and quite free from anxious carefulness, yet not discoloured by stains acquired through neglect. Lastly, let them be so far removed from this world's fashions as to remain altogether common property for the use of the servants of God. For whatever is claimed by one or a few among the servants of God and is not the common property of the whole body. Of the brethren alike is either superfluous or vain, and for that reason to be considered harmful, and affording an appearance of vanity rather than virtue. And, therefore, whatever models we see were not taught either by the saints of old who laid the foundations of the monastic life, or by the fathers of our own time who in their turn keep up at the present day their customs, these we also should reject as superfluous and useless: wherefore they utterly disapproved of a robe of sackcloth as being visible to all and conspicuous, and what from this very fact will not only confer no benefit on the soul but rather minister to vanity and pride, and as being inconvenient and unsuitable for the performance of necessary work for which a monk ought always to go ready and unimpeded. But even if we hear of some respectable persons who have been dressed in this garb, a rule for the monasteries is not, therefore, to be passed by us, nor should the ancient decrees of the holy fathers be upset because we do not think that a few men, presuming on the possession of other virtues, are to be blamed even in regard of those things which they have practiced not in accordance with the Catholic rule. For the opinion of a few ought not to be preferred to or to interfere with the general rule for all. For we ought to give unhesitating allegiance and unquestioning obedience, not to those customs and rules which the will of a few have introduced, but to those which a long standing antiquity and numbers of the holy fathers have passed on by an unanimous decision to those that come after. Nor, indeed, ought this to influence us as a precedent for our daily life, that Joram, the wicked king of Israel, when surrounded by bands of his foes, rent his clothes, and is said to have had sackcloth inside them; or that the Ninevites, in order to mitigate the sentence of God, which had been pronounced against them by the prophet, were clothed in rough sackcloth. The former is shown to have been clothed with it secretly underneath, so that unless the upper garment had been rent it could not possibly have been known by any one, and the latter tolerated a covering of sackcloth at a time when, since all were mourning over the approaching destruction of the city and were clothed with the same garments, none could be accused of ostentation. For where there is no special difference and all are alike no harm is done.

CHAPTER 3
OF THE HOODS OF THE EGYPTIANS

THERE ARE SOME THINGS BESIDES IN THE DRESS OF THE Egyptians which concern not the care of the body so much as the regulation of the character, that the observance of simplicity and innocence may be preserved by the very character of the clothing. For they constantly use both by day and by night very small hoods coming down to the end of the neck and shoulders, which only cover the head, in order that they may constantly be moved to preserve the simplicity and innocence of little children by imitating their actual dress. And these men have returned to childhood in Christ and sing at all hours with heart and soul: "Lord, my heart is not exalted nor are mine eyes lofty. Neither have I walked in great matters nor in wonderful things above me. If I was not humbly minded, but exalted my soul: as a child that is weaned is towards his mother."

CHAPTER 4
OF THE TUNICS OF THE EGYPTIANS

THEY WEAR ALSO LINEN TUNICS WHICH SCARCELY REACH to the elbows, and for the rest leave their hands bare, that the cutting off of the sleeves may suggest that they have cut off all the deeds and works of this world, and the garment of linen teach that they are dead to all earthly conversation, and that hereby they may hear the Apostle saying day by day to them: "Mortify your members which are upon the earth;" their very dress also declaring this: "For ye are dead, and your life is hid with Christ in God;" and again: "And I live, yet now not I but Christ liveth in me. To me indeed the world is crucified, and I to the world."

CHAPTER 5
OF THEIR CORDS

THEY ALSO WEAR DOUBLE SCARVES WOVEN OF WOOLLEN yarn which the Greeks call ἀνάλαβοι, but which we should name girdles or strings, or more properly cords. These falling down over the top of the neck and divided on either side of the throat go round the folds (of the robe) at the armpits and gather them up on either side, so that they can draw up and tuck in close to the body the wide folds of the dress, and so with their arms girt they are made active and ready for all kinds of work, endeavoring with all their might to fulfill the Apostle's charge: "For these hands have ministered not only to me but to those also who are with me," "Neither have we eaten any man's bread for nought, but with labor and toil working night and day that we should not be burdensome to any of you." And: "If any will not work neither let him eat."

CHAPTER 6
OF THEIR CAPES

NEXT THEY COVER THEIR NECKS AND SHOULDERS WITH A narrow cape, aiming at modesty of dress as well as cheapness and economy; and this is called in our language as well as theirs mafors; and so they avoid both the expense and the display of cloaks and great coats.

CHAPTER 7
OF THE SHEEPSKIN AND THE GOATSKIN.

THE LAST ARTICLE OF THEIR DRESS IS THE GOAT-SKIN, WHICH is called melotes, or pera, and a staff, which they carry in imitation of those who foreshadowed the lines of the monastic life in the Old Testament, of whom the Apostle says: "They wandered about in sheepskins and goatskins, being in want, distressed, afflicted; of whom the world was not worthy; wandering in deserts, and in mountains, and in dens, and in caves of the earth." And this garment of goatskin signifies that having destroyed all wantonness of carnal passions they ought to continue in the utmost sobriety of virtue, and that nothing of the wantonness or heat of youth, or of their old lightmindedness, should remain in their bodies.

CHAPTER 8
OF THE STAFF OF THE EGYPTIANS

FOR ELISHA, HIMSELF ONE OF THEM, TEACHES THAT THE SAME men used to carry a staff; as he says to Gehazi, his servant, when sending him to raise the woman's son to life: "Take my staff and run and go and place it on the lad's face that he may live." And the prophet would certainly not have given it to him to take unless he had been in the habit of constantly carrying it about in his hand. And the carrying of the staff spiritually teaches that they ought never to walk unarmed among so many barking dogs of faults and invisible beasts of spiritual wickedness (from which the blessed David, in his longing to be free, says: "Deliver not, O Lord, to the beasts the soul that trusteth in Thee"), but when they attack them they ought to beat them off with the sign of the cross and drive them far away; and when they rage furiously against them they should annihilate them by the constant recollection of the Lord's passion and by following the example of His mortified life.

CHAPTER 9
OF THEIR SHOES

BUT REFUSING SHOES, AS FORBIDDEN BY THE COMMAND OF the gospel, if bodily weakness or the morning cold in winter or the scorching heat of midday compels them, they merely protect their feet with sandals, explaining that by the use of them and the Lord's permission it is implied that if, while we are still in this world we cannot be completely set free from care and anxiety about the flesh, nor can we be altogether released from it, we should at least provide for the wants of the body with as little fuss and as slight an entanglement as possible: and as for the feet of our soul which ought to be ready for our spiritual race and always prepared for preaching the peace of the gospel (with which feet we run after the odour of the ointments of Christ, and of which David says: "I ran in thirst," and Jeremiah: "But I am not troubled, following Thee"), we ought not to suffer them to be entangled in the deadly cares of this world, filling our thoughts with those things which concern not the supply of the wants of nature, but unnecessary and harmful pleasures. And this we shall thus fulfill if, as the Apostle advises, we "make not provision for the flesh with its lusts." But though lawfully enough they make use of these sandals, as permitted by the Lord's command, yet they never suffer them to remain on their feet when they approach to celebrate or to receive the holy mysteries, as they think that they ought to observe in the letter that which was said to Moses and to Joshua, the son of Nun: "Loose the latchet of thy shoe: for the place whereon thou standest is holy ground."

CHAPTER 10
OF THE MODIFICATION IN THE OBSERVANCES WHICH MAY BE PERMITTED IN ACCORDANCE WITH THE CHARACTER OF THE CLIMATE OR THE CUSTOM OF THE DISTRICT

SO MUCH MAY BE SAID, THAT WE MAY NOT APPEAR TO HAVE left out any article of the dress of the Egyptians. But we need only keep to those which the situation of the place and the customs of the district permit. For the severity of the winter does not allow us to be satisfied with slippers or tunics or a single frock; and the covering of tiny hoods or the wearing of a sheepskin would afford a subject for derision instead of edifying the spectators. Wherefore we hold that we ought to introduce only those things which we have described above, and which are adapted to the humble character of our profession and the nature of the climate, that the chief thing about our dress maybe not the novelty of the garb, which might give some offense to men of the world, but its honorable simplicity.

BOOK 2

OF THE CANONICAL SYSTEM OF THE NOCTURNAL PRAYERS AND PSALMS

CHAPTER 1
OF THE CANONICAL SYSTEM OF THE NOCTURNAL PRAYERS AND PSALMS

GIRT, THEREFORE, WITH THIS TWOFOLD GIRDLE OF WHICH we have spoken, the soldier of Christ should next learn the system of the canonical prayers and Psalms which was long ago arranged by the holy fathers in the East. Of their character, however, and of the way in which we can pray, as the Apostle directs, "without ceasing," we shall treat, as the Lord may enable us, in the proper place, when we begin to relate the Conferences of the Elders.

CHAPTER 2
OF THE DIFFERENCE OF THE NUMBER OF PSALMS APPOINTED TO BE SUNG IN ALL THE PROVINCES

FOR WE HAVE FOUND THAT MANY IN DIFFERENT COUNTRIES, according to the fancy of their mind (having, indeed, as the Apostle says, "a zeal, for God but not according to Knowledge", have made for themselves different rules and arrangements in this matter. For some have appointed that each night twenty or thirty Psalms should be said, and that these should be prolonged by the music of antiphonal singing, and by the addition of some modulations as well. Others have even tried to go beyond this number. Some use eighteen. And in this way we have found different rules appointed in different places, and the system and regulations that we have seen are almost as many in number as the monasteries and cells which we have visited. There are some, too, to whom it has seemed good that in the day offices of prayer, viz., Tierce, Sext, and Nones, the number of Psalms and prayers should be made to correspond exactly to the number of the hours at which the services are offered up to the Lord. Some have thought fit that six Psalms should be assigned to each service of the day. And so I think it best to set forth the most ancient system of the fathers which is still observed by the servants of God throughout the whole of Egypt, so that your new monastery in its untrained infancy in Christ may be instructed in the most ancient institutions of the earliest fathers.

CHAPTER 3

OF THE OBSERVANCE OF ONE UNIFORM RULE THROUGHOUT THE WHOLE OF EGYPT, AND OF THE ELECTION OF THOSE WHO ARE SET OVER THE BRETHREN

AND SO THROUGHOUT THE WHOLE OF EGYPT AND THE Thebaid, where monasteries are not rounded at the fancy of every man who renounces the world, but through a succession of fathers and their traditions last even to the present day, or are rounded so to last, in these we have noticed that a prescribed system of prayers is observed in their evening assemblies and nocturnal vigils. For no one is allowed to preside over the assembly of the brethren, or even over himself, before he has not only deprived himself of all his property but has also learnt the fact that he is not his own maker and has no authority over his own actions. For one who renounces the world, whatever property or riches he may possess, must seek the common dwelling of a Coenobium, that he may not flatter himself in any way with what he has forsaken or what he has brought into the monastery. He must also be obedient to all, so as to learn that he must, as the Lord says, become again a little child, arrogating nothing to himself on the score of his age and the number of the years which he now counts as lost while they were spent to no purpose in the world and, as he is only a beginner, and because of the novelty of the apprenticeship, which he knows he is serving in Christ's service, he should not hesitate to submit himself even to his juniors. Further, he is obliged to habituate himself to work and toil, so as to prepare with his own hands; in accordance with the Apostle's command, daily supply of food, either for his own use or for the wants of strangers; and that he may also forget the pride and luxury of his past life, and gain by grinding toil humility of heart. And so no one is chosen to be set over a congregation of brethren before that he who is to be placed in authority has learnt by obedience what he ought to enjoin on those who are to submit to him, and has discovered from the rules of the Elders what he ought to teach to his juniors. For they. say that to rule or to be ruled well needs a wise man, and they call it the greatest gift and grace of the Holy Spirit, since no one can enjoin salutary precepts on those who submit to him but one who has previously been trained in all the rules of virtue; nor can any one obey an Elder but one who has been filled with the love of God and perfected in the virtue of humility. And so we see that there is a variety of rules and regulations in use throughout other districts, because we often have the audacity to preside over a monastery without even having learnt the system of the Elders, and appoint ourselves Abbots before we have, as we ought, professed ourselves disciples, and are readier to require the observance of our own inventions than to preserve the well-tried teaching of our predecessors. But, while we meant to explain the best system of prayers to be observed, we have in our eagerness for the institutions of the fathers anticipated by a hasty digression the account which we were keeping back for its proper place. And so let us now return to the subject before us.

CHAPTER 4

HOW THROUGHOUT THE WHOLE OF EGYPT AND THE THEBAID THE NUMBER OF PSALMS IS FIXED AT TWELVE

SO, AS WE SAID, THROUGHOUT THE WHOLE OF EGYPT AND the Thebaid the number of Psalms is fixed at twelve both at Vespers and in the office of Nocturns, in such a way that at the close two lessons follow, one from the Old and the other from the New Testament. And this arrangement, fixed ever so long ago, has continued unbroken to the present day throughout so many ages, in all the monasteries of those districts, because it is said that it was no appointment of man's invention, but was brought down from heaven to the fathers by the ministry of an angel.

CHAPTER 5

HOW THE FACT THAT THE NUMBER OF THE PSALMS WAS TO BE TWELVE WAS RECEIVED FROM THE TEACHING OF AN ANGEL

FOR IN THE EARLY DAYS OF THE FAITH WHEN ONLY A FEW, and those the best of men, were known by the name of monks, who, as they received that mode of life from the Evangelist Mark of blessed memory, the first to preside over the Church of Alexandria as Bishop, not only preserved those grand characteristics for which we read, in the Acts of the Apostles, that the Church and multitude of believers in primitive times was famous ("The multitude of believers had one heart and one soul. Nor did any of them say that any of the things which he possessed was his own: but they had all things common; for as many as were owners of lands or houses sold them, and brought the price of the things which they sold, and laid it at the feet of the Apostles, and distribution was made to every man as he had need"), but they added to these characteristics others still more sublime. For withdrawing into more secluded spots outside the cities they led a life marked by such rigorous abstinence that even to those of another creed the exalted character of their life was a standing marvel. For they gave themselves up to the reading of Holy Scripture and to prayers and to manual labor night and day with such fervor that they had no desire or thoughts of food — unless on the second or third day bodily hunger reminded them, and they took their meat and drink not so much because they wished for it as because it was necessary for life; and even then they took it not before sunset, in order that they might connect the hours of daylight with the practice of spiritual meditations, and the care of the body with the night, and might perform other things much more exalted than these. And about these matters, one who has never heard anything from one who is at home in such things, may learn from ecclesiastical history. At that time, therefore, when the perfection of the primitive Church remained unbroken, and was still preserved fresh in the memory by their followers and successors, and when the fervent faith of the few had not yet grown lukewarm by being dispersed among the many, the venerable fathers with watchful care made provision for those to come after them, and met together to discuss the daily worship throughout the whole body of the brethren; that they might hand on to those who should succeed them a legacy of piety and peace that was free from all dispute and dissension, for they were afraid that in regard of the daily services some difference or dispute might arise among those who joined together in the same worship, and at some time or other it might send forth a poisonous root of error or jealousy or schism among those who came after. And when each man in proportion to his own fervor — and unmindful of the weakness of others —

thought that that should be appointed which he judged was quite easy by considering his own faith and strength, taking too little account of what would be possible for the great mass of the brethren in general (wherein a very large proportion of weak ones is sure to be found); and when in different degrees they strove, each according to his own powers, to fix an enormous number of Psalms, and some were for fifty, others sixty, and some, not content with this number, thought that they actually ought to go beyond it, — there was such a holy difference of opinion in their pious discussion on the rule of their religion that the time for their Vesper office came before the sacred question was decided; and, as they were going to celebrate their daily rites and prayers, one rose up in the midst to chant the Psalms to the Lord.what plan should be adopted for

And while they were all sitting (as is still the custom in Egypt), with their minds intently fixed on the words of the chanter, when he had sung eleven Psalms, separated by prayers introduced between them, verse after verse being evenly enunciated, he finished the twelfth with a response of Alleluia, and then, by his sudden disappearance from the eyes of all, put an end at once to their discussion and their service.

CHAPTER 6
OF THE CUSTOM OF HAVING TWELVE PRAYERS

WHEREUPON THE VENERABLE ASSEMBLY OF THE FATHERS understood that by Divine Providence a general rule had been fixed for the congregations of the brethren through the angel's direction, and so decreed that this number should be preserved both in their evening and in their nocturnal services; and when they added to these two lessons, one from the Old and one from the New Testament, they added them simply as extras and of their own appointment, only for those who liked, and who were eager to gain by constant study a mind well stored with Holy Scripture. But on Saturday and Sunday they read them both from the New Testament; viz., one from the Epistles or the Acts of the Apostles, and one from the Gospel. And this also those do whose concern is the reading and the recollection of the Scriptures, from Easter to Whitsuntide.

CHAPTER 7
OF THEIR METHOD OF PRAYING

THESE AFORESAID PRAYERS, THEN, THEY BEGIN AND FINISH in such a way that when the Psalm is ended they do not hurry at once to kneel down, as some of us do in this country, who, before the Psalm is fairly ended, make haste to prostrate themselves for prayer, in their hurry to finish the service as quickly as possible. For though we have chosen to exceed the limit which was anciently fixed by our predecessors, supplying the number of the remaining Psalms, we are anxious to get to the end of the service, thinking of the refreshment of the wearied body rather than looking for profit and benefit from the prayer. Among them, therefore, it is not so, but before they bend their knees they pray for a few moments, and while they are standing up spend the greater part of the time in prayer. And so after this, for the briefest space of time, they prostrate themselves to the ground, as if but adoring the Divine Mercy, and as soon as possible rise up, and again standing erect with outspread hands — just as they had been standing to pray before — remain with thoughts intent upon their prayers. For when you lie prostrate for any length of time upon the ground you are more open to an attack, they say, not only of wandering thoughts but also slumber.

And would that we too did not know the truth of this by experience and daily practice — we who when prostrating ourselves on the ground too often wish for this attitude to be prolonged for some time, not for the sake of our prayer so much as for the sake of resting. But when he who is to "collect" the prayer rises from the ground they all start up at once, so that no one would venture to bend the knee before he bows down, nor to delay when he has risen from the ground, lest it should be thought that he has offered his own prayer independently instead of following the leader to the close.

CHAPTER 8
OF THE PRAYER WHICH FOLLOWS THE PSALM

THAT PRACTICE TOO WHICH WE HAVE OBSERVED IN THIS country — viz., that while one sings. to the end of the Psalm, all standing up stag together with a loud voice, "Glory be to the Father and to the Son and to the Holy Ghost" — we have never heard anywhere throughout " the East, but there, while all keep silence when the Psalm is finished, the prayer that follows is offered up by the singer. But with this hymn in honor of the Trinity only the whole Psalmody is usually ended.

CHAPTER 9
OF THE CHARACTERISTICS OF THE PRAYER, THE FULLER TREATMENT OF WHICH IS RESERVED FOR THE CONFERENCES OF THE EIDERS

AND AS THE PLAN OF THESE INSTITUTES LEADS US TO THE system of the canonical prayers, the fuller treatment of which we will however reserve for the Conferences of the Elders (where we shall speak of them at greater length when we have begun to tell in their own words of the character of their prayers, and how continuous they are), still I think it well, as far as the place and my narrative permit, as the occasion offers itself, to glance briefly for the present at a few points, so that by picturing in the meanwhile the movements of the outer man, and by now laying the foundations, as it were, of the prayer, we may afterwards, when we come to speak of the inner man, with less labor build up the complete edifice of his prayers; providing, above all for this, that if the end of life should overtake us and cut us off from finishing the narration which we are anxious (D.V.) fitly to compose, we may at least leave in this work the beginnings of so necessary a matter to you, to whom everything seems a delay, by reason of the fervor of your desire: so that, if a few more years of life are granted to us, we may at least mark out for you some outlines of their prayers, that those above all who live in monasteries may have some information about them; providing also, at the same time, that those who perhaps may meet only with this book, and be unable to procure the other, may find that they are supplied with some sort of information about the nature of their prayers; and as they are instructed about the dress and clothing of the outer man, so too they may not be ignorant what his behavior ought to be in offering spiritual sacrifices. Since, though these books, which we are now arranging with the Lord's help to write, are mainly taken up with what belongs to the outer man and the customs of the Coenobia, yet those will rather be concerned with the training of the inner man and the perfection of the heart, and the life and doctrine of the Anchorites.

CHAPTER 10
OF THE SILENCE AND CONCISENESS WITH WHICH THE COLLECTS ARE OFFERED UP BY THE EGYPTIANS

WHEN, THEN, THEY MEET TOGETHER TO CELEBRATE THE aforementioned rites, which they term synaxes, they are all so perfectly silent that, though so large a number of the brethren is assembled together, you would not think a single person was present except the one who stands up and chants the Psalm in the midst; and especially is this the case when the prayer is offered up, for then there is no spitting, no clearing of the throat, or noise of coughing, no sleepy yawning with open mouths, and gaping, and no groans or sighs are uttered, likely to distract those standing near. No voice is beard save that of the priest concluding the prayer, except perhaps one that escapes the lips through aberration of mind and unconsciously takes the heart by surprise, inflamed as it is with an uncontrollable and irrepressible fervor of spirit, while that which the glowing mind is unable to keep to itself strives through a sort of unutterable groaning to make its escape from the inmost chambers of the breast. But if any one infected with coldness of mind prays out loud or emits any of those sounds we have mentioned, or is overcome by a fit of yawning, they declare that he is guilty of a double fault. He is blameworthy, first, as regards his own prayer because he offers it to God in a careless way; and, secondly, because by his unmannerly noise he disturbs the thoughts of another who would otherwise perhaps have been able to pray with greater attention. And so their rule is that the prayer ought to be brought to an end with a speedy conclusion, lest while we are lingering over it some superfluity of spittle or phlegm should interfere with the close of our prayer. And, therefore, while it is still glowing the prayer is to be snatched as speedily as possible out of the jaws of the enemy, who, although he is indeed always hostile to us, is yet never more hostile than when he sees that we are anxious to offer up prayers to God against his attacks; and by exciting wandering thoughts and all sorts of rheums he endeavors to distract our minds from attending to our prayers, and by this means tries to make it grow cold, though begun with fervor. Wherefore they think it best for the prayers to be short and offered up very frequently: on the one hand that by so often praying to the Lord we may be able to cleave to Him continually; on the other, that when the devil is lying in wait for us, we may by their terse brevity avoid the darts with which he endeavors to wound us especially when we are saying our prayers,

CHAPTER 11
OF THE SYSTEM ACCORDING TO WHICH THE PSALMS ARE SAID AMONG THE EGYPTIANS.

AND, THEREFORE, THEY DO NOT EVEN ATTEMPT TO FINISH the Psalms, which they sing in the service, by an unbroken and continuous recitation. But they repeat them separately and bit by bit, divided into two or three sections, according to the number of verses, with prayers in between. For they do not care about the quantity of verses, but about the intelligence of the mind; aiming with all their might at this: "I will sing with the spirit: I will sing also with the understanding." And so they consider it better for ten verses to be sung with understanding and thought than for a whole Psalm to be poured forth with a bewildered mind. And this is sometimes caused by the hurry of the speaker, when, thinking of the character and number of the remaining Psalms to be sung, he takes no pains to make the meaning clear to his hearers, but hastens on to get to the end of the service. Lastly, if any of the younger monks, either through fervor of spirit or because he has not yet been properly taught, goes beyond the proper limit of what is to be sung, the one who is singing the Psalm is stopped by the senior clapping his hands where he sits in his stall, and making them all rise for prayer. Thus they take every possible care that no weariness may creep in among them as they sit through the length of the Psalms, as thereby not only would the singer himself lose the fruits of understanding, but also loss would be incurred by those whom he made to feel the service a weariness by going on so long. They also observe this with the greatest care; viz., that no Psalm should be said with the response of Alleluia except those which are marked with the inscription of Alleluia in their title. But the aforesaid number of twelve Psalms they divide in such a way that. if there are two brethren they each sing six; if there are three, then four; and if four, three each. A smaller number than this they never sing in the congregation, and accordingly, however large a congregation is assembled, not more than four brethren sing in the service.

CHAPTER 12

OF THE REASON WHY WHILE ONE SINGS THE PSALMS THE REST SIT DOWN DURING THE SERVICE; AND OF THE ZEAL WITH WHICH THEY AFTERWARDS PROLONG THEIR VIGILS IN THEIR CELLS TILL DAYBREAK

THIS CANONICAL SYSTEM OF TWELVE PSALMS, OF WHICH we have spoken, they render easier by such bodily rest that when, after their custom, they celebrate these services, they all, except the one who stands up in the midst to recite the Psalms, sit in very low stalls and follow the voice of the singer with the utmost attention of heart. For they are so worn out with fasting and working all day and night that, unless they were. helped by some such indulgence, they could not possibly get through this number standing up. For they allow no time to pass idly without the performance of some work, because not only do they strive with all earnestness to do with their hands those things which can be done in daylight, but also with anxious minds they examine into those sorts of work which not even the darkness of night can put a stop to, as they hold that they will gain a far deeper insight into subjects of spiritual contemplation With purity of heart, the more earnestly that they devote themselves to work and labor. And therefore they consider that a moderate allowance of canonical prayers was divinely arranged in order that for those who are very ardent in faith room might be left in which their never-tiring flow of virtue might spend itself, and notwithstanding no loathing arise in their wearied and weak bodies from too large a quantity. And so, when the offices of the canonical prayers have been duly finished, every one returns to his own cell (which he inhabits alone, or is allowed to share with only one other whom partnership in work or training in discipleship and learning has joined with him, or perhaps similarity of character has made his companion), and again they offer with greater earnestness the same service of prayer, as their special private sacrifice, as it were; nor do any of them give themselves up any further to rest and sleep till when the brightness of day comes on the labors of the day succeed the labors and meditations of the night.

CHAPTER 13
THE REASON WHY THEY ARE NOT ALLOWED TO GO TO SLEEP AFTER THE NIGHT SERVICE.

AND THESE LABORS THEY KEEP UP FOR TWO REASONS, besides this consideration, — that they believe that when they are diligently exerting themselves they are offering to God a sacrifice of the fruit of their hands. And, if we are aiming at perfection; we also ought to observe this with the same diligence. First, lest our envious adversary, jealous of our purity against which he is always plotting, and ceaselessly hostile to us, should by some illusion in a dream pollute the purity which has been gained by the Psalms and prayers of the night: for after that satisfaction which we have offered for our negligence and ignorance, and the absolution implored with profuse sighs in our confession, he anxiously tries, if he finds some time given to repose, to defile us; then above all endeavoring to overthrow and weaken our trust in God when he sees by the purity of our prayers that we are making most fervent efforts towards God: so that sometimes, when he has been unable to injure some the whole night long, he does his utmost to disgrace them in that short hour. Secondly, because, even if no such dreaded illusion of the devil arises, even a pure sleep in the interval produces laziness in the case of the monk who ought soon to wake up; and, bringing on a sluggish torpor in the mind, it dulls his vigor throughout the whole day, and deadens that keenness of perception and exhausts that energy of heart which would be capable of keeping us all day long more watchful against all the snares of the enemy and more robust. Wherefore to the Canonical Vigils them are added these private watchings, and they submit to them with the greater care, both in order that the purity which has been gained by Psalms and prayers may not be lost, and also that a more intense carefulness to guard us diligently through the day may be secured beforehand by the meditation of the night.

CHAPTER 14
OF THE WAY IN WHICH THEY DEVOTE THEMSELVES IN THEIR CELLS EQUALLY TO MANUAL LABOR AND TO PRAYER

AND THEREFORE THEY SUPPLEMENT THEIR PRAYER BY THE addition of labor, lest slumber might steal upon them as idlers. For as they scarcely enjoy any time of leisure, so there is no limit put to their spiritual meditations. For practising equally the virtues of the body and of the soul, they balance what is due to the outer by what is profitable to the inner man steadying the slippery motions of the heart and the shifting fluctuations of the thoughts by the weight of labor, like some strong and immoveable anchor, by which the changeableness and wanderings of the heart, fastened within the barriers of the cell, may be shut up in some perfectly secure harbour, and so, intent only on spiritual meditation and watchfulness over the thoughts, may not only forbid the watchful mind to give a hasty consent to any evil suggestions, but may also keep it safe from any unnecessary and idle thoughts: so that it is not easy to say which depends on the other — I mean, whether they practice their incessant manual labor for the sake of spiritual meditation, or whether it is for the sake of their continuous labors that they acquire such remarkable spiritual proficiency and light of knowledge.

CHAPTER 15
OF THE DISCREET RULE BY WHICH EVERY ONE MUST RETIRE TO HIS CELL AFTER THE CLOSE OF THE PRAYERS; AND OF THE REBUKE TO WHICH ANY ONE WHO DOES OTHERWISE IS SUBJECT

AND SO, WHEN THE PSALMS ARE FINISHED, AND THE DAILY assembly, as we said above, is broken up, none of them dares to loiter ever so little or to gossip with another: nor does he presume even to leave his cell throughout the whole day, or to forsake the work which he is wont to carry on in it, except when they happen to be called out for the performance of some necessary duty, which they fulfill by going out of doors so that there may not be any chattering at all among them. But every one does the work assigned to him in such a way that, by repeating by heart some Psalm or passage of Scripture, he gives no opportunity or time for dangerous schemes or evil designs, or even for idle talk, as both mouth and heart are incessantly taken up with spiritual meditations. For they are most particular in observing this rule, that none of them, and especially of the younger ones, may be caught stopping even for a moment or going anywhere together with another, or holding his hands in his. But, if they discover any who in defiance of the discipline of this rule have perpetrated any of these forbidden things, they pronounce them guilty of no slight fault, as contumacious and disobedient to the rules; nor are they free from suspicion of plotting and nefarious designs. And, unless they expiate their fault by public penance when all the brethren are gathered together, none of them is allowed to be present at the prayers of the brethren.

CHAPTER 16
HOW NO ONE IS ALLOWED TO PRAY WITH ONE WHO HAS BEEN SUSPENDED FROM PRAYER

FURTHER, IF ONE OF THEM HAS BEEN SUSPENDED FROM prayer for some fault which he has committed, no one has any liberty of praying with him before he performs his penance on the ground, and reconciliation and pardon for his offense has been publicly granted to him by the Abbot before all the brethren. For by a plan of this kind they separate and cut themselves off from fellowship with him in prayer for this reason — because they believe that one who is suspended from prayer is, as the Apostle says, "delivered unto Satan:" and if any one, moved by an ill-considered affection, dares to hold communion with him in prayer before he has been received by the Elder, he makes himself partaker of his damnation, and delivers himself up of his own free will to Satan, to whom the other had been consigned for the correction of his guilt. And in this he falls into a more grievous offense because, by uniting with him in fellowship either in talk or in prayer, he gives him grounds for still greater arrogance, and only encourages and makes worse the obstinacy of the offender. For, by giving him a consolation that is only hurtful, he will make his heart still harder, and not let him humble himself for the fault for which he was excommunicated; and through this he will make him hold the Elder's rebuke as of no consequence, and harbour deceitful thoughts about satisfaction and absolution.

CHAPTER 17
HOW HE WHO ROUSES THEM FOR PRAYER OUGHT TO CALL THEM AT THE USUAL TIME.

BUT HE WHO HAS BEEN ENTRUSTED WITH THE OFFICE OF summoning the religious assembly and with the care of the service should not presume to rouse the brethren for their daily vigils irregularly, as he pleases, or as he may wake up in the night, or as the accident of his own sleep or sleeplessness may incline him. But, although daily habit may constrain him to wake at the usual hour, yet by often and anxiously ascertaining by the course of the stars the right hour for service, he should summon them to the office of prayer, lest he be found careless in one of two ways: either if, overcome with sleep, he lets the proper hour of the night go by, or if, wanting to go to bed and impatient for his sleep, he anticipates it, and so may be thought to have secured is own repose instead of attending to the spiritual office and the rest of all the others.

CHAPTER 18
HOW THEY DO NOT KNEEL FROM THE EVENING OF SATURDAY TILL THE EVENING OF SUNDAY

THIS, TOO, WE OUGHT TO KNOW, — THAT FROM THE evening of Saturday which precedes the Sunday, up to the following evening, among the Egyptians they never kneel, nor from Easter to Whitsuntide; nor do they at these times observe a rule of fasting, the reason for which shall be Explained in its proper place in the Conferences of the Elders, if the Lord permits. At present we only propose to run through the causes very briefly, lest our book exceed its due limits and prove tiresome or burdensome to the reader.

BOOK 3

OF THE CANONICAL SYSTEM OF THE DAILY PRAYERS AND PSALMS

CHAPTER 1
OF THE SERVICES OF THE THIRD, SIXTH, AND NINTH HOURS, WHICH ARE OBSERVED IN THE REGIONS OF SYRIA

THE NOCTURNAL SYSTEM OF PRAYERS AND PSALMS AS observed throughout Egypt has been, I think, by God's help, explained so far as our slender ability was able; and now we must speak of the services of Tierce, Sext, and None, according to the rule of the monasteries of Palestine and Mesopotamia, as we said in the Preface, and must moderate by the customs of these the perfection and inimitable rigour of the discipline of the Egyptians.

CHAPTER 2
HOW AMONG THE EGYPTIANS THEY APPLY THEMSELVES ALL DAY LONG TO PRAYER AND PSALM CONTINUALLY, WITH THE ADDITION OF WORK, WITHOUT DISTINCTION OF HOURS

FOR AMONG THEM (VIZ., THE EGYPTIANS) THESE OFFICES which we are taught to render to the Lord at separate hours and at intervals of time, with a reminder from the converter, are celebrated continuously throughout the whole day, with the addition of work, and that of their own free will. For manual labor is incessantly practiced by them in their cells in such a way that meditation on the Psalms and the rest of the Scriptures is never entirely omitted. And as with it at every moment they mingle suffrages and prayers, they spend the whole day in those offices which we celebrate at fixed times. Wherefore, except Vespers and Nocturns, there are no public services among them in the day except on Saturday and Sunday, when they meet together at the third hour (or the purpose of Holy Communion. For that which is continuously offered is more than what is rendered at intervals of time; and more acceptable as a free gift than the duties which are performed by the compulsion of a rule: as David for this rejoices somewhat exultingly when he says, "Freely will I sacrifice unto Thee;" and, "Let the free will offerings of my mouth be pleasing to Thee, O Lord."

CHAPTER 3
HOW THROUGHOUT ALL THE EAST THE SERVICES OF TIERCE, SEXT, AND NONE ARE ENDED WITH ONLY THREE PSALMS AND PRAYERS EACH; AND THE REASON WHY THESE SPIRITUAL OFFICES ARE ASSIGNED MORE PARTICULARLY TO THOSE HOURS

AND SO IN THE MONASTERIES OF PALESTINE AND Mesopotamia and all the East the services of the above-mentioned hours are ended each day with three Psalms apiece, so that constant prayers may be offered to God at the appointed times, and yet, the spiritual duties being completed with due moderation, the necessary offices of work may not be in any way interfered with: for at these three seasons we know that Daniel the prophet also poured forth his prayers to God day by day in his chamber with the windows open. Nor is it without good reasons that these times are more particularly assigned to religious offices, since at them what completed the promises and summed up our salvation was fulfilled. For we can show that at the third hour the Holy Spirit, who had been of old promised by the prophets, descended in the first instance on the Apostles assembled together for prayer. For when in their astonishment at the speaking with tongues, which proceeded from them through the outpouring of the Holy Ghost upon them, the unbelieving people of the Jews mocked and said that they were full of new wine, then Peter, standing up in the midst of them, said: "Men of

Israel, and all ye who dwell at Jerusalem, let this be known unto you, and consider my words. For these men are not, as ye imagine, drunk, since it is the third hour of the day; but this is that which was spoken by the prophet Joel: and it shall come to pass in the last days, saith the Lord, I will pour out of my Spirit upon all flesh, and your sons and your daughters shall prophesy, and your young men shall see visions and your old men shall dream dreams. And indeed upon my servants and my handmaids in those days I will pour out of my Spirit, and they shall prophesy." And all of this was fulfilled at the third hour, when the Holy Spirit, announced before by the prophets, came at that hour and abode upon the Apostles. But at the sixth hour the spotless Sacrifice, our Lord and Savior, was offered up to the Father, and, ascending the cross for the salvation of the whole world, made atonement for the sins of mankind, and, despoiling principalities and powers, led them away openly; and all of us who were liable to death and bound by the debt of the handwriting that could not be paid, He freed, by taking it away out of the midst and affixing it to His cross for a trophy, At the same hour, too, to Peter, in an ecstasy of mind, there was divinely revealed both the calling of the Gentiles by the letting down of the Gospel vessel from heaven, and also the cleansing of all the living creatures contained in it, when a voice came to him and said to him: "Rise, Peter; kill and eat; " which vessel, let down from heaven by the four corners, is plainly seen to signify nothing else than the Gospel. For although, as it is divided by the fourfold narrative of the Evangelists, it seems to have "four corners" (or beginnings), yet the body of the Gospel is but one; embracing, as it does, the birth as well as the Godhead, and the miracles as well as the passion of one and the same Christ. Excellently, too, it says not "of linen" but "as if of linen." For linen signifies death. Since, then, our Lord's death and passion were not undergone by the law of human nature, but of His own free will, it says "as if of linen." For when dead according to the flesh He was not dead according to the spirit, because "His soul was not left in hell, neither did His flesh see corruption." And again He says: "No man taketh My life from Me but I lay it down of Myself. I have power to lay it down, and I have power to take it again." And so in this vessel of the Gospels let down from heaven, that is written by the Holy Ghost, all the nations which were formerly outside the observance of the law and reckoned as unclean now flow together through belief in the faith that they may to their salvation be turned away from the worship of idols and be serviceable for health-giving food, and are brought to Peter and cleansed by the voice of the Lord. But at the ninth hour, penetrating to hades, He there by the brightness of His splendor extinguished the indescribable darkness of hell, and, bursting its brazen gates and breaking the iron bars brought away with Him to the skies the captive band of saints which was there shut up and detained in the darkness of inexorable hell, and, by taking away the fiery sword, restored to paradise its original inhabitants by his pious confession. At the same hour, too, Cornelius, the centurion, continuing with his customary devotion in his prayers, is made aware through the converse of the angel with him that his prayers and alms are remembered before the Lord, and at the ninth hour the mystery of the calling of the Gentiles is clearly shown to him, which had been revealed to Peter in his ecstasy of mind at the sixth hour. In another passage, too, in the Acts of the Apostles, we are told as follows about the same time: "But Peter and John went up into the temple at the hour of prayer, the ninth hour." And by these notices it is clearly proved that these hours were not without good reason consecrated with religious services by holy and apostolic men, and ought to be observed in like manner by us, who, unless we are compelled, as it were, by some rule to discharge these pious offices at least at stated times, either through sloth or through forgetfulness, or being absorbed in business, spend the whole day without engaging in prayer. But concerning the evening sacrifices what is to be said, since even in the Old Testament these are ordered to be offered continually by the Law of Moses? For that the morning whole-burnt offerings and evening sacrifices were offered every day continually in the temple, although with figurative offerings, we can show from that which is sung by David: "Let my prayer be set forth in Thy sight as the incense, and let the lifting up of my hands be an evening sacrifice," in which place we can understand it in a still higher sense of that true evening sacrifice which was given by the Lord our Savior in the evening to the Apostles at the Supper, when He instituted the holy mysteries of the Church, and of that evening sacrifice which He Himself, on the following day, in the end of the ages, offered up to the Father by the lifting up of His hands for the salvation of the whole world; which spreading forth of His hands on the Cross is quite correctly called a "lifting up." For when we were all lying in hades He raised us to heaven, according to the word of His own promise when He says: "When I am lifted up from the earth, I will draw all men unto Me." But concerning Martins, that also teaches us which it is customary every day to sing at it: "O God, my God, to Thee do I watch at break of day;" and "I will meditate on Thee in the morning;" and "I prevented the dawning of the. day and cried;" and again, " Mine eyes to Thee have prevented the morning, that I might meditate on Thy words." At these hours too that householder in the Gospel hired laborers into his vineyard. For thus also is he described as having hired them in the early morning, which time denotes the Mattin office; then at the third hour; then at the sixth; after this, at the ninth; and last of all, at the eleventh, by which the hour of the lamps is denoted.

CHAPTER 4
HOW THE MATTIN OFFICE WAS NOT APPOINTED BY AN ANCIENT TRADITION BUT WAS STARTED IN OUR OWN DAY FOR A DEFINITE REASON.

BUT YOU MUST KNOW THAT THIS MATTINS, WHICH IS NOW very generally observed in Western countries, was appointed as a canonical office in our own day, and also in our own monastery, where our Lord Jesus Christ was born of a Virgin and deigned to submit to growth in infancy as man, and where by His Grace He supported our own infancy, still tender in religion, and, as it were, fed with milk. For up till that time we find that when this office of Mattins (which is generally celebrated after a short interval after the Psalms and prayers of Nocturns in the monasteries of Gaul) was finished, together with the daily vigils, the remaining hours were assigned by our Elders to bodily refreshment. But when some rather carelessly abused this indulgence and prolonged their time for sleep too long, as they were not obliged by the requirements of any service to leave their cells or rise from their beds till the third hour; and when, as well as losing their labor, they were drowsy from excess of sleep in the daytime, when they ought to have been applying themselves to some duties, (especially on those days when an unusually oppressive weariness was caused by their keeping watch from the evening till the approach of morning), a complaint was brought to the Elders by some of the brethren who were ardent in spirit and in no slight measure disturbed by this carelessness, and it was determined by them after long discussion and anxious consideration that up till sunrise, when they could without harm be ready to read or to undertake manual labor, time for rest should be given to their wearied bodies, and after this they should all be summoned to the observance of this service and should rise from their beds, and by reciting three Psalms and prayers (after the order anciently fixed for the observance of Tierce and Sext, to signify the confession of the Trinity) should at the same time by an uniform arrangement put an end to their sleep and make a beginning to their work. And this form, although it may seem to have arisen out of an accident and to have been appointed within recent memory for the reason given above, yet it clearly makes up according to the letter that number which the blessed David indicates (although it can be taken spiritually): "Seven times a day do I praise Thee because of Thy righteous judgments." For by the addition of this service we certainly hold these spiritual assemblies seven times a day, and are shown to sing praises to God seven times in it. Lastly, though this same form, starting from the East, has most beneficially spread to these parts, yet still in some long-established monasteries In the East, which will not brook the slightest violation of the old rules of the Fathers, it seems never to have been introduced.

CHAPTER 5
HOW THEY OUGHT NOT TO GO BACK TO BED AGAIN AFTER THE MATTIN PRAYERS.

BUT SOME IN THIS PROVINCE, NOT KNOWING THE REASON why this office was appointed and introduced, go back again to bed after their Mattin prayers are finished, and in spite of it fall into that very habit to check which our Elders instituted this service. For they are eager to finish it at that hour, that an opportunity maybe given, to those who are inclined to be indifferent and not careful enough, to go back to bed again, which most certainly ought not to be done (as we showed more fully in the previous book when describing the service of the Egyptians), for fear least the force of our natural passions should be aroused and stain that purity of ours which was gained by humble confession and prayers before the dawn, or some illusion of the enemy pollute us, or even the repose of a pure and natural sleep interfere with the fervor of our spirit and make us lazy and slothful throughout the whole day, as we are chilled by the sluggishness caused by sleep. And to avoid this the Egyptians, and especially as they are in the habit of rising at fixed times even before the cock-crow, when the canonical office has been celebrated, afterwards prolong their vigils even to daylight, that the morning light when it comes on them may find them established in fervor of spirit, and keep them still more careful and fervent all through the day, as it has found them prepared for the conflict and strengthened against their daily struggle with the devil by the practice of nocturnal vigils and spiritual meditation.

CHAPTER 6
HOW NO CHANGE WAS MADE BY THE ELDERS IN THE ANCIENT SYSTEM OF PSALMS WHEN THE MATTIN OFFICE WAS INSTITUTED

BUT THIS TOO WE OUGHT TO KNOW, VIZ., THAT NO CHANGE was made in the ancient arrangement of Psalms by our Elders who decided that this Mattin service should be added; but that office was always celebrated in their nocturnal assemblies according to the same order as it had been before. For the hymns which in this country they used at the Mattin service at the close of the nocturnal vigils, which they are accustomed to finish after the cock-crowing and before dawn, these they still sing in like manner; viz., Ps. 148, beginning "O praise the Lord from heaven," and the rest which follow; but the 50th Psalm and the 62nd, and the 89th have, we know, been assigned to this new service. Lastly, throughout Italy at this day, when the Mattin hymns are ended, the 50th Psalm is sung in all the churches, which I have no doubt can only have been derived from this source.

CHAPTER 7
HOW ONE WHO DOES NOT COME TO THE DAILY PRAYER BEFORE THE END OF THE FIRST PSALM IS NOT ALLOWED TO ENTER THE ORATORY; BUT AT NOCTURNS A LATE ARRIVAL UP TO THE END OF THE SECOND PSALM CAN BE OVERLOOKED

BUT ONE WHO AT TIERCE, SEXT, OR NONE HAS NOT COME to prayer before the Psalm is begun and finished does not venture further to enter the Oratory nor to join himself to those singing the Psalms; but, standing outside, he awaits the breaking-up of the congregation, and while they are all coming out does penance lying on the ground, and obtains absolution for his carelessness and lateness, knowing that he can in no other way expiate the fault of his sloth, nor can ever be admitted to the service which will follow three hours later, unless he has been quick to make satisfaction at once for his present negligence by the help of true humility. But in the nocturnal assemblies a late arrival up to the second Psalm is allowed, provided that before the Psalm is finished and the brethren bow down in prayer he makes haste to take his place in the congregation and join them; but he will most certainly be subjected to the same blame and penance which we mentioned before if he has delayed ever so little beyond the hour permitted for a late arrival.

CHAPTER 8

OF THE VIGIL SERVICE WHICH IS CELEBRATED ON THE EVENING PRECEDING THE SABBATH; OF ITS LENGTH, AND THE MANNER IN WHICH IT IS OBSERVED

IN THE WINTER TIME, HOWEVER, WHEN THE NIGHTS ARE longer, the Vigils, which are celebrated every week on the evening at the commencing the Sabbath, are arranged by the elders in the monasteries to last till the fourth cock-crowing, for this reason, viz., that after the watch through the whole night they may, by resting their bodies for the remaining time of nearly two hours, avoid flagging through drowsiness the whole day long, and be content with repose for this short time instead of resting the whole night. And it is proper for us, too, to observe this with the utmost care, that we may be content with the sleep which is allowed us after the office of Vigils up to daybreak, — i.e., till the Mattin Psalms, — and afterwards spend the whole day in work and necessary duties, lest through weariness from the Vigils, and feebleness, we might be forced to take by day the sleep which we cut off from the night, and so be thought not to have cut short our bodily rest so much as to have changed our time for repose and nightly retirement. For our feeble flesh could not possibly be defrauded of the whole night's rest and yet keep its vigor unshaken throughout the following day without sleepiness of mind and heaviness of spirit, as it will be hindered rather than helped by this unless after Vigils are over it enjoys a short slumber. And, therefore, if, as we have suggested, at least an hour's sleep is snatched before daybreak, we shall save all the hours of Vigils which we have spent all through the night in prayer, granting to nature what is due to it, and having no necessity of taking back by day what we have cut off from the night. For a man will certainly have to give up everything to this flesh if he tries, not in a rational manner to withhold a part only, but to refuse the whole, and (to speak candidly) is anxious to cut off not what is superfluous but what is necessary. Wherefore Vigils have to be made up for with greater interest if they are prolonged with ill-considered and unreasonable length till daybreak. And so they divide them into an office in three parts, that by this variety the effort may be distributed and the exhaustion of the body relieved by some agreeable relaxation. For when standing they have sung three Psalms antiphonally, after this, sitting on the ground or in very low stalls, one of them repeats three Psalms, while the rest respond, each Psalm being assigned to one of the brethren, who succeed each other in turn; and to these they add three lessons while still sitting quietly. And so, by lessening their bodily exertion, they manage to observe their Vigils with greater attention of mind.

CHAPTER 9

THE REASON WHY A VIGIL IS APPOINTED AS THE SABBATH DAY DAWNS, AND WHY A DISPENSATION FROM FASTING IS ENJOYED ON THE SABBATH ALL THROUGH THE EAST

AND THROUGHOUT THE WHOLE OF THE EAST IT HAS BEEN settled, ever since the time of the preaching of the Apostles, when the Christian faith and religion was founded, that these Vigils should be celebrated as the Sabbath dawns, for this reason, — because, when our Lord and Savior had been crucified on the sixth day of the week, the disciples, overwhelmed by the freshness of His sufferings, remained watching throughout the whole night, giving no rest or sleep to their eyes. Wherefore, since that time, a service of Vigils has been appointed for this night, and is still observed in the same way up to the present day all through the East. And so, after the exertion of the Vigil, a dispensation from fasting, appointed in like manner for the Sabbath by apostolic men, is not without reason enjoined in all the churches of the East, in accordance with that saying of Ecclesiastes, which, although it has another and a mystical sense, is not misapplied to this, by which we are charged to give to both days — that is, to the seventh and eighth equally— the same share of the service, as it says: "Give a portion to these seven and also to these eight." For this dispensation from fasting must not be understood as a participation in the Jewish festival by those above all who are shown to be free from all Jewish superstition, but as contributing to that rest of the wearied body of which we have spoken; which, as it fasts continually for five days in the week all through the year, would easily be worn out and fail, unless it were revived by an interval of at least two days.

CHAPTER 10

HOW IT WAS BROUGHT ABOUT THAT THEY FAST ON THE SABBATH IN THE CITY.

BUT SOME PEOPLE IN SOME COUNTRIES OF THE WEST, AND especially in the city, not knowing the reason of this indulgence, think that a dispensation from fasting ought certainly not to be allowed On the Sabbath, because they say that on this day the Apostle Peter fasted before his encounter with Simon. But from this it is quite clear that he did this not in accordance with a canonical rule, but rather through the needs of his impending struggle. Since there, too, for the same purpose, Peter seems to have imposed on his disciples not a general but a special fast, which he certainly would not have done if he had known that it was wont to be observed by canonical rule: just as he would surely have been ready to appoint it even on Sunday, if the occasion of his struggle had fallen upon it: but no canonical rule of fasting would have been made general from this, because it was no general observance that led to it, but a matter of necessity, which forced it to be observed on a single occasion

CHAPTER 11

OF THE POINTS IN WHICH THE SERVICE HELD ON SUNDAY DIFFERS FROM WHAT IS CUSTOMARY ON OTHER DAYS

BUT WE OUGHT TO KNOW THIS, TOO, THAT ON SUNDAY ONLY one office is celebrated before dinner, at which, out of regard for the actual service and the Lord's communion, they use a more solemn and a longer service of Psalms and prayers and lessons, and so consider that Tierce and Sext are included in it. And hence it results that, owing to the addition of the lessons, there is no diminution of the amount of their devotions, and yet some difference is made, and an indulgence over other times seems to be granted to the brethren out of reverence for the Lord's resurrection; and this seems to lighten the observance all through the week, and, by reason of the difference which is interposed, it makes the day to be looked forward to more solemnly as a festival, and owing to the anticipation of it the fasts of the coming week are less felt. For any weariness is always borne with greater equanimity, and labor undertaken without aversion, if some variety is interposed or change of work succeeds.

CHAPTER 12

OF THE DAYS ON WHICH, WHEN SUPPER IS PROVIDED FOR THE BRETHREN, A PSALM IS NOT SAID AS THEY ASSEMBLE FOR THE MEALS AS IS USUAL AT DINNER

LASTLY, ALSO, ON THOSE DAYS, — I.E., ON SATURDAY AND Sunday, — and on holy days, on which it is usual for both dinner and supper to be provided for the brethren, a Psalm is not said in the evening, either when they come to supper or when they rise from it, as is usual at their ordinary dinner and the canonical refreshment on fast days, which the customary Psalms usually precede and follow. But they simply make a plain prayer and come to supper, and again, when they rise from it, conclude with prayer alone; because this repast is something special among the monks: nor are they all obliged to come to it, but it is only for strangers who have come to see the brethren, and those whom bodily weakness or their own inclination invites to it.

BOOK 4

OF THE INSTITUTES OF THE RENUNCIANTS

CHAPTER 1

OF THE TRAINING OF THOSE WHO RENOUNCE THIS WORLD, AND OF THE WAY IN WHICH THOSE ARE TAUGHT AMONG THE MONKS OF TABENNA AND THE EGYPTIANS WHO ARE RECEIVED INTO THE MONASTERIES,

FROM THE CANONICAL SYSTEM OF PSALMS AND PRAYERS which ought to be observed in the daily services throughout the monasteries, we pass, in the due course of our narrative, to the training. of one who renounces this world endeavoring first, as well as we can, to embrace, in a short account, the terms on which those who desire to turn to the Lord can be received in the monasteries; adding some things from the rule of the Egyptians, some from that of the monks of Tabenna, whose monastery in the Thebaid is better filled as regards numbers, as it is stricter in the rigour of its system, than all others, for there are in it more than five thousand brethren under the rule of one Abbot; and the obedience with which the whole number of monks is at all times subject to one Elder is what no one among us would render to another even for a short time, or would demand from him.

CHAPTER 2

OF THE WAY IN WHICH AMONG THEM MEN REMAIN IN THE MONASTERIES EVEN TO EXTREME OLD AGE

AND I THINK THAT BEFORE ANYTHING ELSE WE OUGHT TO touch on their untiring perseverance and humility and subjection, — how it lasts for so long, and by what system it is formed, through which they remain in the monasteries till they are bent double with old age; for it is so great that we cannot recollect any one who joined our monasteries keeping it up unbroken even for a year: so that when we have seen the beginning of their renunciation of the world, we shall understand how it came about that, starting from such a commencement, they reached such a height of perfection.

CHAPTER 3
OF THE ORDEAL BY WHICH ONE WHO IS TO BE RECEIVED IN THE MONASTERY IS TESTED

ONE, THEN, WHO SEEKS TO BE ADMITTED TO THE DISCIPLINE of the monastery is never received before he gives, by lying outside the doors for ten days or even longer, an evidence of his perseverance and desire, as well as of humility and patience. And when, prostrate at the feet of all the brethren that pass by, and of set purpose repelled and scorned by all of them, as if he was wanting to enter the monastery not for the sake of religion but because he was obliged; and when, too, covered with many insults and affronts, he has given a practical proof of his steadfastness, and has shown what he will be like in temptations by the way he has borne the disgrace; and when, with the ardor of his soul thus ascertained, he is admitted, then they enquire with the utmost care whether he is contaminated by a single coin from his former possessions clinging to him. For they know that he cannot stay for long under the discipline of the monastery, nor ever learn the virtue of humility and obedience, nor be content with the poverty and difficult life of the monastery, if he knows that ever so small a sum of money has been kept hid; but, as soon as ever a disturbance arises on some occasion or other, he will at once dart off from the monastery like a stone from a sling, impelled to this by trusting in that sum of money.

CHAPTER 4
THE REASON WHY THOSE WHO ARE RECEIVED IN THE MONASTERY ARE NOT ALLOWED TO BRING ANYTHING IN WITH THEM

AND FOR THESE REASONS THEY DO NOT AGREE TO TAKE from him money to be used even for the good of the monastery: First, in case he may be puffed up with arrogance, owing to this offering, and so not deign to put himself on a level with the poorer brethren; and next, lest he fail through this pride of his to stoop to the humility of Christ, and so, when he cannot hold out under the discipline of the monastery, leave it, and afterwards, when he has cooled down, want in a bad spirit to receive and get back — not without loss to the monastery — what he had contributed in the early days of his renunciation, when he was aglow with spiritual fervor. And that this rule should always be kept they have been frequently taught by many instances. For in some monasteries where they are not so careful some who have been received unreservedly have afterwards tried most sacrilegiously to demand a return of that which they had contributed and which had been spent on God's work.

CHAPTER 5
THE REASON WHY THOSE WHO GIVE UP THE WORLD, WHEN THEY ARE RECEIVED IN THE MONASTERIES, MUST LAY ASIDE THEIR OWN CLOTHES AND BE CLOTHED IN OTHERS BY THE ABBOT

WHEREFORE EACH ONE ON HIS ADMISSION IS STRIPPED of all his former possessions, so that he is not allowed any longer to keep even the clothes which he has on his back: but in the council of the brethren he is brought forward into the midst and stripped of his own clothes, and clad by the

Abbot's hands in the dress of the monastery, so that by this he may know not only that he has been despoiled of all his old things, but also that he has laid aside all worldly pride, and come down to the want and poverty of Christ, and that he is now to be supported not by wealth sought for by the world's arts, nor by anything reserved from his former state of unbelief, but that he is to receive out of the holy and sacred funds of the monastery his rations for his service; and that, as he knows that he is thence to be clothed and fed and that he has nothing of his own, he may learn, nevertheless, not to be anxious about the morrow, according to the saying of the Gospel, and may not be ashamed to be on a level with the poor, that is with the body of the brethren, with whom Christ was not ashamed to be numbered, and to call him-self their brother, but that rather he may glory that he has been made to share the lot of his own servants.

CHAPTER 6
THE REASON WHY THE CLOTHES OF THE RENUNCIANTS WITH WHICH THEY JOINED THE MONASTERY ARE PRESERVED BY THE STEWARD

BUT THOSE CLOTHES, WHICH HE LAID ASIDE, ARE CONSIGNED to the care of the steward and kept until by different sorts of temptations and trials they can recognize the excellence of his progress and life and endurance. And if they see that he can continue therein as time goes on, and remain in that fervor with which he began, they give them away to the poor. But if they find that he has been guilty of any fault of murmuring, or of even the smallest piece of disobedience, then they strip off from him the dress of the monastery in which he had been clad, and reclothe him in his old garments which had been confiscated, and send him away. For it is not right for him to go away with those which he had received, nor do they allow anyone to be any longer dressed in them if they have seen him once grow cold in regard to the rule of their institution. Wherefore, also, the opportunity of going out openly is not given to any one, unless he escapes like a runaway slave by taking advantage of the thickest shades of night, or is judged unworthy of this order and profession and lays aside the dress of the monastery and is expelled with shame and disgrace before all the brethren.

CHAPTER 7
THE REASON WHY THOSE WHO ARE ADMITTED TO A MONASTERY ARE NOT PERMITTED TO MIX AT ONCE WITH THE CONGREGATION OF THE BRETHREN, BUT ARE FIRST COMMITTED TO THE GUEST HOUSE

WHEN, THEN, ANY ONE HAS BEEN RECEIVED AND PROVED by that persistence of which we have spoken, and, laying aside his own garments, has been clad in those of the monastery, he is not allowed to mix at once with the congregation of the brethren, but is given into the charge of an Elder, who lodges apart not far from the entrance of the monastery, and is entrusted with the care of strangers and guests, and bestows all his diligence in receiving them kindly. And when he has served there for a whole year without any complaint, and has given evidence of service towards strangers, being thus initiated in the first rudiments of humility and patience, and by long practice in it acknowledged, when he is to be admitted from this into the congregation of the brethren he is handed over to another Elder, who is placed over ten of the juniors, who are entrusted to him by the Abbot, and whom he both teaches and governs in accordance with the arrangement which we read of in Exodus as made by Moses.

CHAPTER 8
OF THE PRACTICES IN WHICH THE JUNIORS ARE FIRST EXERCISED THAT THEY MAY BECOME PROFICIENT IN OVERCOMING ALL THEIR DESIRES

AND HIS ANXIETY AND THE CHIEF PART OF HIS INSTRUCTION — through which the juniors brought to him may be able in due course to mount to the greatest heights of perfection — will be to teach him first to conquer his own wishes; and, anxiously and diligently practising him in this, he will of set purpose contrive to give him such orders as he knows to be contrary to his liking; for, taught by many examples, they say that a monk, and especially the younger ones, cannot bridle the desire of his concupiscence unless he has first learnt by obedience to mortify his wishes. And so the lay it down that the man who has not first learnt to overcome his desires cannot possibly stamp out anger or sulkiness, or the spirit of fornication; nor can he preserve true humility of heart, or lasting unity with the brethren, or a stable and continuous concord; nor remain for any length of time in the monastery.

CHAPTER 9
THE REASON WHY THE JUNIORS ARE ENJOINED NOT TO KEEP BACK ANY OF THEIR THOUGHTS FROM THE SENIOR.

BY THESE PRACTICES, THEN, THEY HASTEN TO IMPRESS AND instruct those whom they are training with the alphabet, as it were, and first syllables in the direction of perfection, as they can clearly see by these whether they are grounded in a false and imaginary or in a true humility. And, that they may easily arrive at this, they are next taught not to conceal by a false shame any itching thoughts in their hearts, but, as soon as ever such arise, to lay them bare to the senior, and, in forming a judgment about them, not trust anything to their own discretion, but to take it on trust that that is good or bad which is considered and pronounced so by the examination of the senior. Thus it results that our cunning adversary cannot in any way circumvent a young and inexperienced monk, or get the better of his ignorance, or by any craft deceive one whom he sees to be protected not by his own discretion but by that of his senior, and who cannot be persuaded to hide from his senior those suggestions of his which like fiery darts he has shot into his heart; since the devil, subtle as he is, cannot ruin or destroy a junior unless he has enticed him either through pride or through shame to conceal his thoughts. For they lay it down as an universal and clear proof that a thought is from the devil if we are ashamed to disclose it to the senior.

CHAPTER 10

HOW THOROUGH IS THE OBEDIENCE OF THE JUNIORS EVEN IN THOSE THINGS WHICH ARE MATTERS OF COMMON NECESSITY

NEXT, THE RULE IS KEPT WITH SUCH STRICT OBEDIENCE THAT, without the knowledge and permission of their superior, the juniors not only do not dare to leave their cell but on their own authority do not venture to satisfy their common and natural needs. And so they are quick to fulfill without any discussion all those things that are ordered by him, as if they were commanded by God from heaven; so that sometimes, when impossibilities are commanded them, they undertake them with such faith and devotion as to strive with all their powers and without the slightest hesitation to fulfill them and carry them out; and out of reverence for their senior they do not even consider whether a command is an impossibility. But of their obedience I omit at present to speak more particularly, for we propose to speak of it in the proper place a little later on, with instances of it, if through your prayers the Lord carry us safely through. We now proceed to the other regulations, passing over all account of those which cannot be imposed on or kept in the monasteries in this country, as we promised to do in our Preface; for instance, how they never use woollen garments, but only cotton, and these not double, changes of which each superior gives out to the ten monks under his care when he sees that those which they are wearing are dirty.

CHAPTER 11

THE KIND OF FOOD WHICH IS CONSIDERED THE GREATER DELICACY BY THEM

I PASS OVER, TOO, THAT DIFFICULT AND SUBLIME SORT OF self-control, through which it is considered the greatest luxury if the plant called cherlock, prepared with salt and steeped in water, is set on the table for the repast of the brethren; and many other things like this, which in this country neither the climate nor the weakness of our constitution would permit. And I shall only follow up those matters which cannot be interfered with by any weakness of the flesh or local situation, if only no weakness of mind or coldness of spirit gets rid of them.

CHAPTER 12

HOW THEY LEAVE OFF EVERY KIND OF WORK AT THE SOUND OF SOME ONE KNOCKING AT THE DOOR, IN THEIR EAGERNESS TO ANSWER AT ONCE,

AND SO, SITTING IN THEIR CELLS AND DEVOTING THEIR energies equally to work and to meditation, when they hear the sound of some one knocking at the door and striking on the cells of each, summoning them to prayer or some work, every one eagerly dashes out from his cell, so that one who is practising the writer's art, although he may have just begun to form a letter, does not venture to finish it, but runs out with the utmost speed, at the very moment when the sound of the knocking reaches his ears, without even waiting to finish the letter he has begun; but, leaving the lines of the letter incomplete, he aims not at abridging and saving his labor, but rather hastens with the utmost earnestness and zeal to attain the virtue of obedience, which they put not merely before manual labor and reading and silence and quietness in the cell, but even before all virtues, so that they consider that everything should be postponed to it, and are content to undergo any amount of inconvenience if only it may be seen that they have in no way neglected this virtue.

CHAPTER 13
HOW WRONG IT IS CONSIDERED FOR ANY ONE TO SAY THAT ANYTHING, HOWEVER TRIFLING, IS HIS OWN.

AMONG THEIR OTHER PRACTICES I FANCY THAT IT IS unnecessary even to mention this virtue, viz., that no one is allowed to possess a box or basket as his special property, nor any such thing which he could keep as his own and secure with his own seal, as we are well aware that they are in all respects stripped so bare that they have nothing whatever except their shirt, cloak, shoes, sheepskin, and rush mat; for in other monasteries as well, where some indulgence and relaxation is granted, we see that this rule is still most strictly kept, so that no one ventures to say even in word that anything is his own: and it is a great offense if there drops from the mouth of a monk such an expression as "my book," " my tablets," " my pen," " my coat," or "my shoes;" and for this he would have to make satisfaction by a proper penance, if by accident some such expression escaped his lips through thoughtlessness or ignorance.

CHAPTER 14
HOW, EVEN IF A LARGE SUM OF MONEY IS AMASSED BY THE LABOR OF EACH, STILL NO ONE MAY VENTURE TO EXCEED THE MODERATE LIMIT OF WHAT IS APPOINTED AS ADEQUATE

AND ALTHOUGH EACH ONE OF THEM MAY BRING IN DAILY BY his work and labor so great a return to the monastery that he could out of it not only satisfy his own moderate demands but could also abundantly supply the wants of many, yet he is no way puffed up, nor does he flatter himself on account of his toil and this large gain from his labor, but, except two biscuits, which are sold there for scarcely threepence, no one thinks that he has a right to anything further. And among them there is nothing (and I am ashamed to say this, and heartily wish it was unknown in our own monasteries) which is claimed by any of them, I will not say in deed but even in thought, as his special property. And though he believes that the whole granary of the monastery forms his substance, and, as Lord of all, devotes his whole care and energy to it all, yet nevertheless, in order to maintain that excellent state of want and poverty which he has secured and which he strives to preserve to the very last in unbroken perfection, he regards himself as a foreigner and an alien to them all, so that he conducts himself as a stranger and a sojourner in this world, and considers himself a pupil of the monastery and a servant instead of imagining that he is Lord and master of anything.

CHAPTER 15
OF THE EXCESSIVE DESIRE OF POSSESSION AMONG US

TO THIS WHAT SHALL WE WRETCHED CREATURES SAY, WHO though living in Coenobia and established under the government and care of an Abbot yet carry about our own keys, and trampling under foot all feeling of shame and disgrace which should spring from our profession, are not ashamed actually to wear openly upon our fingers rings with which to seal what we have stored up; and in whose case not merely boxes and baskets, but not even chests and closets are sufficient for those things which we collect or which we reserved when we forsook the world; and who sometimes get so angry over trifles and mere nothings (to which however we lay claim as if they were our own) that if any one dares to lay a finger on any of them, we are so filled with rage against him that we cannot keep the wrath of our heart from being expressed on our lips and in bodily excitement.

But, passing by our faults and treating with silence those things of which it is a shame even to speak, according to this saying: "My mouth shall not speak the deeds of men," let us in accordance with the method of our narration which we have begun proceed to those virtues which are practiced among them, and which we ought to aim at with all earnestness; and let us briefly and hastily set down the actual rules and systems that afterwards, coming to some of the deeds and acts of the elders which we propose carefully to preserve for recollection, we may support by the strongest testimonies what we have set forth in our treatise, and still further confirm everything that we have said by examples and instances from life.

CHAPTER 16
ON THE RULES FOR VARIOUS REBUKES

IF THEN ANY ONE BY ACCIDENT BREAKS AN EARTHENWARE jar (which they call "baucalis"), he can only expiate his carelessness by public penance; and when all the brethren are assembled for service he must lie on the ground and ask for absolution until the service of the prayers is finished; and will obtain it when by the Abbot's command he is bidden to rise from the ground. The same satisfaction must be given by one who when summoned to some work or to the usual service comes rather late, or who when singing a Psalm hesitates ever so little. Similarly if he answers unnecessarily or roughly or impertinently, if he is careless in carrying out the services enjoined to him, if he makes a slight complaint, if preferring reading to work or obedience he is slow in performing his appointed duties, if when service is over he does not make haste to go back at once to his cell, if he stops for ever so short a time with someone else, if he goes anywhere else even for a moment, if he takes anyone else by the hand, if he ventures to discuss anything however small with one who is not the joint-occupant of his cell, if he prays with one who is suspended from prayer, if he sees any of his relations or friends in the world and talks with them without his senior, if he tries to receive a letter from any one or to write back without his Abbot's leave.

To such an extent does spiritual censure proceed and in such matters and faults like these. But as for other things which when indiscriminately committed among us are treated by us too as blameworthy, viz.: open wrangling, manifest contempt, arrogant contradictions, going out from the monastery freely and without check, familiarity with women, wrath, quarrelling, jealousies, disputes, claiming something as one's own property, the infection of covetousness, the desire and acquisition of unnecessary things which are not possessed by the rest of the brethren, taking food between meals and by stealth, and things like these — they are dealt with not by that spiritual censure of which we spoke, but by stripes; or are atoned for by expulsion.

CHAPTER 17
OF THOSE WHO INTRODUCED THE PLAN THAT THE HOLY LESSONS SHOULD BE READ IN THE COENOBIA WHILE THE BRETHREN ARE EATING, AND OF THE STRICT SILENCE WHICH IS KEPT AMONG THE EGYPTIANS

BUT WE HAVE BEEN INFORMED THAT THE PLAN THAT, WHILE the brethren are eating, the holy lessons should be read in the Coenobia did not originate in the Egyptian system but in the Cappadocian. And there is no doubt that they meant to establish it not so much for the sake of the spiritual exercise as for the sake of putting a stop to unnecessary and idle conversation, and especially discussions, which so often arise at meals; since they saw that these could not be prevented among them in any other way. For among the Egyptians and especially those of Tabenna so strict a silence is observed by all that when so large a number of the brethren has sat down together to a meal, no one ventures to talk even in a low tone except the dean, who however if he sees that anything is wanted to be put on or taken off the table, signifies it by a sign rather than a word. And while they are eating, the rule of this silence is so strictly kept that with their hoods drawn down over their eyelids (to prevent their roving looks having the opportunity of wandering inquisitively) they can see nothing except the table, and the food that is put on it, and which they take from it; so that no one notices what another is eating.

CHAPTER 18
HOW IT IS AGAINST THE RULE FOR ANY ONE TO TAKE ANYTHING TO EAT OR DRINK EXCEPT AT THE COMMON TABLE.

IN BETWEEN THEIR REGULAR MEALS IN COMMON THEY ARE especially careful that no one should presume to gratify his palate with any food: so that when they are walking casually through gardens or orchards, when the fruit hanging enticingly on the trees not only knocks against their breasts as they pass through, but is also lying on the ground and offering itself to be trampled underfoot, and (as it is all ready to be gathered) would easily be able to entice those who see it to gratify their appetite, and by the chance offered to them and the quantity of the fruit, to excite even the most severe and abstemious to long for it; still they consider it wrong not merely to taste a single fruit, but even to touch one with the hand, except what is put on the table openly for the common meal of all, and supplied publicly by the steward's catering through the service of the brethren, for their enjoyment.

CHAPTER 19
HOW THROUGHOUT PALESTINE AND MESOPOTAMIA A DAILY SERVICE IS UNDERTAKEN BY THE BRETHREN.

IN ORDER THAT WE MAY NOT APPEAR TO OMIT ANY OF THE Institutes of the Coenobia I think that it should be briefly mentioned that in other countries as well there is a daily service undertaken by the brethren. For throughout the whole of Mesopotamia, Palestine, and Cappadocia and all the East the brethren succeed one another in turn every week for the performance of certain duties, so that the number serving is told off according to the whole number of monks in the Coenobium. And they hasten to fulfill these duties with a zeal and humility such as no slave bestows on his service even to a most harsh and powerful master; so that not satisfied only with these services which are rendered by canonical rule, they actually rise by night in their zeal and relieve those whose special duty this is; and secretly anticipating them try to finish those duties which these others would have to do. But each one who undertakes these weeks is on duty and has to serve until supper on Sunday, and when this is done, his duty for the whole week is finished, so that, when all the brethren come together to chant the Psalms (which according to custom they sing before going to bed) those whose turn is over wash the feet of all in turn, seeking faithfully from them the reward of this blessing for their work during the whole week, that the prayers offered up by all the brethren together may accompany them as they fulfill the command of Christ. The prayer, to wit, that intercedes for their ignorances and for their sins committed through human frailty, and may commend to God the complete service of their devotion like some rich offering. And so on Monday after the Martin hymns they hand over to others who take their place the vessels and utensils with which they have ministered, which these receive and keep with the utmost care and anxiety, that none of them may be injured or destroyed, as they believe that even for the smallest vessels they must give an account, as sacred things, not only to a present steward, but to the Lord, if by chance any of them is injured through their carelessness. And what limit there is to this discipline, and what fidelity and care there is in keeping it up, you may see from one instance which I will give as an example. For while we are anxious to satisfy that fervor of yours through which you ask for a full account of everything, and want even what you know perfectly well to be repeated to you in this treatise, we are also afraid of exceeding the limits of brevity.

CHAPTER 20
OF THE THREE LENTIL BEANS WHICH THE STEWARD FOUND

DURING THE WEEK OF A CERTAIN BROTHER THE STEWARD passing by saw lying on the ground three lentil beans which had slipped out of the hand of the monk on duty for the week as he was hastily preparing them for cooking, together with the water in which he was washing them; and immediately he consulted the Abbot on the subject; and by him the monk was adjudged a pilferer and careless about sacred property, and so was suspended from prayer. And the offense of his negligence was only pardoned when he had atoned for it by public penance. For they believe not only that they themselves are not their own, but also that everything that they possess is consecrated to the Lord. Wherefore if anything whatever has once been brought into the monastery they hold that it ought to be treated with the utmost reverence as a holy thing. And they attend to and arrange everything with great fidelity, even in the case of things which are considered unimportant or regarded as common and paltry, so that if they change their position and put them in a better place, or if they fill a bottle with water, or give anybody something to drink out of it, or if they remove a little dust from the oratory or from their cell they believe with implicit faith that they will receive a reward from the Lord.

CHAPTER 21
OF THE SPONTANEOUS SERVICE OF SOME OF THE BRETHREN

WE HAVE BEEN TOLD OF BRETHREN IN WHOSE WEEK THERE was such a scarcity of wood that they had not enough to prepare the usual food for the brethren; and when it had been ordered by the Abbot's authority that until more could be brought and fetched, they should content themselves with dried food, though this was agreed to by all and no one could expect any cooked food; still these men as if they were cheated of the fruit and reward of their labor and service, if they did not prepare the food for their brethren according to custom in the order of their turn — imposed upon themselves such uncalled-for labor and care that in those dry and sterile regions where wood cannot possibly be procured unless it is cut from the fruit trees (for there are no wild shrubs found there as with us), they wander about through the wide deserts, and traversing the wilderness which stretches towards the Dead Sea, collect in their lap and the folds of their dress the scanty stubble and brambles which the wind carries hither and thither, and so by their voluntary service prepare all their usual food for the brethren, so that they suffer nothing to be diminished of the ordinary supply; discharging these duties of theirs towards their brethren with such fidelity that though the scarcity of wood and the Abbot's order would be a fair excuse for them, yet still out of regard for their profit and reward they will not take advantage of this liberty.

CHAPTER 22

THE SYSTEM OF THE EGYPTIANS, WHICH IS APPOINTED FOR THE DAILY SERVICE OF THE BRETHREN

THESE THINGS HAVE BEEN TOLD IN ACCORDANCE WITH the system, as we remarked before, of the whole East, which also we say should be observed as a matter of course in our own country. But among the Egyptians whose chief care is for work there is not the mutual change of weekly service, for fear lest owing to the requirements of office they might all be hindered from keeping the rule of work. But one of the most approved brethren is given the care of the larder and kitchen, and he takes charge of that office for good and all as long as his strength and years permit. For he is exhausted by no great bodily labor, because no great care is expended among them in preparing food or in cooking, as they so largely make use of dried and uncooked food, and among them the leaves of leeks cut each month, and cherlock, table salt, olives, tiny little salt fish which they call sardines, form the greatest delicacy.

CHAPTER 23

THE OBEDIENCE OF ABBOT JOHN BY WHICH HE WAS EXALTED EVEN TO THE GRACE OF PROPHECY

AND SINCE THIS BOOK IS ABOUT THE TRAINING OF ONE who renounces this world, whereby, making a beginning of true humility and perfect obedience, he may be enabled to ascend the heights of the other virtues as well, I think it well to set down just by way of specimen, as we promised, some of the deeds of the elders whereby they excelled in this virtue, selecting a few only out of many instances, that, if any are anxious to aim at still greater heights, they may not only receive from these an incitement towards the perfect life, but may also be furnished with a model of what they purpose. Wherefore, to make this book as short as possible we will produce and set down two or three out of the whole number of the Fathers; and first of all Abbot John who lived near Lycon which is a town in the Thebaid; and who was exalted even to the grace of prophecy for his admirable obedience, and was so celebrated all the world over that he was by his merits rendered famous even among kings of this world. For though, as we said, he lived in the most remote parts of the Thebaid, still the Emperor Theodosius did not venture to declare war against the most powerful tyrants before he was encouraged by his utterances and replies: trusting in which as if they had been brought to him from heaven he gained victories over his foes in battles which seemed hopeless.

CHAPTER 24

OF THE DRY STICK WHICH, AT THE BIDDING OF HIS SENIOR, ABBOT JOHN KEPT ON WATERING AS IF IT WOULD GROW

AND SO THIS BLESSED JOHN FROM HIS YOUTH UP EVEN TO a full and ripe age of manhood was subject to his senior as long as he continued living in this world, and carried out his commands with such humility that his senior himself was utterly astounded at his obedience; and as he wanted to make sure whether this virtue came from genuine faith and profound simplicity of heart, or whether it was put on and as it were constrained and only shown in the presence of the bidder, he often laid upon him many superfluous and almost unnecessary or even impossible commands. From which I will select three to show to those who wish to know how perfect was his disposition and subjection. For the old man took from his woodstack a stick which had previously been cut and got ready to make the fire with, and which, as no opportunity for cooking had come, was lying not merely dry but even mouldy from the lapse of time. And when he had stuck it into the ground before his very eyes, he ordered him to fetch water and to water it twice a day that by this daily watering it might strike roots and be restored to life as a tree, as it was before, and spread out its branches and afford a pleasant sight to the eyes as well as a shade for those who sat under it in the heat of summer. And this order the lad received with his customary veneration, never considering its impossibility, and day by day carried it out so that he constantly carried water for nearly two miles and never ceased to water the stick; and for a whole year no bodily infirmity, no festival services, no necessary business (which might fairly have excused him from carrying out the command), and lastly no severity of winter could interfere and hinder him from obeying this order. And when the old man had watched this zeal of his on the sly without saying anything for several days and had seen that he kept this command of his with simple willingness of heart, as if it had come from heaven, without any change of countenance or consideration of its reasonableness — approving the unfeigned obedience of his humility and at the same time commiserating his tedious labor which in the zeal of his devotion he had continued for a whole year — he came to the dry stick, and "John," said he, "has this tree put forth roots or no?" And when the other said that he did not know, then the old man as if seeking the truth of the matter and trying whether it was yet depending on its roots, pulled up the stick before him with a slight disturbance of the earth, and throwing it away told him that for the future he might stop watering it.

CHAPTER 25
OF THE UNIQUE VASE OF OIL THROWN AWAY BY ABBOT JOHN AT HIS SENIOR'S COMMAND.

THUS THE YOUTH, TRAINED UP BY EXERCISES OF THIS SORT, daily increased in this virtue of obedience, and shone forth more and more with the grace of humility; and when the sweet odour of his obedience spread throughout all the monasteries, some of the brethren, coming to the older for the sake of testing him or rather of being edified by him, marvelled at his obedience of which they had heard; and so the older called him suddenly, and said, "Go up and take this cruse of oil" (which was the only one in the desert and which furnished a very scanty supply of the rich liquid for their own use and for that of strangers) "and throw it down out of window." And he flew up stairs when summoned and threw it out of window and cast it down to the ground and broke it in pieces without any thought or consideration of the folly of the command, or their daily wants, and bodily infirmity, or of their poverty, and the trials and difficulties of the wretched desert in which, even if they had got the money for it, oil of that quality, once lost, could not be procured or replaced.

CHAPTER 26

HOW ABBOT JOHN OBEYED HIS SENIOR BY TRYING TO ROLL A HUGE STONE, WHICH A LARGE NUMBER OF MEN WERE UNABLE TO MOVE

AGAIN, WHEN SOME OTHERS WERE ANXIOUS TO BE EDIFIED by the example of his obedience, the elder called him and said: "John, run and roll that stone hither as quickly as possible;" and he forthwith, applying now his neck, and now his whole body, tried with all his might and main to roll an enormous stone which a great crowd of men would not be able to move, so that not only were his clothes saturated with sweat from his limbs, but the stone itself was wetted by his neck; in this too never weighing the impossibility of the command and deed, out of reverence for the old man and the unfeigned simplicity of his service, as he believed implicitly that the old man could not command him to do anything vain or without reason.

CHAPTER 27
OF THE HUMILITY AND OBEDIENCE OF ABBOT PATERMUCIUS, WHICH HE DID NOT HESITATE TO MAKE PERFECT BY THROWING HIS LITTLE BOY INTO THE RIVER AT THE COMMAND OF HIS SENIOR

SO FAR LET IT SUFFICE FOR ME TO HAVE TOLD A FEW THINGS out of many concerning Abbot John: now I will relate a memorable deed of Abbot Patermucius. For he, when anxious to renounce the world, remained lying before the doors of the monastery for a long time until by his dogged persistence he induced them — contrary to all the rules of the Coenobia — to receive him together with his little boy who was about eight years old. And when they were at last admitted they were at once not only committed to the care of different superiors, but also put to live in separate cells that the father might not be reminded by the constant sight of the little one that out of all his possessions and carnal treasures, which he had cast off and renounced, at least his son remained to him; and that as he was already taught that he was no longer a rich man, so he might also forget the fact that he was a father. And that it might be more thoroughly tested whether he would make affection and love for his own flesh and blood of more account than obedience and Christian mortification (which all who renounce the world ought out of love to Christ to prefer), the child was on purpose neglected and dressed in rags instead of proper clothes; and so covered and disfigured with dirt that he would rather disgust than delight the eyes of his father whenever he saw him. And further, he was exposed to blows and slaps from different people, which the father often saw inflicted without the slightest reason on his innocent child under his very eyes, so that he never saw his cheeks without their being stained with the dirty marks of tears. And though the child was treated thus day afterday before his eyes, yet still out of love for Christ and the virtue of obedience the father's heart stood firm and unmoved. For he no longer regarded him as his own son, as he had offered him equally with himself to Christ; nor was he concerned about his present injuries, but rather rejoiced because he saw that they were endured, not without profit; thinking little of his son's tears, but anxious about his own humility and perfection. And when the Superior of the Coenobium saw his steadfastness of mind and immovable inflexibility, in order thoroughly to prove the constancy of his purpose, one day when he had seen the child crying, he pretended that he was annoyed with him and told the father to throw him into the river.

Then he, as if this had been commanded him by the Lord, at once snatched up the child as quickly as possible, and carried him in his arms to the river's bank to throw him in. And straightway in the fervor of his faith and obedience this would have been carried out in act, had not some of the brethren been purposely set to watch the banks of the river very carefully, and when the child was thrown in, had somehow snatched him from the bed of the stream, and prevented the command, which was really fulfilled by the obedience and devotion of the father, from being consummated in act and result.

CHAPTER 28

HOW IT WAS REVEALED TO THE ABBOT CONCERNING PATERMUCIUS THAT HE HAD DONE THE DEED OF ABRAHAM; AND HOW WHEN THE SAME ABBOT DIED, PATERMUCIUS SUCCEEDED TO THE CHARGE OF THE MONASTERY

AND THIS MAN'S FAITH AND DEVOTION WAS SO ACCEPTABLE to God that it was immediately approved by a divine testimony. For it was forthwith revealed to the Superior that by this obedience of his he had copied the deed of the patriarch

Abraham. And when shortly afterwards the same Abbot of the monastery departed out of this life to Christ, he preferred him to all the brethren, and left him as his successor and as Abbot to the monastery.

CHAPTER 29

OF THE OBEDIENCE OF A BROTHER WHO AT THE ABBOT'S BIDDING CARRIED ABOUT IN PUBLIC TEN BASKETS AND SOLD THEM BY RETAIL

WE WILL ALSO NOT BE SILENT ABOUT A BROTHER WHOM WE knew, who belonged to a high family according to the rank of this world, for he was sprung from a father who was a count and extremely wealthy, and had been well brought up with a liberal education. This man, when he had left his parents and fled to the monastery, in order to prove the humility of his disposition and the ardor of his faith was at once ordered by his superior to load his shoulders with ten baskets (which there was no need to sell publicly), and to hawk them about through the streets for sale: this condition being attached, so that he might be kept longer at the work, viz.: that if anyone should chance to want to buy them all together, he was not to allow it, but was to sell them to purchasers separately. And this he carried out with the utmost zeal, and trampling under foot all shame and confusion, out of love for Christ, and for His Name's sake, he put the baskets on his shoulders and sold them by retail at the price fixed and brought back the money to the monastery; not in the least upset by the novelty of so mean and unusual a duty, and paying no attention to the indignity of the thing and the splendor of his birth, and the disgrace of the sale, as he was aiming at gaining through the grace of obedience that humility of Christ which is the true nobility.

CHAPTER 30

OF THE HUMILITY OF ABBOT PINUFIUS, WHO LEFT A VERY FAMOUS COENOBIUM OVER WHICH HE PRESIDED AS PRESBYTER, AND OUT OF THE LOVE OF SUBJECTION SOUGHT A DISTANT MONASTERY WHERE HE COULD BE RECEIVED AS A NOVICE

THE LIMITS OF THE BOOK COMPEL US TO DRAW TO A CLOSE; but the virtue of obedience, which holds the first place among other good qualities, will not allow us altogether to pass over in silence the deeds of those who have excelled by it. Wherefore aptly combining these two together, I mean, consulting brevity as well as the wishes and profit of those who are in earnest, we will only add one example of humility, which, as it was shown by no novice but one already perfect and an Abbot, may not only instruct the younger, but also incite the elders to the perfect virtue of humility, as they read it. Thus we saw Abbot Pinufius who when he was presbyter of a huge Coenobium which is in Egypt not far from the city of Panephysis, was held in honor and respect by all men out of reverence either for his life or for his age or for his priesthood; and when he saw that for this reason he could not practice that humility which he longed for with all the ardor of his disposition, and had no opportunity of exercising the virtue of subjection which he desired, he fled secretly from the Coenobium and withdrew alone into the furthest parts of the Thebaid, and there laid aside the habit of the monks and assumed a secular dress, and thus sought the Coenobium of Tabenna, which he knew to be the strictest of all, and in which he fancied that he would not be known owing to the distance of the spot, or else that he could easily lie hid there in consequence of the size of the monastery and the number of brethren. There he remained for a long time at the entrance, and as a suppliant at the knees of the brethren sought with most earnest prayers to gain admission. And when he was at last with much scorn admitted as a feeble old man who had lived all his life in the world, and had asked in his old age to be allowed to enter a Coenobium when he could no longer gratify his passions, — as they said that he was seeking this not for the sake of religion but because he was compelled by hunger and want, they gave him the care and management of the garden, as he seemed an old man and not specially fitted for any particular work. And this he performed under another and a younger brother who kept him by him as entrusted to him, and he was so subordinate to him, and cultivated the desired virtue of humility so obediently that he daily performed-with the utmost diligence not only everything that had to do with the care and management of the garden, but also all those duties which were looked on by the other as hard and degrading, and disagreeable. Rising also by night he did many things secretly, without anyone looking on or knowing it, when darkness concealed him so that no one could discover the author of the deed.

And when he had hidden himself there for three years and had been sought for high and low by the brethren all through Egypt, he was at last seen by one who had come from the parts of Egypt, but could scarcely be recognized owing to the meanness of his dress and the humble character of the duty he was performing. For he was stooping down and hoeing the ground for vegetables and bringing dung on his shoulders and laying it about their roots. And seeing this the brother for a long time hesitated about recognizing him, but at last he came nearer, and taking careful note not only of his looks but also of the tone of his voice, straightway fell at his feet: and at first all who saw it were struck with the greatest astonishment why he should do this to one who was looked up. on by them as the lowest of all, as being. a novice and one who had but lately forsaken the world: but afterwards they were struck with still greater wonder when he forthwith announced his name, which was one that had been well known amongst them also by repute. And all the brethren asking his pardon for their former ignorance because they had for so long classed him with the juniors and children, brought him back to his own Coenobium, against his will and in tears because by the envy of the devil he had been cheated out of a worthy mode of life and the humility which he was rejoicing in having discovered after his long search, and because he had not succeeded in ending his life in that state of subjection which he had secured. And so they guarded him with the utmost care lest he should slip away again in the same sort of way and escape from them also.

CHAPTER 31
HOW WHEN ABBOT PINUFIUS WAS BROUGHT BACK TO HIS MONASTERY HE STAYED THERE FOR A LITTLE WHILE AND THEN FLED AGAIN INTO THE REGIONS OF SYRIAN PALESTINE

AND WHEN HE HAD STOPPED THERE FOR A LITTLE WHILE, again he was seized with a longing and desire for humility, and, taking advantage of the silence of night, made his escape in such a way that this time he sought no neighboring district, but regions which were unknown and strange and separated by a wide distance. For embarking in a ship he managed to travel to Palestine, believing that he would more securely lie hid if he betook himself to those places in which his name had never been heard. And when he had come thither, at once he sought out our own monastery which was at no great distance from the cave in which our Lord vouchsafed to be born of a virgin. And though he concealed himself here for some time, yet like "a city set on an hill" (to use our Lord's expression) he could not long be hid. For presently some of the brethren who had come to the holy places from Egypt to pray there recognized him and recalled him with most fervent prayers to his own Coenobium.

CHAPTER 32
THE CHARGE WHICH THE SAME ABBOT PINUFIUS GAVE TO A BROTHER WHOM HE ADMITTED INTO HIS MONASTERY IN OUR PRESENCE

THIS OLD MAN, THEN, WE AFTERWARDS DILIGENTLY SOUGHT out in Egypt because we had been intimate with him in our own monastery; and I propose to insert in this work of mine an exhortation which he gave in our presence to a brother whom he admitted into the monastery, because I think that it may be useful. You know, said he, that after lying for so many days at the entrance you are to-day to be admitted. And to begin with you ought to know the reason of the difficulty put in your way. For it may be of great service to you in this road on which you are desirous to enter, if you understand the method of it and approach the service of Christ accordingly, and as you ought.

CHAPTER 33
HOW IT IS THAT, JUST AS A GREAT REWARD IS DUE TO THE MONK WHO LABORS ACCORDING TO THE REGULATIONS OF THE FATHERS, SO LIKEWISE PUNISHMENT MUST HE INFLICTED ON AN IDLE ONE; AND THEREFORE NO ONE SHOULD BE ADMITTED INTO A MONASTERY TOO EASILY

FOR AS UNBOUNDED GLORY HEREAFTER IS PROMISED TO those who faithfully serve God and cleave to Him according to the rule of this system; so the severest penalties are in store for those who have carried it out carelessly and coldly, and have failed to show to Him fruits of holiness corresponding to what they professed or what they were believed by men to be. For "it is better," as Scripture says, "that a man should not vow rather than that he should vow and not pay;" and "Cursed is he that doeth the work of the Lord carelessly." Therefore you were for a long while declined by us, not as if we did not des re with all our hearts to secure your salvation and the salvation of all, nor as if we did not care to go to meet even afar off those who are longing to be converted to Christ; but for fear lest if we received you rashly we might make ourselves guilty in the sight of God of levity, and make you incur a yet heavier punishment, if, when you had been too easily admitted by us without realizing the responsibility of this profession, you had afterwards turned out a deserter or lukewarm. Wherefore you ought in the first instance to learn the actual reason for the renunciation of the world, and when you have seen this, you can be taught more plainly what you ought to do, from the reason for it.

CHAPTER 34
OF THE WHY IN WHICH OUR RENUNCIATION IS NOTHING BUT MORTIFICATION AND THE IMAGE OF THE CRUCIFIED.

RENUNCIATION IS NOTHING BUT THE EVIDENCE OF THE cross and of mortification. And so you must know that to-day you are dead to this world and its deeds and desires, and that, as the Apostle says, you are crucified to this world and this world to you. Consider therefore the demands of the cross under the sign of which you ought henceforward to live in this life; because you no longer live but He lives in you who was crucified for you. We must therefore pass our time in this life in that fashion and form in which He was crucified for us on the cross so that (as David says) piercing our flesh with the fear of the Lord, we may have all our wishes and desires not subservient to our own lusts but fastened to His mortification. For so shall we fulfill the command of the Lord which says: "He that taketh not up his cross and followeth me is not worthy of me." But perhaps you will say: How can a man carry his cross continually? or how can anyone who is alive be crucified? Hear briefly how this is.

CHAPTER 35
HOW THE FEAR OF THE LORD IS OUR CROSS

THE FEAR OF THE LORD IS OUR CROSS. AS THEN ONE WHO IS crucified no longer has the power of moving or turning his limbs in any direction as he pleases, so we also ought to affix our wishes and desires — not in accordance with what is pleasant and delightful to us now, but in accordance with the law of the Lord, where it constrains us. And as he who is fastened to the wood of the cross no longer considers things present, nor thinks about his likings, nor is perplexed by anxiety and care for the morrow, nor disturbed by any desire of possession, nor inflamed by any pride or strife or rivalry, grieves not at present injuries, remembers not past ones, and while he is still breathing in the body considers that he is dead to all earthly things, sending the thoughts of his heart on before to that place whither he doubts not that he is shortly to come: so we also, when crucified by the fear of the Lord ought to be dead indeed to all these things, i.e. not only to carnal vices but also to all earthly things, having the eye of our minds fixed there whither we hope at each moment that we are soon to pass. For in this way we can have all our desires and carnal affections mortified.

CHAPTER 36
HOW OUR RENUNCIATION OF THE WORLD IS OF NO USE IF WE ARE AGAIN ENTANGLED IN THOSE THINGS WHICH WE HAVE RENOUNCED

BEWARE THEREFORE LEST AT ANY TIME YOU TAKE AGAIN any of those things which you renounced and forsook, and, contrary to the Lord's command, return from the field of evangelical work, and be found to have clothed yourself again in your coat which you had stripped off; neither sink back to the low and earthly lusts and desires of this world, and in defiance of Christ's word come down from the rod of perfection and dare to take up again any of those things which you have renounced and forsaken. Beware that you remember nothing of your kinsfolk or of your former affections, and that you are not called back to the cares and anxieties of this world, and (as our Lord says) putting your hand to the plough and looking back be found unfit for the kingdom of heaven. Beware lest at any time, when you have begun to dip into the knowledge of the Psalms and of this life, you be little by little puffed up and think of reviving that pride which now at your beginning you have trampled underfoot in the ardor of faith and in fullest humility; and thus (as the Apostle says) building again those things which you had destroyed, you make yourself a backslider. But rather take heed to continue even to the end in that state of nakedness of which you made profession in the sight of God and of his angels. In this humility too and patience, with which you persevered for ten days before the doors and entreated with many tears to be admitted into the monastery, you should not only continue but also increase and go forward. For it is too bad that when you ought to be carried on from the rudiments and beginnings, and go forward to perfection, you should begin to fall back from these to worse things. For not he who begins these things, but he who endures in them to the end, shall be saved.

CHAPTER 37

HOW THE DEVIL ALWAYS LIES IN WAIT FOR OUR END, AND HOW WE OUGHT CONTINUALLY TO WATCH HIS HEAD.

FOR THE SUBTLE SERPENT IS EVER "WATCHING OUR HEEL," that is, is lying in wait for the close, and endeavoring to trip us up right to the end of our life. And therefore it will not be of any use to have made a good beginning and to have eagerly taken the first step towards renouncing the world with all fervor, if a corresponding end does not likewise set it off and conclude it, and if the humility and poverty of Christ, of which you have now made profession in His sight, are not preserved by you even to the close of your life, as they were first secured. And that you may succeed in doing this, do you ever "watch his head," i.e. the first rise of thoughts, by bringing them at once to your superior. For thus you will learn to "bruise" his dangerous beginnings, if you are not ashamed to disclose any of them to your superior.

CHAPTER 38

OF THE RENUNCIANT'S PREPARATION AGAINST TEMPTATION, AND OF THE FEW WHO ARE WORTHY OF IMITATION.

WHEREFORE, AS SCRIPTURE SAYS, "WHEN YOU GO FORTH to serve the Lord stand in the fear of the Lord, and prepare your mind" not for repose or carelessness or delights, but for temptations and troubles. For "through much tribulation we must enter into the kingdom of God." For "strait is the gate and narrow is the way which leadeth unto life, and few there be which find it." Consider therefore that you belong to the few and elect; and do not grow cold after the examples of the lukewarmness of many: but live as the few, that with the few you may be worthy of a place in the kingdom of God: for "many are called, but few chosen, and it is a "little flock to which it is the Father's good pleasure to give" an inheritance. You should therefore realize that it is no light sin for one who has made profession of perfection to follow after what is imperfect. And to this state of perfection you may attain by the following steps and in the following way.

CHAPTER 39

OF THE WAY IN WHICH WE SHALL MOUNT TOWARDS PERFECTION, WHEREBY WE MAY AFTERWARDS ASCEND FROM THE FEAR OF GOD UP TO LOVE

"THE beginning" of our salvation and the safeguard of it is, as I said, "the fear of the Lord." For through this those who are trained in the way of perfection can gain a start in, conversion as well as purification from vices and security in virtue. And when this has gained an entrance into a man's heart it produces contempt of all things, and begets a forgetfulness of kinsfolk and a horror of the world itself. But by the contempt for the loss of all possessions humility is gained. And humility is attested by these signs: First of all if a man has all his desires mortified; secondly, if he conceals none of his actions or even of his thoughts from his superior; thirdly, if he puts no trust in his own opinion, but all in the judgment of his superior, and listens eagerly and willingly to his directions; fourthly, if he maintains in everything obedience and gentleness and constant patience; fifthly, if he not only hurts nobody else, but also is not annoyed or vexed at wrongs done to himself; sixthly, if he does nothing and ventures on nothing to which he is not urged by the Common Rule or by the example of our elders; seventhly, if he is contented with the lowest possible position, and considers himself as a bad workman and unworthy in the case of everything enjoined to him; eighthly, if he does not only outwardly profess with his lips that he is inferior to all, but really believes it in the inmost thoughts of his heart; ninthly, if he governs his tongue, and is not over talkative; tenthly, if he is not easily moved or too ready to laugh. For by such signs and the like is true humility recognised. And when this has once been genuinely secured, then at once it leads you on by a still higher step to love which knows no fear; and through this you begin, without any effort and as it were naturally, to keep up everything that you formerly observed not without fear of punishment; no longer now from regard of punishment or fear of it but from love of goodness itself, and delight in virtue.

CHAPTER 40
THAT THE MONK SHOULD SEEK FOR EXAMPLES OF PERFECTION NOT FROM MANY INSTANCES BUT FROM ONE OR A VERY FEW.

AND THAT YOU MAY THE MORE EASILY ARRIVE AT THIS, THE examples of the perfect life of one dwelling in the congregation, which you may imitate, should be sought from a very few or indeed from one or two only and not from too many. For apart from the fact that a life which is tested and refined and purified is only to be found in a few, there is this also to be gained, viz.: that a man is more thoroughly instructed and formed by the example of some one, towards the perfection which he sets before him, viz.: that of the Coenobite life

CHAPTER 41
THE APPEARANCE OF WHAT INFIRMITIES ONE WHO LIVES IN A COENOBIUM OUGHT TO EXHIBIT.

AND THAT YOU MAY BE ABLE TO ATTAIN ALL THIS, AND continually remain subject to this spiritual rule, you must observe these three things in the congregation: viz.: that as the Psalmist says: "I was like a deaf man and heard not and as one that is dumb who doth not open his mouth; and I became as a man that heareth not, and in whose mouth there are no reproofs," so you also should walk as one that is deaf and dumb and blind, so that — putting aside the contemplation of him who has been rightly chosen by you as your model of perfection — you should be like a blind man and not see any of those things which you find to be unedifying, nor be influenced by the authority or fashion of those who do these things, and give yourself up to what is worse and what you formerly condemned. If you hear any one disobedient or insubordinate or disparaging another or doing anything different from what was taught to you, you should not go wrong and be led astray by such an example to imitate him; but, "like a deaf man," as if you had never heard it, you should pass it all by. If insults are offered to you or to anyone else, or wrongs done, be immovable, and as far as an answer in retaliation is concerned be silent "as one that is dumb," always singing in your heart this verse of the Psalmist: "I said I will take heed to my ways that I offend not with my tongue. I set a guard to my mouth when the sinner stood before me. I was dumb and was humbled and kept silence from good things." But cultivate above everything this fourth thing which adorns and graces those three of which we have spoken above; viz.: make yourself, as the Apostle directs, a fool in this world that you may become wise, exercising no discrimination and judgment of your own on any of those matters which are commanded to you, but always showing obedience with all simplicity and faith, judging that alone to be holy, useful, and wise which God's law or the decision of your superior declares to you to be such. For built up on such a system of instruction you may continue forever under this discipline, and not fall away from the monastery in consequence of any temptations or devices of the enemy.

CHAPTER 42
HOW A MONK SHOULD NOT LOOK FOR THE BLESSING OF PATIENCE IN HIS OWN CASE AS A RESULT OF THE VIRTUE OF OTHERS, BUT RATHER AS A CONSEQUENCE OF HIS OWN LONGSUFFERING

YOU SHOULD THEREFORE NOT LOOK FOR PATIENCE IN YOUR own case from the virtue of others, thinking that then only can you secure it when you are not irritated by any (for it is not in your own power to prevent this from happening); but rather you should look for it as the consequence of your own humility and long-suffering which dues depend on your own will.

CHAPTER 43
RECAPITULATION OF THE EXPLANATION HOW A MONK CAN MOUNT UP TOWARDS PERFECTION

AND IN ORDER THAT ALL THESE THINGS WHICH HAVE BEEN set forth in a somewhat lengthy discourse may be more easily stamped on your heart and may stick in your thoughts with all tenacity, I will make a summary of them so that you may be able to learn all the changes by heart by reason of their brevity and conciseness. Hear then in few words how you can mount up to the heights of perfection without an effort or difficult "The beginning" of our salvation and of wisdom" is, according to Scripture, "the fear of the Lord." From the fear of the Lord arises salutary compunction. From compunction of heart springs renunciation, i.e. nakedness and contempt of all possessions. From nakedness is begotten humility; from humility the mortification of desires. Through mortification of desires all faults are extirpated and decay. By driving out faults virtues shoot up and increase. By the budding of virtues purity of heart is gained. By purity of heart the perfection of apostolic love is acquired.

BOOK 5

OF THE SPIRIT OF GLUTTONY

CHAPTER 1
THE TRANSITION FROM THE INSTITUTES OF THE MONKS TO THE STRUGGLE AGAINST THE EIGHT PRINCIPAL FAULTS

THIS FIFTH BOOK OF OURS IS NOW BY THE HELP OF GOD TO be produced. For after the four books which have been composed on the customs of the monasteries, we now propose, being strengthened by God through your prayers, to approach the struggle against the eight principal faults, i.e. first, Gluttony or the pleasures of the palate; secondly, Fornication; thirdly, Covetousness, which means Avarice, or, as it may more properly be called, the love of money, fourthly, Anger; fifthly, Dejection; sixthly, "Accidie," which is heaviness or weariness of heart; seventhly, κενοδοξία which means foolish or vain glory; eighthly, pride. And on entering upon this difficult task we need your prayers, O most blessed Pope Castor, more than ever; that we may be enabled in the first place worthily to investigate the nature of these in all points however trifling or hidden or obscure: and next to explain with sufficient clearness the causes of them and thirdly to bring forward fitly the cures and remedies for them.

CHAPTER 2
HOW THE OCCASIONS OF THESE FAULTS, BEING FOUND IN EVERYBODY, ARE IGNORED BY EVERYBODY; AND HOW WE NEED THE LORD'S HELP TO MAKE THEM PLAIN

AND OF THESE PASSIONS AS THE OCCASIONS ARE RECOGNIZED by everybody as soon as they are laid open by the teaching of the elders, so before they are revealed, although we are all overcome by them, and they exist in every one, yet nobody knows of them. But we trust that we shall be able in some measure to explain them, if by your prayers that word of the Lord, which was announced by Isaiah, may apply to us also — "I will go before thee, and bring low the mighty ones of the land, I will break the gates of brass, and cut asunder the iron bars, and I will open to thee concealed treasures and hidden secrets" — so that the word of the Lord may go before us also, and first may bring low the mighty ones of our land, i.e. these same evil passions which we are desirous to overcome, and which claim for themselves dominion and a most horrible tyranny in our mortal body; and may make them yield to our investigation and explanation, and thus breaking the gates of our ignorance, and cutting asunder the bars of vices which shut us out from true knowledge, may lead to the hiddenthings of our secrets, and reveal to us who have been illuminated, according to the Apostle's word, "the hidden things of darkness, and may make manifest the counsels of the hearts," that thus penetrating with pure eyes of the mind to the foul darkness of vices, we may be able to disclose them and drag them forth to light; and may succeed in explaining their occasions and natures to those who are either free from them, or are still tied and bound by them, and so passing as the prophet says, through the fire of vices which terribly inflame our minds, we may be able forthwith to pass also through the water of virtues which extinguish them unharmed, and being bedewed (as it were) with spiritual remedies may be found worthy to be brought in purity of heart to the consolations of perfection.

CHAPTER 3
HOW OUR FIRST STRUGGLE MUST BE AGAINST THE SPIRIT OF GLUTTONY, I.E. THE PLEASURES OF THE PALATE.

AND SO THE FIRST CONFLICT WE MUST ENTER UPON IS THAT against gluttony, which we have explained as the pleasures of the palate: and in the first place as we are going to speak of the system of fasts, and the quality of food, we must again recur to the traditions and customs of the Egyptians, as everybody knows that they contain a more advanced discipline in the matter of self-control, and a perfect method of discrimination.

CHAPTER 4
THE TESTIMONY OF ABBOT ANTONY IN WHICH HE TEACHES THAT EACH VIRTUE OUGHT TO BE SOUGHT FOR FROM HIM WHO PROFESSES IT IN A SPECIAL DEGREE

FOR IT IS AN ANCIENT AND EXCELLENT SAYING OF THE blessed Antony that when a monk is endeavoring after the plan of the monastic life to reach the heights of a more advanced perfection, and, having learned the consideration of discretion, is able now to stand in his own judgment, and to arrive at the very summit of the anchorite's life, he ought by no means to seek for all kinds of virtues from one man however excellent. For one is adorned with flowers of knowledge, another is more strongly fortified with methods of discretion, another is established in the dignity of patience, another excels in the virtue of humility, another in that of continence, another is decked with the grace of simplicity. This one excels all others in magnanimity, that one in pity, another in vigils, another in silence, another in earnestness of work. And therefore the monk who desires to gather spiritual honey, ought like a most careful bee, to suck out virtue from those who specially possess it, and should diligently store it up in the vessel of his own breast: nor should he investigate what any one is lacking in, but only regard and gather whatever virtue he has. For if we want to gain all virtues from some one person, we shall with great difficulty or perhaps never at all find suitable examples for us to imitate. For though we do not as yet see that even Christ is made "all things in all," as the Apostle says; still in this way we can find Him bit by bit in all. For it is said of Him, "Who was made of God to you wisdom and righteousness and sanctification and redemption." While then in one there is found wisdom, in another righteousness, in another sanctification, in another kindness, in another chastity, in another humility, in another patience, Christ is at the present time divided, member by member, among all of the saints. But when all come together into the unity of the faith and virtue, He is formed into the "perfect man," completing the fullness of His body, in the joints and properties of all His members. Until then that time arrives when God will be "all in all," for the present God can in the way of which we have spoken be "in all," through particular virtues, although He is not yet "all in all" through the fullness of them. For although our religion has but one end and aim, yet there are different ways by which we approach God, as will be more fully shown in the Conferences of the Elders. And so we must seek a model of discretion and continence more particularly from those from whom we see that those virtues flow forth more abundantly through the grace of the Holy Spirit; not that anyone can alone acquire those things which are divided among many, but in order that in those good qualities of which we are capable we may advance towards the imitation of those who especially have acquired them.

CHAPTER 5
THAT ONE AND THE SAME RULE OF FASTING CANNOT BE OBSERVED BY EVERYBODY.

AND SO ON THE MANNER OF FASTING A UNIFORM RULE CANNOT easily be observed, because everybody has not the same strength; nor is it like the rest of the virtues, acquired by steadfastness of mind alone. And therefore, because it does not depend only on mental firmness, since it has to do with the possibilities of the body, we have received this explanation concerning it which has been handed down to us, viz.: that there is a difference of time, manner, and quality of the refreshment in proportion to the difference of condition of the body, the age, and sex: but that there is one and the same rule of restraint to everybody as regards continence of mind, and the virtue of the spirit. For it is impossible for everyone to prolong his fast for a week, or to postpone taking refreshment during a two or three days' abstinence. By many people also who are worn out with sickness and especially with old age, a fast even up to sunset cannot be endured without suffering. The sickly food of moistened beans does not agree with everybody: nor does a sparing diet of fresh vegetables suit all, nor is a scanty meal of dry bread permitted to all alike. One man does not feel satisfied with two pounds, for another a meal of one pound, or six ounces, is too much; but there is one aim and object of continence in the case of all of these, viz.: that no one may be overburdened beyond the measure of his appetite, by gluttony. For it is not only the quality, but also the quantity of food taken which dulls the keenness of the mind, and when the soul as well as the flesh is surfeited, kindles the baneful and fiery incentive to vice.

CHAPTER 6
THAT THE MIND IS NOT INTOXICATED BY WINE ALONE

THE BELLY WHEN FILLED WITH ALL KINDS OF FOOD GIVES birth to seeds of wantonness, nor can the mind, when choked with the weight of food, keep the guidance and government of the thoughts. For not only is drunkenness with wine wont to intoxicate the mind, but excess of all kinds of food makes it weak and uncertain, and robs it of all its power of pure and clear contemplation. The cause of the overthrow and wantonness of Sodom was not drunkenness through wine, but fullness of bread. Hear the Lord rebuking Jerusalem through the prophet. "For how did thy sister Sodom sin, except in that she ate her bread in fullness and abundance?" And because through fullness of bread they were inflamed with uncontrollable lust of the flesh, they were burnt up by the judgment of God with fire and brimstone from heaven. But if excess of bread alone drove them to such a headlong downfall into sin through the vice of satiety, what shall we think of those who with a vigorous body dare to partake of meat and wine with unbounded licence, taking not just what their bodily frailty demands, but what the eager desire of the mind suggests.

CHAPTER 7
HOW BODILY WEAKNESS NEED NOT INTERFERE WITH PURITY OF HEART

BODILY WEAKNESS IS NO HINDRANCE TO PURITY OF HEART, if only so much food is taken as the bodily weakness requires, and not what pleasure asks for. It is easier to find men who altogether abstain from the more fattening kinds of foods than men who make a moderate use of what is allowed to our necessities; and men who deny themselves everything out of love of continence than men who taking food on the plea of weakness preserve the due measure of what is sufficient. For bodily weakness has its glory of self-restraint, where though food is permitted to the failing body, a man deprives himself of his refreshment. Although he needs it, and only indulges in just so much food as the strict judgment of temperance decides to be sufficient for the necessities of life, and not what the longing appetite asks for. The more delicate foods, as they conduce to bodily health, so they need not destroy the purity of chastity, if they are taken in moderation. For whatever strength is gained by partaking of them is used up in the toil and waste of car. Wherefore as no state of life can be deprived of the virtue of abstinence, so to none is the crown of perfection denied.

CHAPTER 8
HOW FOOD SHOULD BE TAKEN WITH REGARD TO THE AIM AT PERFECT CONTINENCE.

AND SO IT IS A VERY TRUE AND MOST EXCELLENT SAYING OF the Fathers that the right method of fasting and abstinence lies in the measure of moderation and bodily chastening; and that this is the aim of perfect virtue for all alike, viz.: that though we are still forced to desire it, yet we should exercise self-restraint in the matter of the food, which we are obliged to take owing to the necessity of supporting the body. For even if one is weak in body, he can attain to a perfect virtue and one equal to that of those who are thoroughly strong and healthy, if with firmness of mind he keeps a check upon the desires and lusts which are not due to weakness of the flesh. For the Apostle says: "And take not care for the flesh in its lusts." He does not forbid care for it in every respect: but says that care is not to be taken in regard to its desires and lusts. He cuts away the luxurious fondness for the flesh: he does not exclude the control necessary for life: he does the former, lest through pampering the flesh we should be involved in dangerous entanglements of the desires; the latter lest the body should be injured by our fault and unable to fulfill its spiritual and necessary duties.

CHAPTER 9
OF THE, MEASURE OF THE CHASTISEMENT TO BE UNDERTAKEN, AND THE REMEDY OF FASTING.

THE PERFECTION THEN OF ABSTINENCE IS NOT TO BE gathered from calculations of time alone, nor only from the quality of the food; but beyond everything from the judgment of conscience. For each one should impose such a sparing diet on himself as the battle of his bodily struggle may require. The canonical observance of fasts is indeed valuable and by all means to be kept. But unless this is followed by a temperate partaking of food, one will not be able to arrive at the goal of perfection. For the abstinence of prolonged fasts — where repletion of body follows — produces weariness for a time rather than purity and chastity. Perfection of mind indeed depends upon the abstinence of the belly. He has no lasting purity and chastity, who is not contented always to keep to a well-balanced and temperate diet. Fasting, although severe, yet if unnecessary relaxation follows, is rendered useless, and presently leads to the vice of gluttony. A reasonable supply of food partaken of daily with moderation, is better than a severe and long fast at intervals. Excessive fasting has been known not only to undermine the constancy of the mind, but also to weaken the power of prayers through sheer weariness of body.

CHAPTER 10
THAT ABSTINENCE FROM FOOD IS NOT OF ITSELF SUFFICIENT FOR PRESERVATION OF BODILY AND MENTAL PURITY

IS ORDER TO PRESERVE THE MIND AND BODY IN A PERFECT condition abstinence from food is not alone sufficient: unless the other virtues of the mind as well are joined to it. And so humility must first be learned by the virtue of obedience, and grinding toil and bodily exhaustion. The possession of money must not only be avoided, but the desire for it must be utterly rooted out. For it is not enough not to possess it — a thing which comes to many as a matter of necessity - but we ought, if by chance it is offered, not even to admit the wish to have it. The madness of anger should be controlled; the downcast look of dejection be overcome; vainglory should be despised, the disdainfulness of pride trampled underfoot, and the shifting and wandering thoughts of the mind restrained by continual recollection of God. And the slippery wanderings of our heart should be brought back again to the contemplation of God as often as our crafty enemy, in his endeavor to lead away the mind a captive from this consideration, creeps into the innermost recesses of the heart.

CHAPTER 11
THAT BODILY LUSTS ARE NOT EXTINGUISHED EXCEPT BY THE ENTIRE ROOTING OUT OF VICE

FOR IT IS AN IMPOSSIBILITY THAT THE FIERY MOTIONS OF THE body can be extinguished, before the incentives of the other chief vices are utterly rooted out: concerning which we will speak in their proper place, if God permits, separately, in different books. But now we have to deal with Gluttony, which is the desire of the palate, against which our first battle is. He then will never be able to check the motions of a burning lust, who cannot restrain the desires of the appetite. The chastity of the inner man is shown by the perfection of this virtue. For you will never feel sure that he can strive against the opposition of a stronger enemy, whom you have seen overcome by weaker ones in a higher conflict. For of all virtues the nature is but one and the same, although they appear to be divided into many different kinds and names: just as there is but one substance of gold, although it may seem to be distributed through many different kinds of jewelry according to the skill of the goldsmith. And so he is proved to possess no virtue perfectly, who is known to have broken down in some part of them. For how can we believe that that man has extinguished the burning heats of concupiscence (which are kindled not only by bodily incitement but by vice of the mind), who could not assuage the sharp stings of anger which break out from intemperance of heart alone? Or how can we think that he has repressed the wanton desires of the flesh and spirit, who has not been able to conquer the simple fault of pride? Or how can we believe that one has trampled underfoot a wantonness which is ingrained in the flesh, who has not been able to disown the love of money, which is something external and outside our own substance? In what way will he triumph in the war of flesh and spirit, who has not been man enough to cure the disease of dejection? However great a city may be protected by the height of its walls and the strength of its closed gates, yet it is laid waste by the giving up of one postern however small. For what difference does it make whether a dangerous foe makes his way into the heart of the city over high walls, and through the wide spaces of the gate, or through secret and narrow passages?

CHAPTER 12
THAT IN OUR SPIRITUAL CONTEST WE OUGHT TO DRAW AN EXAMPLE FROM THE CARNAL CONTESTS

"ONE WHO STRIVES IN THE GAMES IS NOT CROWNED UNLESS he has contended lawfully." One who wants to extinguish the natural desires of the flesh, should first hasten to overcome those vices whose seat is outside our nature. For if we desire to make trial of the force of the Apostle's saying, we ought first to learn what are the laws and what the discipline of the world's contest, so that finally by a comparison with these, we may be able to know what the blessed Apostle meant to teach to us who are striving in a spiritual contest by this illustration. For in these conflicts, which, as the same Apostle says, hold out "a corruptible crown" to the victors, this rule is kept, that he who aims at preparing himself for the crown of glory, which is embellished with the privilege of exemption, and who is anxious to enter the highest struggle in the contest, should first in the Olympic and Pythian games give evidence of his abilities as a youth, and his strength in its first beginnings; since in these the younger men who want to practice this training are tested as to whether they deserve or ought to be admitted to it, by the judgment both of the president of the games and of the whole multitude.

And when any one has been carefully tested, and has first been proved to be stained by no infamy of life, and then has been adjudged not ignoble through the yoke of slavery, and for this reason unworthy to be admitted to this training and to the company of those who practice it, and when thirdly he produces sufficient evidence of his ability and prowess and by striving with the younger men and his own compeers has shown both his skill and valor as a youth, and going forward from the contests of boys has been by the scrutiny of the president permitted to mix with full-grown men and those of approved experience, and has not only shown himself their equal in valor by constant striving with them, but has also many a time carried off the prize of victory among them, then at last he is allowed to approach the most illustrious conflict of the games, permission to contend in which is granted to none but victors and those who are decked with many crowns and prizes. If we understand this illustration from a carnal contest, we ought by a comparison with it to know what is the system and method of our spiritual conflict as well.

CHAPTER 13
THAT WE CANNOT ENTER THE BATTLE OF THE INNER MAN UNLESS WE HAVE BEEN SET FREE FROM THE VICE OF GLUTTONY

WE ALSO OUGHT FIRST TO GIVE EVIDENCE OF OUR FREEDOM from subjection to the flesh. For "of whom a man is overcome, of the same is he the slave." And "every one that doeth sin slave of sin." And when the scrutiny is the of the president of the contest finds that we are stained by no infamy of disgraceful lust, and when we are judged by him not to be slaves of the flesh, and ignoble and unworthy of the Olympic struggle against our vices, then we shall be able to enter the lists against our equals, that is the lusts of the flesh and the motions and disturbances of the soul. For it is impossible for a full belly to make trial of the combat of the inner man: nor is he worthy to be tried in harder battles, who can be overcome in a slight skirmish.

CHAPTER 14
HOW GLUTTONOUS DESIRES CAN BE OVERCOME

FIRST THEN WE MUST TRAMPLE UNDER FOOT GLUTTONOUS desires, and to this end the mind must be reduced not only by fasting, but also by vigils, by reading, and by frequent compunction of heart for those things in which perhaps it recollects that it has been deceived or overcome, sighing at one time with horror at sin, at another time inflamed with the desire of perfection and saintliness: until it is fully occupied and possessed by such cares and meditations, and recognizes the participation of food to be not so much a concession to pleasure, as a burden laid upon it; and considers it to be rather a necessity for the body than anything desirable for the soul. And, preserved by this zeal of mind and continual compunction, we shall beat down the wantonness of the flesh (which becomes more proud and haughty by being fomented with food) and its dangerous incitement, and so by the copiousness of our tears and the weeping of our heart we shall succeed in extinguishing the fiery furnace of our body, which is kindled by the Babylonish king who continually furnishes us with opportunities for sin, and vices with which we burn more fiercely, instead of naphtha and pitch — until, through the grace of God, instilled like dew by His Spirit in our hearts, the heats of fleshly lusts can be altogether deadened. This then is our first contest, this is as it were our first trial in the Olympic games, to extinguish the desires of the palate and the belly by the longing for perfection.

On which account we must not only trample down all unnecessary desire for food by the contemplation of the virtues, but also must take what is necessary for the support of nature, not without anxiety of heart, as if it were opposed to chastity. And so at length we may enter on the course of our life, so that there may be no time in which we feel that we are recalled from our spiritual studies, further than when we are obliged by the weakness of the body to descend for the needful care of it. And when we are subjected to this necessity — of attending to the wants of life rather than the desires, of the soul — we should hasten to withdraw as quickly as possible from it, as if it kept us back from really health-giving studies. For we cannot possibly scorn the gratification of food presented to us, unless the mind is fixed on the contemplation of divine things, and is the rather entranced with the love of virtue and the delight of things celestial. And so a man will despise all things present as transitory, when he has securely fixed his mental gaze on, those things which are immovable and eternal, and already contemplates in heart — though still in the flesh — the blessedness of his future life.

CHAPTER 15
HOW A MONK MUST ALWAYS BE EAGER TO PRESERVE HIS PURITY OF HEART

IT IS LIKE THE CASE WHEN ONE ENDEAVORS TO STRIKE SOME mighty prize of virtue on high. pointed out by some very small mark; with the keenest eyesight he points the aim of his dart, knowing that large rewards of glory and prizes depend on his hitting it; and he turns away his gaze from every other consideration, and must direct it thither, where he sees that the reward and prize is placed, because he would be sure to lose the prize of his skill and the reward of his prowess if the keenness of his gaze should be diverted ever so little.

CHAPTER 16

HOW, AFTER THE FASHION OF THE OLYMPIC GAMES, A MONK SHOULD NOT ATTEMPT SPIRITUAL CONFLICTS UNLESS HE HAS WON BATTLES OVER THE FLESH

AND SO WHEN THE DESIRES OF THE BELLY AND OF THE palate have been by these considerations overcome, and when we have been declared, as in the Olympic contests, neither slaves of the flesh nor infamous through the brand of sin, we shall be adjudged to be worthy of the contest in higher struggles as well, and, leaving behind lessons of this kind, may be believed capable of entering the lists against spiritual wickednesses, against which only victors and those who are allowed to contend in a spiritual conflict are deemed worthy to struggle. For this is so to speak a most solid foundation of all the conflicts, viz.: that in the first instance the impulses of carnal desires should be destroyed. For no one can lawfully strive unless his own flesh has been overcome. And one who does not strive lawfully certainly cannot take a share in the contest, nor win a crown of glory and the grace of victory. But if we have been overcome in this battle, having been proved as it were slaves of carnal lusts, and thus displaying the tokens neither of freedom nor of strength, we shall be straightway repulsed from the conflicts with spiritual hosts, as unworthy and as slaves, with every mark of confusion. For "every one that doeth sin is the servant of sin." And this will be addressed to us by the blessed Apostle, together with those among whom fornication is named. "Temptation does not overtake you, except such as is human." For if we do not seek for strength of mind we shall not deserve to make trial of severer contest against wickedness on high, if we have been unable to subdue our weak flesh which resists the spirit. And some not understanding this testimony of the Apostle, have read the subjunctive instead of the indicative mood, i.e.,

"Let no temptation overcome you, except such as is human." But it is clear that it is rather said by him with the meaning not of a wish but of a declaration or rebuke.

CHAPTER 17
THAT THE FOUNDATION AND BASIS OF THE SPIRITUAL COMBAT MUST BE LAID IN THE STRUGGLE AGAINST GLUTTONY

WOULD YOU LIKE TO HEAR A TRUE ATHLETE OF CHRIST striving according to the rules and laws of the conflict? "I," said he, "so run, not as uncertainly; I so fight, not as one that beateth the air: but I chastise my body and bring it into subjection, lest by any means when I have preached to others I myself should be a castaway." You see how he made the chief part of the struggle depend upon himself, that is upon his flesh, as if on a most sure foundation, and placed the result of the battle simply in the chastisement of the flesh and the subjection of his body. "I then so run not as uncertainly." He does not run uncertainly, because, looking to the heavenly Jerusalem, he has a mark set, towards which his heart is swiftly directed without swerving. He does not run uncertainly, because, "forgetting those things which are behind, he reaches forth to those that are before, pressing towards the mark for the prize of the high calling of God in Christ Jesus," whither he ever directs his mental gaze, and hastening towards it with all speed of heart, proclaims with confidence, "I have fought a good fight, I have finished my course, I have kept the faith." And because he knows he has run unweariedly "after the odour of the ointment" a of Christ with ready devotion of heart, and has won the battle of the spiritual combat by the chastisement of the flesh, he boldly concludes and says, "Henceforth there is laid up for me a crown of righteousness, which the Lord, the righteous judge, will give to me in that day." And that he might open up to us also a like hope of reward, if we desire to imitate him in the struggle of his course, he added: "But not to me only, but to all also who love His coming;" declaring that we shall be sharers of his crown in the day of judgment, if we love the coming of Christ — not that one only which will be manifest to men even against their will; but also this one which daily comes to pass in holy souls — and if we gain the victory in the fight by chastising the body. And of this coming it is that the Lord speaks in the Gospel. "I," says He, "and my Father will come to him, and will make our abode with him." And again: "Behold, I stand at the door and knock: if any man hear my voice and open the gate, I will come in to him and will sup with him, and he with me."

CHAPTER 18

OF THE NUMBER OF DIFFERENT CONFLICTS AND VICTORIES THROUGH WHICH THE BLESSED APOSTLE ASCENDED TO THE CROWN OF THE HIGHEST

BUT HE DOES NOT MEAN THAT HE HAS ONLY FINISHED THE contest of a race when he says "I so run, not as uncertainly" (a phrase which has more particularly to do with the intention of the mind and fervor of his spirit, in which he followed Christ with all zeal, crying out with the Bride, "We will run after thee for the odour of thine ointments;" and again, "My soul cleaveth unto thee:" but he also testifies that he has conquered in another kind of contest, saying, "So fight I, not as one that beateth the air, but I chastise my body and bring it into subjection." And this properly has to do with the pains of abstinence, and bodily fasting and affliction of the flesh: as he means by this that he is a vigorous bruiser of his own flesh, and points out that not in vain has he planted his blows of Continence against it; but that he has gained a battle triumph by mortifying his own body; for when it is chastised with the blows of continence and struck down with the boxing-gloves of fasting, he has secured for his victorious spirit the crown of immortality and the prize of incorruption. You see the orthodox method of the contest, and consider the issue of spiritual combats: how the athlete of Christ having gained a victory over the rebellious flesh, having cast it as it were under his feet, is carried forward as triumphing on high. And therefore "he does not run uncertainly," because he trusts that he will forthwith enter the holy city, the heavenly Jerusalem. He "so fights," that is with fasts and humiliation of the flesh, "not as one that beateth the air," that is, striking into space with blows of continence, through which he struck not the empty air, but those spirits who inhabit it, by the chastisement of his body. For one who says "not as one that beateth the air," shows that he strikes — not empty and void air, but certain beings in the air. And because he had overcome in this kind of contest, and marched on enriched with the rewards of many crowns, not undeservedly does he begin to enter the lists against still more powerful foes, and having triumphed over his former rivals, he boldly makes proclamation and says, "Now our striving is not against flesh and blood, but against principalities, against powers, against world-rulers of this darkness, against spiritual wickedness in heavenly places."

CHAPTER 19

THAT THE ATHLETE OF CHRIST, SO LONG AS HE IS IN THE BODY, IS NEVER WITHOUT A BATTLE

THE ATHLETE OF CHRIST, AS LONG AS HE IS IN THE BODY, is never in want of a victory to be gained in contests: but in proportion as he grows by triumphant successes, so does a severer kind of struggle confront him. For when the flesh is subdued and conquered, what swarms of foes, what hosts of enemies are incited by his triumphs and rise up against the victorious soldier of Christ! for fear lest in the ease of peace the soldier of Christ might relax his efforts and begin to forget the glorious struggles of his contests, and be rendered slack through the idleness which is caused by immunity from danger, and be cheated of the reward of his prizes and the recompense of his triumphs. And so if we want to rise with ever-growing virtue to these stages of triumph we ought also in the same way to enter the lists of battle and begin by saying with the Apostle: "I so fight, not as one that beateth the air, but I chastise my body and bring it into subjection," that when this conflict is ended we may once more be able to say with him: "we wrestle not against flesh and blood, but against principalities, against powers, against world-rulers of this darkness, against spiritual wickedness in heavenly places." For otherwise we cannot possibly join battle with them nor deserve to make trial of spiritual combats if we are baffled in a carnal contest, and smitten down in a struggle with the belly: and deservedly will it be said of us by the Apostle in the language of blame: "Temptation does not overtake you, except what is common to man."

CHAPTER 20

HOW A MONK SHOULD NOT OVERSTEP THE PROPER HOURS FOR TAKING FOOD, IF HE WANTS TO PROCEED TO THE STRUGGLE OF INTERIOR CONFLICTS

A MONK THEREFORE WHO WANTS TO PROCEED TO THE struggle of interior conflicts should lay down this as a precaution for himself to begin with: viz.: that he will not in any case allow himself to be overcome by any delicacies, or take anything to eat or drink before the fast is over and the proper hour for refreshment has come, outside meal times; nor, when the meal is over, will he allow himself to take a morsel however small; and likewise that he will observe the canonical time and measure of sleep. For that self-indulgence must be cut off in the same way that the sin of unchastity has to be rooted out. For if a man is unable to check the unnecessary desires of the appetite how will he be able to extinguish the fire of carnal lust? And if a man is not able to control passions, which are openly manifest and are but small, how will he be able with temperate discretion to fight against those which are secret, and excite him, when none are there to see? And therefore strength of mind is tested in separate impulses and in any sort of passion: and if it is overcome in the case of very small and manifest desires, how it will endure in those that are really great and powerful and hidden, each man's conscience must witness for himself.

CHAPTER 21
OF THE INWARD PEACE OF A MONK, AND OF SPIRITUAL ABSTINENCE

FOR IT IS NOT AN EXTERNAL ENEMY WHOM WE HAVE TO dread. Our foe is shut up within ourselves: an internal warfare is daily waged by us: and if we are victorious in this, all external things will be made weak, and everything will be made peaceful and subdued for the soldier of Christ. We shall have no external enemy to fear, if what is within is overcome and subdued to the spirit. And let us not believe that that external fast from visible food alon can possibly be sufficient for perfection of heart and purity of body unless with it there has also been united a fast of the soul. For the soul also has its foods which are harmful, fattened on which, even without superfluity of meats, it is involved in a downfall of wantonness. Slander is its food, and indeed one that is very dear to it. A burst of anger also is its food, even if it be a very slight one; yet supplying it with miserable food for an hour, and destroying it as well with its deadly savor. Envy is a food of the mind, corrupting it with its poisonous juices and never ceasing to make it wretched and miserable at the prosperity and success of another. Kenodoxia, i.e., vainglory is its food, which gratifies it with a delicious meal for a time; but afterwards strips it clear and bare of all virtue, and dismisses it barren and void of all spiritual fruit, so that it makes it not only lose the rewards of huge labors, but also makes it incur heavier punishments. All lust and shifty wanderings of heart are a sort of food for the soul, nourishing it on harmful meats, but leaving it afterwards without share of the heavenly bread and of really solid food. If then, with all the powers we have, we abstain from these in a most holy fast, our observance of the bodily fast will be both useful and profitable. For labor of the flesh, when joined with contrition of the spirit, will produce a sacrifice that is most acceptable to God, and a worthy shrine of holiness in the pure and undefiled inmost chambers of the heart. But if, while fasting as far as the body is concerned, we are entangled in the most dangerous vices of the soul, our humiliation of the flesh will do us no good whatever, while the most precious part of us is defiled: since we go wrong through that substance by virtue of which we are made a shrine of the Holy Ghost. For it is not so much the corruptible flesh as the clean heart, which is made a shrine for God, and a temple of the Holy Ghost. We ought therefore, whenever the outward man fasts, to restrain the inner man as well from food which is bad for him: that inner man, namely, which the blessed Apostle above all urges us to present pure before God, that it may be found worthy to receive Christ as a guest within, saying "that in the inner man Christ may dwell in your hearts through faith. "

CHAPTER 22
THAT WE SHOULD FOR THIS REASON PRACTICE BODILY ABSTINENCE THAT WE MAY BY IT ATTAIN TO A SPIRITUAL FAST

AND SO WE KNOW THAT WE OUGHT THEREFORE TO BESTOW attention on bodily abstinence, that we may by this fasting attain to purity of heart. Otherwise our labors will be spent in vain, if we endure this without weariness, in contemplating the end, but are unable to reach the end for which we have endured such trials; and it would have been better to have abstained from the forbidden foods of the soul than to have fasted with the body from things indifferent and harmless, for in the case of these latter there is a simple and harmless reception of a creature of God, which in itself has nothing wrong about it: but in the case of the former there is at the very first a dangerous tendency to devour the brethren; of which it is said, "Do not love backbiting lest thou be rooted out." And concerning anger and jealousy the blessed Job says: "For anger slayeth a fool, and envy killeth a child." And at the same time it should be noticed that he who is angered is set down as a fool; and he who is jealous, as a child. For the former is not undeservedly considered a fool, since of his own accord he brings death upon himself, being goaded by the stings of anger; and the latter, while he is envious, proves that he is a child and a minor, for while he envies another he shows that the one at whose prosperity he is vexed, is greater than he.

CHAPTER 23
WHAT SHOULD BE THE CHARACTER OF THE MONK'S FOOD

WE SHOULD THEN CHOOSE FOR OUR FOOD, NOT ONLY THAT which moderates the heat of burning lust, and avoids kindling it; but what is easily got ready, and what is recommended by its cheapness, and is suitable to the life of the brethren and their common use. For the nature of gluttony is threefold: first, there is that which forces us to anticipate the proper hour for a meal, next that which delights in stuffing the stomach, and gorging all kinds of food; thirdly, that which takes pleasure in more refined and delicate feasting. And so against it a monk should observe a threefold watch: first, he should wait till the proper time for breaking the fast; secondly, he should not give way to gorging; thirdly, he should be contented with any of the commoner sorts of food. For anything that is taken over and above what is customary and the common use of all, is branded by the ancient tradition of the fathers as defiled with the sin of vanity and glorying and ostentation. Nor of those whom we have seen to be deservedly eminent for learning and discretion, or whom the grace of Christ has singled out as shining lights for every one to imitate, have we known any who have abstained from eating bread which is accounted cheap and easily to be obtained among them; nor have we seen that any one who has rejected this rule and given up the use of bread and taken to a diet of beans or herbs or fruits, has been reckoned among the most esteemed, or even acquired the grace of knowledge and discretion. For not only do they lay it down that a monk ought not to ask for foods which are not customary for others, lest his mode of life should be exposed publicly to all and rendered vain and idle and so be destroyed by the disease of vanity; but they insist that the common chastening discipline of fasts ought not lightly to be disclosed to any one, but as far as possible concealed and kept secret. But when any of the brethren arrive they rule that we ought to show the virtues of kindness and charity instead of observing a severe abstinence and our strict daily rule: nor should we consider what our own wishes and profit or the ardor of our desires may require, but set before us and gladly fulfill whatever the refreshment of the guest, or his weakness may demand from us.

CHAPTER 24

HOW IN EGYPT WE SAW THAT THE DAILY FAST WAS BROKEN WITHOUT SCRUPLE ON OUR ARRIVAL

WHEN we had come from the region of Syria and had sought the province of Egypt, in our desire to learn the rules of the Eiders, we were astonished at the alacrity of heart with which we were there received so that no rule forbidding refreshment till the appointed hour of the fast was over was observed, such as we had been brought up to observe in the monasteries of Palestine; but except in the case of the regular days, Wednesdays and Fridays, wherever we went the daily fast was broken: and when we asked why the daily fast was thus ignored by them without scruple one of the elders replied: "The opportunity for fasting is always with me. But as I am going to conduct you on your way, I cannot always keep you with me. And a fast, although it is useful and advisable, is yet a free-will offering. But the exigencies of a command require the fulfillment of a work of charity. And so receiving Christ in you I ought to refresh Him but when I have sent you on your way I shall be able to balance the hospitality offered for His sake by a stricter fast on my own account. For 'the children of the bridegroom cannot fast while the bridegroom is with them:' but when he has departed, then they will rightly fast."

CHAPTER 25

OF THE ABSTINENCE OF ONE OLD MAN WHO TOOK FOOD SIX TIMES SO SPARINGLY THAT HE WAS STILL HUNGRY

WHEN ONE OF THE ELDERS WAS PRESSING ME TO EAT A little more as I was taking refreshment, and I said that I could not, he replied: "I have already laid my table six times for different brethren who had arrived, and, pressing each of them, I partook of food with him, and am still hungry, and do you, who now partake of refreshment for the first time, say that you cannot eat any more?"

CHAPTER 26

OF ANOTHER OLD MAN, WHO NEVER PARTOOK OF FOOD ALONE IN HIS CELL

WE HAVE SEEN ANOTHER WHO LIVED ALONE, WHO DECLARED that he had never enjoyed food by himself alone, but that even if for five days running none of the brethren came to his cell he constantly put off taking food until on Saturday or Sunday he went to church for service and found some stranger whom he brought home at once to his cell, and together with him partook of refreshment for the body not so much by reason of his own needs, as for the sake of kindness and on his brother's account. And so as they know that the daily fast is broken without scruple on the arrival of brethren, when they leave, they compensate for the refreshment which has been enjoyed on their account by a greater abstinence, and sternly make up for the reception of even a very little food by a severer chastisement not only as regards bread, but also by lessening their usual amount of sleep.

CHAPTER 27
WHAT THE TWO ABBOTS PAESIUS AND JOHN SAID OF THE FRUITS OF THEIR ZEAL

WHEN THE AGED JOHN, WHO WAS SUPERIOR OF A LARGE monastery and of a quantity of brethren, had come to visit the aged Paesius, who was living in a vast desert, and had been asked of him as of a very old friend, what he had done in all the forty years in which he had been separated from him and had scarcely ever been disturbed in his solitude by the brethren: "Never," said he, "has the sun seen me eating," "nor me angry," said the other.

CHAPTER 28
THE LESSON AND EXAMPLE WHICH ABBOT JOHN WHEN DYING LEFT TO HIS DISCIPLES

WHEN THE SAME OLD MAN, AS ONE WHO WAS READILY going to depart to his own, was lying at his last gasp, and the brethren were standing round, they implored and intreated that he would leave them, as a sort of legacy, some special charge by which they could attain to the height of perfection, the more easily from the brevity of the charge: he sighed and said, "I never did my own will, nor taught any one what I had not first done myself.

CHAPTER 29

OF ABBOT MACHETES, WHO NEVER SLEPT DURING THE SPIRITUAL CONFERENCES, BUT ALWAYS WENT TO SLEEP DURING EARTHLY TALES

WE KNEW AN OLD MAN, MACHETES BY NAME, WHO LIVED AT a distance from the crowds of the brethren, and obtained by his daily prayers. this grace from the Lord, that as often as a spiritual conference was held, whether by day or by night, he never was at all overcome by sleep: but if any one tried to introduce a word of detraction, or idle talk, he dropped off to sleep at once as if the poison of slander could not possibly penetrate to pollute his ears.

CHAPTER 30

A SAYING OF THE SAME OLD MAN ABOUT NOT JUDGING ANY ONE

THE SAME OLD MAN, WHEN HE WAS TEACHING US THAT NO one ought to judge another, remarked that there were three points on which he had charged and rebuked the brethren, viz.: because some allowed their uvula to be cut off, or kept a cloak in their cell, or blessed oil and gave it to those dwelling in the world who asked for it: and he said that he had done all these things himself. For having contracted some malady of the uvula, I wasted away, said he, for so long, through its weakness, that at last I was driven by stress of the pain, and by the persuasion of all the elders, to allow it to be cut off. And I was forced too by reason of this illness, to keep a cloak. And I was also compelled to bless oil and give it to those who prayed for it — a thing which I execrated above everything, since that I thought that it proceeded from great presumption of heart — when suddenly many who were living in the world surrounded me, so that I could not possibly escape them in any other way, had they not extorted from me with no small violence, and entreaties that I would lay my hand on a vessel offered by them, and sign it with the sign of the cross: and so believing that they had secured blessed oil, at last they let me go. And by these things I plainly discovered that a monk was in the same case and entangled in the same faults for which he had ventured to judge others. Each one therefore ought only to judge himself, and to be on the watch, with care and circumspection in all things not to judge the life and conduct of others in accordance with the Apostle's charge, "But thou, why dost thou judge thy brother? to his own master he standeth or falleth." And this: "Judge not, that ye be not judged. For with what judgment ye judge, ye shall be judged." For besides the reason of Which we have spoken, it is for this cause also dangerous to judge concerning others because in those matters in which we are offended — as we do not know the need or the reason for which they are really acting either rightly in the sight of God, or at any rate in a pardonable manner — we are found to have judged them rashly and in this commit no light sin, by forming an opinion of our brethren different from what we ought.

CHAPTER 31

THE SAME OLD MAN'S REBUKE WHEN HE SAW HOW THE BRETHREN WENT TO SLEEP DURING THE SPIRITUAL CONFERENCES, AND WOKE UP WHEN SOME IDLE STORY WAS TOLD

THE SAME OLD MAN MADE CLEAR BY THIS PROOF THAT IT was the devil who encouraged idle tales, and showed himself always as the enemy of spiritual conferences. For when he was discoursing to some of the brethren on necessary matters and spiritual things, and saw that they were weighed down with a sound slumber, and could not drive away the weight of sleep from their eyes, he suddenly introduced an idle tale. And when he saw that at once they woke up, delighted with it, and pricked up their ears, he groaned and said, "Up till now we were speaking of celestial things and all your eyes were overpowered with a sound slumber; but as soon as an idle tale was introduced, we all woke up and shook off the drowsiness of sleep which had overcome us. And from this therefore consider who is the enemy of that spiritual conference, and who has shown himself the suggester of that useless and carnal talk. For it is most evidently shown that it is he who, rejoicing in evil, never ceases to encourage the latter and to oppose the former."

CHAPTER 32
OF THE LETTERS WHICH WERE BURNT WITHOUT BEING READ

NOR DO I THINK IT LESS NEEDFUL TO RELATE THIS ACT OF a brother who was intent on purity of heart, and extremely anxious with regard to the contemplation of things divine. When after an interval of fifteen years a large number of letters had been brought to him from his father and mother and many friends in the province of Pontus, he received the huge packet of letters, and turning over the matter in his own mind for some time, "What thoughts," said he, "will the reading of these suggest to me, which will incite me either to senseless joy or to useless sadness! for how many days will they draw off the attention of my heart from the contemplation I have set before me, by the recollection of those who wrote them! How long will it take for the disturbance of mind thus created to be calmed, and what an effort will it cost for that former state of peacefulness to be restored, if the mind is once moved by the sympathy of the letters, and by recalling the words and looks of those whom it has left for so long begins once more in thought and spirit to revisit them, to dwell among them and to be with them. And it will be of no use to have forsaken them in the body, if one begins to look on them with the heart, and readmits and revives that memory which on renouncing this world every one gave up, as if he were dead. Turning this over in his mind, he determined not only not to read a single letter, but not even to open the packet, for fear lest, at the sight of the names of the writers, or on recalling their appearance, the purpose of his spirit might give way. And so he threw it into the fire to be burnt, all tied up just as he had received it, crying, "Away, O ye thoughts of my home, be ye burnt up, and try no further to recall me to those things from which I have fled."

CHAPTER 33

OF THE SOLUTION OF A QUESTION WHICH ABBOT THEODORE OBTAINED BY PRAYER

WE KNEW ALSO ABBOT THEODORE, A MAN GIFTED WITH the utmost holiness and with perfect knowledge not only in practical life, but also in understanding the Scriptures, which he had not acquired so much by study and reading, or worldly education, as by purity of heart alone: since he could with difficulty understand and speak but a very few words of the Greek language. This man when he was seeking an explanation of some most difficult question, continued without ceasing for seven days and nights in prayer until he discovered by a revelation from the Lord the solution of the question propounded.

CHAPTER 34
OF THE SAYING OF THE SAME OLD MAN, THROUGH WHICH HE TAUGHT BY WHAT EFFORTS A MONK CAN ACQUIRE A KNOWLEDGE OF THE SCRIPTURES

THIS MAN THEREFORE, WHEN SOME OF THE BRETHREN WERE wondering at the splendid light of his knowledge and were asking of him some meanings of Scripture, said that a monk who wanted to acquire a knowledge of the Scriptures ought not to spend his labor on the works of commentators, but rather to keep all the efforts of his mind and intentions of his heart set on purifying himself from carnal vices: for when these are driven out, at once the eyes of the heart, as if the veil of the passions were removed, will begin as it were naturally to gaze on the mysteries of Scripture: since they were not declared to us by the grace of the Holy Spirit in order that they should remain unknown and obscure; but they are rendered obscure by our fault, as the veil of our sins covers the eyes of the heart, and when these are restored to their natural state of health, the mere reading of Holy Scripture is by itself amply sufficient for beholding the true knowledge, nor do they need the aid of commentators, just as these eyes of flesh need no man's teaching how to see, provided that they are free from dimness or the darkness of blindness. For this reason there have arisen so great differences and mistakes among commentators because most of them, paying no sort of attention towards purifying the mind, rush into the work of interpreting the Scriptures, and in proportion to the density or impurity of their heart form opinions that are at variance with and contrary to each other's and to the faith, and so are unable to take in the light of

CHAPTER 35
A REBUKE OF THE SAME OLD MAN, WHEN HE HAD COME TO MY CELL IN THE MIDDLE OF THE NIGHT

THE SAME THEODORE CAME UNEXPECTEDLY TO MY CELL IN the dead of night, with paternal inquisitiveness seeking what I — an unformed anchorite as I was — might be doing by myself; and when he had found me there already, as I had finished my vesper office, beginning to refresh my wearied body, and lying down on a mat, he sighed from the bottom of his heart, and calling me by name, said, "How many, O John, are at this hour communing with God, and embracing Him, and detaining Him with them, while you are deprived of so great light, enfeebled as you are with lazy sleep!"

And since the virtues of the fathers and the grace given to them have tempted us to turn aside to a story like this, I think it well to record in this volume a noteworthy deed of charity, which we experienced from the kindness of that most excellent man Archebius, that the purity of continence grafted on to a work of charity may more readily shine forth, being embellished with a pleasing variety. For the duty of fasting is then rendered acceptable to God, when it is made perfect by the fruits of charity.

CHAPTER 36
A DESCRIPTION OF THE DESERT IN DIOLCOS, WHERE THE ANCHORITES LIVE

AND SO WHEN WE HAD COME, WHILE STILL BEGINNERS, FROM the monasteries of Palestine, to a city of Egypt called Diolcos, and were contemplating a large number of monks bound by the discipline of the Coenobium, and trained in that excellent system of monasteries, which is also the earliest, we were also eager to see with all wisdom of heart another system as well which is still better, viz.: that of the anchorites, as we were incited thereto by the praises of it by everybody. For these men, having first lived for a very long time in Coenobia, and having diligently learnt all the rules of patience and discretion, and acquired the virtues of humility and renunciation, and having perfectly overcome all their faults, in order to engage in most fearful conflicts with devils, penetrate the deepest recesses of the desert. Finding then that men of this sort were living near the river Nile in a place which is surrounded on one side by the same river, on the other by the expanse of the sea, and forms an island, habitable by none but monks seeking such recesses, since the saltness of the soil and dryness of the sand make it unfit for any cultivation — to these men, I say, we eagerly hastened, and were beyond measure astonished at their labors which they endure in the contemplation of the virtues and their love of solitude. For they are hampered by such a scarcity even of water that the care and exactness with which they portion it out is such as no miser would bestow in preserving and hoarding the most precious kind of wine. For they carry it three miles or even further from the bed of the above-mentioned river, for all necessary purposes; and the distance, great as it is, with sandy mountains in between, is doubled by the very great difficulty of the task.

CHAPTER 37

OF THE CELLS WHICH ABBOT ARCHEBIUS GAVE UP TO US WITH THEIR FURNITURE

HAVING THEN SEEN THIS, AS WE WERE INFLAMED WITH the desire of imitating them, the aforesaid Archebius, the most famous among them for the grace of kindness, drew us into his cell, and having discovered our desire, pretended that he wanted to leave the place, and to offer his cell to us, as if he were going away, declaring that he would have done it, even if we had not come. And we, inflamed with the desire of remaining there, and putting unhesitating faith in the assertions of so great a man, willingly agreed to this, and took over his cell with all its furniture and belongings. And so having succeeded in his pious fraud, he left the place for a few days in which to procure the means for constructing a cell, and after this returned, and with the utmost labor built another cell for himself. And after some little time, when some other brethren came inflamed with the same desire to stay there, he deceived them by a similar charitable falsehood, and gave this one up with everything pertaining to it. But he, unweariedly persevering in his act of charity, built for himself a third cell to dwell in.

CHAPTER 38

THE SAME ARCHEBIUS PAID A DEBT OF HIS MOTHER'S BY THE LABOR OF HIS OWN HANDS

IT SEEMS TO ME WORTH WHILE TO HAND DOWN ANOTHER charitable act of the same man, that the monks of our land may be taught by the example of one and the same man to maintain not only a rigorous continence, but also the most unfeigned affection of love. For he, sprung from no ignoble family, while yet a child, scorning the love of this world and of his kinsfolk, fled to the monastery which is nearly four miles distant from the aforementioned town, where he so passed all his life, that never once throughout the whole of fifty years did he enter or see the village from which he had come, nor even look upon the face of any woman, not even his own mother. In the mean while his father was overtaken by death, and left a debt of a hundred solidi. And though he himself was entirely free from all annoyances, since he had been disinherited of all his father's property, yet he found that his mother was excessively annoyed by the creditors. Then he through consideration of duty somewhat moderated that gospel severity through which formerly, while his parents were prosperous, he did not recognize that he possessed a father or mother on earth; and acknowledged that he had a mother, and hastened to relieve her in her distress, without relaxing anything of the austerity he had set himself. For remaining within the cloister of the monastery he asked that the task of his usual work might be trebled. And there for a whole year toiling night and day alike he paid to the creditors the due measure of the debt secured by his toil and labor, and relieved his mother from all annoyance and anxiety; ridding her of the burden of the debt in such a way as not to suffer aught of the severity he had set himself to be diminished on plea of duteous necessity. Thus did he preserve his wonted austerities, without ever denying to his mother's heart the work which duty demanded, as, though he had formerly disregarded her for the love of Christ, he now acknowledged her again out of consideration of duty.

CHAPTER 39
OF THE DEVICE OF A CERTAIN OLD MAN BY WHICH SOME WORK WAS FOUND FOR ABBOT SIMEON WHEN BE HAD NOTHING TO DO

WHEN A BROTHER WHO WAS VERY DEAR TO US, SIMEON BY name, a man utterly ignorant of Greek, had come from the region of Italy, one of the elders, anxious to show to him, as he was a stranger, a work of charity, with some pretense of the benefit being mutual, asked him why he sat doing nothing in his cell, guessing from this that he would not be able to stay much longer in it both because of the roving thoughts which idleness produces and because, of his want of the necessities of life; well knowing that no one can endure the assault: made in solitude, but one who is contented to procure food for himself by the labor of his hands. And when the other replied that he could not do or manage any of the things which were usually done by the brethren there, except write a good hand, if any one in Egypt wanted a Latin book for his use, then he at length seized the opportunity to secure the long wished for work of charity, under color of its being a mutual benefit; and said, "From God this opportunity comes, for I was just looking for some one to write out for me the Epistles in Latin; for I have a brother who is bound in the chains of military service, and is a good Latin scholar, to whom I want to send something from Scripture for him to read for his edification." And so when Simeon gratefully took this as an opportunity offered to him by God, the old man also gladly seized the pretext, under color of which he could freely carry out his work of charity, and at once not only brought him as a matter of business everything he could want for a whole year, but also conveyed to him parchment and everything requisite for writing, and received afterwards the manuscript, which was not of the slightest use (since in those parts they were all utterly ignorant of this language), and did no good to anybody except that which resulted from this device and large outlay, as the one, without shame or confusion, procured his necessary food and sustenance by the reward of his work and labor, and the other carried out his kindness and bounty as it were by the compulsion of a debt: securing for himself a more abundant reward proportioned to the zeal with which he procured for his foreign brother not only his necessary food, but materials for writing, and an opportunity of work.

CHAPTER 40

OF THE BOYS WHO WHEN BRINGING TO A SICK MAN SOME FIGS, DIED IN THE DESERT FROM HUNGER, WITHOUT HAVING TASTED THEM

BUT SINCE IN THE SECTION IN WHICH WE PROPOSED TO SAY something about the strictness of fasting and abstinence, kindly acts and deeds of charity seem to have been intermingled, again returning to our design we will insert in this little book a noteworthy deed of some who were boys in years though not in their feelings. For when, to their great surprise, some one had brought to Abbot John, the steward in the desert of Scete, some figs from Libya Mareotis, as being a thing never before seen in those districts, — (John) who had the management of the church in the days of the blessed Presbyter Paphnutius, by whom it had been intrusted to him, at once sent them by the hands of two lads to an old man who was laid up in ill health in the further parts of the desert, and who lived about eighteen miles from the church. And when they had received the fruit, and set off for the cell of the above-mentioned old man, they lost the right path altogether — a thing which there easily happens even to elders — as a thick fog suddenly came on. And when all day and night they had wandered about the trackless waste of the desert, and could not possibly find the sick man's cell, worn out at last both by weariness from their journey, and from hunger and thirst, they bent their knees and gave up their souls to God in the very act of prayer. And afterwards, when they had been for a long while sought for by the marks of their footsteps which in those sandy regions are impressed as if on snow, until a thin coating of sand blown about even by a slight breeze covers them up again, it was found that they had preserved the figs untouched, just as they had received them; choosing rather to give up their lives, than their fidelity to their charge, and to lose their life on earth than to violate the commands of their senior.

CHAPTER 41
THE SAYING OF ABBOT MACARIUS OF THE BEHAVIOR OF A MONK AS ONE WHO WAS TO LIVE FOR A LONG WHILE, AND AS ONE WHO WAS DAILY AT THE POINT OF DEATH

THERE IS STILL ONE VALUABLE CHARGE OF THE BLESSED Macarius to be brought forward by us, so that a saying of so great a man may close this book of fasts and abstinence. He said then that a monk ought to bestow attention on his fasts, just as if he were going to remain in the flesh for a hundred years; and to curb the motions of the soul, and to forget injuries, and to loathe sadness, and despise sorrows and losses, as if he were daily at the point of death. For in the former case discretion is useful and proper as it causes a monk always to walk with well-balanced care, and does not suffer him by reason of a weakened body to fall from the heights over most dangerous precipices: in the other high-mindedness is most valuable as it will enable him not only to despise the seeming prosperity of this present world, but also not to be crushed by adversity and sorrow, and to despise them as small and paltry matters, since he has the gaze of his mind continually fixed there, whither daily at each moment he believes that he is soon to be summoned.

BOOK 6

ON THE SPIRIT OF FORNICATION

Chapter 1
THE SECOND ENEMY TO FIGHT

THE FATHERS TEACH US THAT OUR SECOND ENEMY IS impurity. This fight we have to fight is longer, more difficult than the others, and very few win a complete victory. It is a cruel war that begins for man from his youth, and that does not end until all other vices are destroyed. The enemy attacks us from both sides, by two different passions, and we must also oppose a double resistance. As its strength comes from the weaknesses of the flesh and the soul, it is also by uniting their efforts to combat it that we will be able to triumph over it. It is not enough for bodily fasting to conquer or preserve perfect purity; first, we must have the contrition of the heart, and fight against the impure spirit by persevering prayer; then to meditate incessantly on the Holy Scripture, to acquire the science of it, and not to neglect the work of the hands, which will stop the distractions of our minds. Above all, it is necessary to establish oneself in a sincere humility, without which one can never fully overcome any vice.

Chapter 2
THE MAIN REMEDY AGAINST IMPURITY

THE MAIN REMEDY AGAINST THIS VICE IS THE CLEANSING OF the heart, where our Lord tells us that lies the seed of this terrible disease. It is from the heart, he says, that evil thoughts, homicides, adulteries, fornications, robberies, and false witness come out (Mt 15:19). It is therefore necessary to purify this source of life and death. Solomon recommends it to us: "Keep your heart with all possible care, for it is he who is the source of life" (Pr 4:23). And, indeed, the flesh is subject to its movements and its empire.

We must, therefore, ardently follow the laws of abstinence, lest the abundance of food should prevent the flesh from obeying the salutary counsels of the spirit, and resisting with insolence against its master. If we apply ourselves only to chastising our body, without at the same time fasting our soul with all its vices and without nourishing it with pious studies and holy meditations, we can never rise to perfect purity, since the principal part of ourselves will defile our body. First of all, as our Lord recommends, purify the inside of the cup and dish so that the outside also becomes pure (Mt 23:26).

Chapter 3
THE REMOTENESS OF THE WORLD HELPS TO OVERCOME IMPURITY

THE OTHER VICES ARE USUALLY CORRECTED BY FREQUENTING men and fighting every day against opportunities. The faults committed are, so to speak, a means of healing. Anger, for example, sadness, envy, impatience, gives way to the reflection and persevering efforts of the one who lives among his brothers and the temptations he encounters there. The more events there are, the more the victory seems quick and easy. This disease, on the contrary, requires, besides the mortification of the body and the contrition of the heart, solitude and separation from the world. It is the way to appease this terrible fever of the senses and to recover a perfect health. In certain diseases, it is avoided to show the patients foods which could be harmful to them, lest this sight should excite in them fatal desires. In order to heal impurity, it is necessary to seek calmness and loneliness so that the soul, no longer troubled by dangerous images, can rise to more holy thoughts and more easily this poisonous plant.

Chapter 4
THE DIFFERENCE BETWEEN CHASTITY AND ABSTINENCE

NOBODY MUST BELIEVE FOR THAT REASON THAT WE CLAIM that there are no religious abstinents living in community. We recognize, on the contrary, that it is very easy to find. But to be abstinent or to be chaste is not the same thing. To be chaste is to live in the love of unalterable purity, and this virtue is the privilege of those who remain virgins of body and spirit, like the two saints John in the New Testament, and like Elijah, Jeremiah and Daniel, in the Old. We can also put in the same rank those who, having experienced the weaknesses of the flesh, have arrived, by dint of pain and vigilance, to recover this purity of soul and body, and not only resist the temptations of lust but no longer experience the movements of nature. It is this chastity that we believe is very difficult to acquire in the society of men. We do not say the impossible thing; but we let everyone think about it and express themselves in their consciousness.

We believe that many abstinents that have, rarely or often, to support the fights of the flesh, resist and triumph for fear of hell or desire of heaven. But the Fathers, while recognizing that they can fight in this way against the ardor of the passions, declaim for they must not believe themselves to be invulnerable; for as long as the war lasts, it is easy to strike and defeat the enemy often, one is never safe from danger.

Chapter 5
MAN'S EFFORTS ARE NOT ENOUGH TO OVERCOME IMPURITY

IF, THEN, WE ARE DETERMINED TO FIGHT A GOOD FIGHT like the Apostle, if we wish with all our soul to overcome the spirit of impurity, let us hasten to do so, by entrusting ourselves, not in our own forces, could never be sufficient, but in the help of divine grace. We will always have to fight this vice, as long as we do not recognize that this war is above our strength, and that despite all our efforts we will not win the victory, if Die does not help us with its all-powerful protection.

Chapter 6
A SPECIAL GRACE OF GOD IS NECESSARY TO PRESERVE CHASTITY

THE GRACE OF GOD IS DOUBTLESS NECESSARY TO TRIUMPH over all vices and to make progress in every virtue; but it is even more so when it comes to impurity. This virtue is a special gift, as evidenced by the testimony of the Fathers and the experience of those who obtained it. Because how to be delivered from the flesh by staying in one's body? and is it not supernatural to be clothed with a fragile flesh, without feeling its ardor? It would be impossible for man to rise on his wings to this celestial purity, if the grace of God did not draw him from the earthly mud by the gift of chastity. There is no virtue that can equal our carnal nature to the spiritual nature of angels, such as that virtue of chastity, which, according to the Apostle, makes us citizens of heaven, when we are still inhabitants of the earth (Phi 3, 20), since we already possess, in our fragile flesh, that peace which is promised to the saints when they are delivered from their mortal bodies.

Chapter 7
EXAMPLE OF THE ATHLETE PROPOSED BY THE APOSTLE

LISTEN TO WHAT THE APOSTLE SAYS: "HE WHO FIGHTS IN the arena abstains from everything" (1 Cor 9:25). Let us seek what is meant by everything in order to be able to apply to our spiritual struggles this comparison drawn from the battles of the world. Athletes who wanted to fight in the arena were not allowed to use all the food that could tempt them. They had to be content with those prescribed by the regulations, and not only were they forced to abstain from forbidden food, drunkenness, and debauchery, but they had to flee laziness, idleness, inaction, in order to increase their strengths by study and continuous exercises. They had to live in celibacy and abstinence to remain strangers to worries, sadness and embarrassment of the world. They had to deal only with their profession, and they were not distracted by any need because they

from the person who presided over the battles they received their daily subsistence, and they thought only of deserving the crown and the honors of victory. When they were preparing for battle, not only did they remain pure from all intercourse with women, but they defended themselves from all unintentional defilements during the night, girding themselves painfully on the reins with lead slings; they thought that they would lose their strength in order to fight well, if some deceptive image of pleasure would alter their purity.

Chapter 8
THE MEANS THAT ATHLETES TOOK TO PREPARE FOR BATTLE

LET US UNDERSTAND WELL THE CONDUCT OF THE ATHLETES of the world, of which St. Paul offers us the example, and observe with what care they observe and guard themselves. What, then, shall we not do to keep unchaste the chastity of the soul and the body, we who are obliged every day to eat the sacred flesh of the Lamb, to which every unclean person could not touch in the old law ! Leviticus says, "He who is pure shall eat meat; but whoever eats the meat of the sacrifice offered to God, though he has contracted some defilement, shall perish before the Lord. "(Lv 7, 19-20). What, then, is the excellence of purity, since without it, under the old law, it was impossible to participate in sacrifices, which were however only figures, and without it also, those who desire in this world a crown corruptible, can not get it!

Chapter 9
HOW MUST WE ALWAYS KEEP OUR HEART PURE IN GOD'S SIGHT

IT IS NECESSARY ABOVE ALL TO PURIFY WITH EXTREME vigilance the folds of our heart; because this purity of body that we desire to have, we must possess it in the secrets of our consciousness. It is there that God resides as referee and judge of our fights. He sees in it our ardor and our efforts; and his presence must prevent us from recklessly admitting in ourselves thoughts which we should have a horror of manifesting abroad, and thereby defiling ourselves secretly with what would blush in front of men. If we could hide from the eyes of men, could we escape those of the holy angels and of God himself, whose science penetrates the deepest night?

Chapter 10
WHAT IS THE SIGN OF PERFECT PURITY?

We will have an obvious mark, a certain proof of our purity, if no deceptive image disturbs our sleep, or can not excite in us, despite its obsessions, the movements of concupiscence. Because, although these movements are not not by themselves a true sin, they show however that the soul is not yet perfect and completely free from vice, since it is always subject to such illusions.

Chapter 11
WHERE DO THE UNINTENTIONAL IMPURITIES COME FROM?

The rest of the night makes known the nature of the thoughts to which we have allowed ourselves during the day. When these illusions of the senses come to us, we must not attribute them to sleep, but to our negligence while we were awake. The hidden evil that manifests itself in us is not based on the darkness of the night; he was already in the recesses of our souls, and when he occurs outside during our sleep, he shows the impure ardours that we had excited during the day, feeding us with dangerous thoughts. Thus the diseases of the body are not formed at the moment when they appear on the outside, their origin is older; they are caused by the carelessness and imprudence of those who take food contrary to their health, and give birth in them moods capable of killing them.

Chapter 12
THE FLESH CAN NOT BE PURE, IF THE HEART IS NOT

GOD, THE AUTHOR AND CREATOR OF THE HUMAN RACE, knows better than anyone the nature of his work and the means of repairing it. So he applied the remedy where he knew that was the main cause of illness, when he said, "He who looks upon a woman with a bad desire, has already committed adultery in his heart" (Mt 5:2). Speaking of these guilty looks, our Lord does not condemn so much those of the body as those of the soul, who abuse their eyes to see; it is the sick and wounded heart of the features of impurity, which conceives this bad desire and uses sight, a benefit of the Creator, to commit the evil. This look only makes concupiscence appear hidden in him. The Divine Physician gives the right remedy to cure this fatal intoxication that comes to us through the eyes. Scripture does not say, "Keep your eyes as safe as possible." It would be above all, however, that they should be watched if they were the principal source of concupiscence; but they are but the servants of the soul, and it is said, "Keep your heart with all possible care" (Pr 4:25). The remedy is applied to what can abuse the eyes.

Chapter 13
WE MUST FIGHT CARNAL THOUGHTS FROM THEIR ORIGIN

THE FIRST CARE WE MUST TAKE TO PURIFY OUR HEART, IS TO banish any memory of a woman, that the tricks of the devil could awaken. We must even away from our mother, our sisters, our parents and the godly people we met. We must hasten to divert our thoughts, lest the tempter take advantage of the opportunity to mislead our minds on other women, and to give rise to dangerous images.

Let us constantly remember the precept of the Lord: "Keep your heart with all possible care" (Gen 3:15), and let us also try to break the serpent's head, that is, to discover the principle of evil thoughts that could slip into our soul; for if the head of the devil penetrated into our heart by our negligence, his body would soon be entirely by our consent; and once established there, we would perish victims of his passions and his tyranny. In the morning we must destroy the sinners who rise from our earth, that is to say, our carnal thoughts at birth; we must break the children of Babylon on the stone when they are still small (Ps 126: 12). For if we do not kill them while they are young, if we let them grow by our fault, they will strengthen and rebel to lose us, and we will be able to overcome them with much difficulty and fighting.

When the strong, that is to say, our spirit, is armed to guard his house, when he defends with the fear of God all the retreats of his heart, he preserves in peace all that he possesses (Lk 11, 21), that is to say the fruit of his labors and the virtues painfully and long acquired. But if a stronger enemy arises and triumphs, that is to say, if the demon takes advantage of his consent, he will seize the weapons in which he trusted, that is to say the fear of God and of the thought of the Holy Scriptures, and he will share his remains by dispelling the merit of his virtues by the vices that are opposed to them.

Chapter 14
PURPOSE OF THE AUTHOR IN SPEAKING OF CHASTITY

I will pass over in silence all the praises that Scripture gives to chastity; my intention is not to praise it, but to explain, according to the tradition of the Fathers, its qualities, how one must acquire or preserve it, and what are its results. It will suffice for me to quote a passage from St. Paul's letter to the Thessalonians, to show how much the Apostle esteemed this virtue among all, and commended it by glorifying it.

Chapter 15
THE APOSTLE CONSIDERS CHASTITY AS HOLINESS

"The will of God," he says, "is your sanctification." And so that we understand what he means by sanctification, if it is only justice, charity, humility, patience, by which we believe to sanctify ourselves, he explains very clearly what he calls Sanctification: "God wills your sanctification, that is to say, that you abstain from all fornication, and that everyone may keep the vessel of his body with honor and holiness, without defiling it with desires, as the Gentiles do, who do not know God "(1 Thess 4: 4-5).

You see how much the Apostle praises this virtue, since he calls it the honor and holiness of our body. On the contrary, he who feels the movements of concupiscence is in the shame of impurity; he is far from holiness. The Apostle, a little later, still gives this virtue the name of holiness. "For God," he says, "has not called us to be unclean, but to be holy; and whoever despises these things despises not a man, but God who has given us his Holy Spirit "(Ib 7). Thus, St. Paul adds to his precept an inviolable sanction, since he says: "He who despises these things, that is to say, what I have just said of purity, do not despise the man who makes you this commandment, but God who speaks to you in me and who has chosen our heart for the abode of the Holy Spirit".

You see how the Apostle exalts purity by his words and his praises, since he first attributes to us our own sanctification, which he then assures us to deliver our body from all defilement, and that after having removed it shame, she keeps it in honor and holiness; finally, which is the height of happiness and reward, he declares that it is through her that the Holy Spirit comes to live in our soul.

Chapter 16

ANOTHER TESTIMONY OF ST. PAUL ON THE SAME SUBJECT

EVEN THOUGH THIS BOOK IS COMING TO AN END, I STILL want to quote another testimony from the Apostle. He says in his letter to the Hebrews, "Try to keep peace with everyone and holiness, without which no one can see God" (Heb 12:14). He clearly states here that without holiness, which, according to him, consists in the purity of mind and body, it is impossible to see God. And he explains the meaning of his words, adding, "Let not a fornicator and a layman be among you like Esau" (Ibid, 16).

Chapter 17

THE HOPE OF REWARD SHOULD MAKE US WATCH OUT MORE CAREFULLY ABOUT CHASTITY

THE MORE THE REWARD OF CHASTITY IS SUBLIME AND heavenly, the more fiercely the enemy attacks it. So we must continually apply ourselves to maintain not only the abstinence of our body, but also the compunction of our heart, by continual moans and prayers, so that this fire of carnal desires, that the King of Babylon never ceases to light in ourselves, to be extinguished by the dew of the Holy Spirit who will descend into our hearts.

Chapter 18
CHASTITY MUST BE BASED ON HUMILITY, AND SCIENCE ON CHASTITY

OUR ELDERS SAY THAT ONE CAN NOT POSSESS PURITY without having given him the humility of the heart as a foundation; but they also affirm that one can not reach true science until one has torn from one's soul the root of vice which is contrary to it. They think that we can meet chaste people who are not learned, but that it is impossible to find the science of holiness without perfect purity. The gifts of God are different, and the grace of the Holy Spirit is not the same in all.

Chapter 19
SENTENCE OF SAINT BASIL ON CHASTITY

THERE IS A REMARKABLE SAYING OF ST. BASIL, BISHOP OF Caesarea: "I have never known women," said he, "and yet I am not a virgin." He understood that purity was not so much in the privation of all commerce with women as in the true purity of heart, which alone preserves the body from all defilement by the fear of God or the love of chastity.

Chapter 20
HOW DOES ONE RECOGNIZE THAT ONE IS REALLY CHASTE OF HEART

We may believe that we have arrived at this purity, if no voluptuous sensation disturbs our sleep, and natural accidents occur without us noticing. It's above the nature of the complete cut off but we must, by virtue of virtue, make them more and more rare.

Chapter 21
HOW CAN WE PRESERVE PERFECT CHASTITY

The way to achieve this and to advance in purity, is to consider that God sees, night and day, not only our hidden actions, but also our most secret thoughts, and that we will have to give him an account of all our works as of all the desires of our heart.

Chapter 22
HOW FAR SHOULD THE PURITY OF THE BODY GO

Let us therefore hasten to fight all the unfortunate movements of our soul and our body, until the sad necessities of nature excite in us no pleasure and do not affect our purity. He who, during sleep, yields to illusions of deceptive images, must recognize that he is not yet perfectly chaste.

Chapter 23
WAYS TO ACQUIRE PURITY OF HEART AND BODY

So that these illusions do not surprise us while sleeping, we must always observe a regular and moderate abstinence; for if we fasted too much, we would soon be drawn into an opposite excess. These inequalities will prevent the peace which is so desirable; we will be either too weakened by fasting, or too heavy with food, and our purity will suffer from these changes of diet.

One must also practice patience and humility of heart, and fight, all day, against anger and other passions. Where fury reigns, the flames of impurity are necessarily ignited. But let us be especially vigilant during the night; for if the purity of the day prepares the chastity of the night, our night watches help us to be calm and strong during the exercises of the day.

BOOK 7

OF THE SPIRIT OF COVETOUSNESS

CHAPTER 1

HOW OUR WARFARE WITH COVETOUSNESS IS A FOREIGN ONE, AND HOW THIS FAULT IS NOT A NATURAL ONE IN MAN, AS THE OTHER FAULTS ARE

OUR THIRD CONFLICT IS AGAINST COVETOUSNESS WHICH we can describe as the love of money; a foreign warfare, and one outside of our nature, and in the case of a monk originating only from the state of a corrupt and sluggish mind, and often from the beginning of his renunciation being unsatisfactory, and his love towards God being lukewarm at its foundation. For the rest of the incitements to sin planted in human nature seem to have their commencement as it were congenital with us, and somehow being deeply rooted in our flesh, and almost coeval with our birth, anticipate our powers of discerning good and evil, and although in very early days they attack a man, yet they are overcome with a long struggle.

CHAPTER 2

HOW DANGEROUS IS THE DISEASE OF COVETOUSNESS

BUT THIS DISEASE COMING UPON US AT A LATER PERIOD, and approaching the soul from without, as it can be the more easily guarded against and resisted, so; if it is disregarded and once allowed to gain an entrance into the heart, is the more dangerous to every one, and with the greater difficulty expelled. For it becomes "a root of all evils," and gives rise to a multiplicity of incitements to sin.

CHAPTER 3
WHAT IS THE USEFULNESS OF THOSE VICES WHICH ARE NATURAL TO

FOR EXAMPLE, DO NOT WE SEE THOSE NATURAL IMPULSES of the flesh not only in boys in whom innocence still anticipates the discernment of good and evil, but even in little children and infants, who although they have not even the slightest approach to lust within them, yet show that the impulses of the flesh exist in them and are naturally excited? Do not we also see that the deadly pricks of anger already exist in full vigor likewise in little children? and before they have learnt the virtue of patience, we see that they are disturbed by wrongs, and feel affronts offered to them even by way of a joke; and sometimes, although strength is lacking to them, the desire to avenge themselves is not wanting, when anger excites them. Nor do I say this to lay the blame on their natural state, but to point out that of these impulses which proceed from us, some are implanted in us for a useful purpose, while some are introduced from without, through the fault of carelessness and the desire of an evil will. For these carnal impulses, of which we spoke above, were with a useful purpose implanted in our bodies by the providence of the Creator, viz.: for perpetuating the race, and raising up children for posterity: and not for committing adulteries and debaucheries, which the authority of the law also condemns. The pricks of anger too, do we not see that they have been most wisely given to us, that being enraged at our sins and mistakes, we may apply ourselves the rather to virtues and spiritual exercises, showing forth all love towards God, and patience towards our brethren? We know too how great is the use of sorrow, which is reckoned among the other vices, when it is turned to an opposite use. For on the one hand, when it is in accordance with the fear of God it is most needful, and on the other, when it is in accordance with the world, most pernicious; as the Apostle teaches us when he says that "the sorrow which is according to God worketh repentance that is steadfast unto salvation, but the sorrow of the world worketh death."

CHAPTER 4

THAT WE CAN SAY THAT THERE EXIST IN US SOME NATURAL FAULTS, WITHOUT WRONGING THE CREATOR

IF THEN WE SAY THAT THESE IMPULSES WERE IMPLANTED IN us by the Creator, He will not on that account seem blameworthy, if we choose wrongly to abuse them, and to pervert them to harmful purposes, and are ready to be made sorry by means of the useless Cains of this world, and not by means of showing penitence and the correction of our faults: or at least if we are angry not with ourselves (which would be profitable) but with our brethren in defiance of God's command. For in the case of iron, which is given us for good and useful purposes, if any one should pervert it for murdering the innocent, one would not therefore blame the maker of the metal because man had used to injure others that which he had provided for good and useful purposes of living happily.

CHAPTER 5

OF THE FAULTS WHICH ARE CONTRACTED THROUGH OUR OWN FAULT, WITHOUT NATURAL IMPULSES

BUT WE AFFIRM THAT SOME FAULTS GROW UP WITHOUT ANY natural occasion giving birth to them, but simply from the free choice of a corrupt and evil will, as envy and this very sin of covetousness; which are caught (so to speak) from without, having no origination in us from natural instincts.

But these, in proportion as they are easily guarded against and readily avoided, just so do they make wretched the mind that they have got hold of and seized, and hardly do they suffer it to get at the remedies which would cure it: either because these who are wounded by persons whom they might either have ignored, or avoided, or easily overcome, do not deserve to be healed by a speedy cure, or else because, having laid the foundations badly, they are unworthy to raise an edifice of virtue and reach the summit of perfection.

CHAPTER 6
HOW DIFFICULT THE EVIL OF COVETOUSNESS IS TO DRIVE AWAY WHEN ONCE IT HAS BEEN ADMITTED

WHEREFORE LET NOT THIS EVIL SEEM OF NO ACCOUNT OR unimportant to anybody: for as it can easily be avoided, so if it has once got hold of any one, it scarcely suffers him to get at the remedies for curing it. For it is a regular nest of sins, and a "root of all kinds of evil," and becomes a hopeless incitement to wickedness, as the Apostle says, "Covetousness," i.e. the love of money, "is a root of all kinds of evil."

CHAPTER 7
OF THE SOURCE FROM WHICH COVETOUSNESS SPRINGS, AND OF THE EVILS OF WHICH IT IS ITSELF THE MOTHER

WHEN THEN THIS VICE HAS GOT HOLD OF THE SLACK AND lukewarm soul of some monk, it begins by tempting him in regard of a small sum of money, giving him excellent and almost reasonable excuses why he ought to retain some money for himself. For he complains that what is provided in the monastery is not sufficient, and can scarcely be endured by a sound and sturdy body. What is he to do if ill health comes on, and he has no special store of his own to support him in his weakness? He says that the allowance of the monastery is but meager, and that there is the greatest carelessness about the sick: and if he has not something of his own so that he can look after the wants of his body, he will perish miserably. The dress which is allowed him is insufficient, unless he has provided something with which to procure another. Lastly, he says that he cannot possibly remain for long in the same place and monastery, and that unless he has secured the money for his journey, and the cost of his removal over the sea, he cannot move when he wants to, and, detained by the compulsion of want, will henceforth drag out a wretched and wearisome existence without making the slightest advance: that he cannot without indignity be supported by another's substance, as a pauper and one in want. And so when he has bamboozled himself with such thoughts as these, he racks his brains to think how he can acquire at least one penny. Then he anxiously searches for some special work which he can do without the Abbot knowing anything about it. And selling it secretly, and so securing the coveted coin, he torments himself worse and worse in thinking how he can double it: puzzled as to where to deposit it, or to whom to intrust it. Then he is oppressed with a still weightier care as to what to buy with it, or by what transaction he can double it. And when this has turned out as he wished, a still more greedy craving for gold springs up, and is more and more keenly excited, as his store of money grows larger and larger. For with the increase of wealth the mania of covetousness increases. Then next he has forebodings of a long life, and an enfeebled old age, and infirmities of all sorts, and long drawn out, which will be insupportable in old age, unless a large store of money has been laid by in youth. And so the wretched soul is agitated, and held fast, as it were, in a serpent's toils, while it endeavors to add to that heap which it has unlawfully secured, by still more unlawful care, and itself gives birth to plagues which inflame it more sorely, and being entirely absorbed in the quest of gain, pays attention to nothing but how to get money with which to fly as quickly as possible from the discipline of the monastery, never keeping faith where there is a gleam of hope of money to be got. For this it shrinks not from the crime of lying, perjury, and theft, of breaking a promise, of giving way to injurious bursts of passion. If the man has dropped away at all from the hope of gain, he has no scruples about transgressing the bounds of humility, and through it all gold and the love of gain become to him his God, as the belly does to others. Wherefore the blessed Apostle, looking out on the deadly poison of this pest, not only says that it is a root of all kinds of evil, but also calls it the worship of idols, saying "And covetousness (which in Greek is called φιλαργυρία) which is the worship of idols." You see then to what a downfall this madness step by step leads, so that by the voice of the Apostle it is actually declared to be the worship of idols and false gods, because passing over the image and likeness of God (which one who serves God with devotion ought to preserve undefiled in himself), it chooses to love and care for images stamped on gold instead of God.

CHAPTER 8
HOW COVETOUSNESS IS A HINDRANCE TO ALL VIRTUES

WITH SUCH STRIDES THEN IN A DOWNWARD DIRECTION HE goes from bad to worse, and at last cares not to retain I will not say the virtue but even the shadow of humility, charity, and obedience; and is displeased with everything, and murmurs and groans over every work; and now having cast off all reverence, like a bad-tempered horse, dashes off headlong and unbridled: and discontented with his daily food and usual clothing, announces that he wall not put up with it any longer. He declares that God is not only there, and that his salvation is not confined to that place, where, if he does not take himself off pretty quickly from it, he deeply laments that he will soon die.

CHAPTER 9
HOW A MONK WHO HAS MONEY CANNOT STAY IN THE MONASTERY

AND SO HAVING MONEY TO PROVIDE FOR HIS WANDERINGS, with the assistance of which he has fitted himself as it were with wings, and now being quite ready for his move, he answers impertinently to all commands, and behaves himself like a stranger and a visitor, and whatever he sees needing improvement, he despises and treats with contempt. And though he has a supply of money secretly hidden, yet he complains that he has neither shoes nor clothes, and is indignant that they are given out to him so slowly. And if it happens that through the management of the superior some of these are given first to one who is known to have nothing whatever, he is still more inflamed with burning rage, and thinks that he is despised as a stranger; nor is he contented to turn his hand to any work, but finds fault with everything which the needs of the monastery require to be done. Then of set purpose he looks out for opportunities of being offended and angry, lest he might seem to have gone forth from the discipline of the monastery for a trivial reason. And not content to take his departure by himself alone, lest it should be thought that he has left as it were from his own fault, he never stops corrupting as many as he can by clandestine conferences.

But if the severity of the weather interferes with his journey and travels, he remains all the time in suspense and anxiety of heart, and never stops sowing and exciting discontent; as he thinks that he will only find consolation for his departure and an excuse for his fickleness in the bad character and defects of the monastery.

CHAPTER 10

OF THE TOILS WHICH A DESERTER FROM A MONASTERY MUST UNDERGO THROUGH COVETOUSNESS, THOUGH HE USED FORMERLY TO MURMUR AT THE VERY SLIGHTEST TASKS

AND SO HE IS DRIVEN ABOUT, AND MORE AND MORE inflamed with the love of his money, which when it is acquired, never allows a monk either to remain in a monastery or to live under the discipline of a rule. And when separating him like some wild beast from the rest of the herd, it has made him through want of companions an animal fit for prey, and caused him to be easily eaten up, as he is deprived of fellow lodgers, it forces him, who once thought it beneath him to perform the slight duties of the monastery, to labor without stopping night and day, through hope of gain; it suffers him to keep no services of prayer, no system of fasting, no rule of vigils; it does not allow him to fulfill the duties of seemly intercession, If only he can satisfy the madness of avarice, and supply his daily wants; inflaming the more the fire of covetousness, while believing that it will be extinguished by getting.

CHAPTER 11

THAT UNDER PRETENSE OF KEEPING THE PURSE WOMEN HAVE TO BE SOUGHT TO DWELL WITH THEM

HENCE MANY ARE LED ON OVER AN ABRUPT PRECIPICE, AND by an irrevocable fall, to death, and not content to possess by themselves that money which they either never had before, or which by a bad beginning they kept back, they seek for women to dwell with them, to preserve what they have unjustifiably amassed.or retained. And they implicate themselves in so many harmful and dangerous occupations, that they are cast down even to the depths of hell, while they refuse to acquiesce in that saying of the Apostle, that "having food and clothing they should be content" with that which the thrift of the monastery supplied, but "wishing to become rich they fall into temptation and the snare of the devil, and many unprofitable and hurtful desires, which drown men in destruction and perdition. For the love of money," i.e. covetousness, "is a root of all kinds of evil, which some coveting have erred from the faith, and have entangled themselves in many sorrows."

CHAPTER 12

AN INSTANCE OF A LUKEWARM MONK CAUGHT IN THE SNARES OF COVETOUSNESS

I KNOW OF ONE, WHO THINKS HIMSELF A MONK, AND what is worse flatters himself on his perfection, who had been received into a monastery, and when charged by his Abbot not to turn his thoughts back to those things which he had given up and renounced, but to free himself from covetousness, the root of all kinds of evil, and from earthly snares; and when told that if he wished to be cleansed from his former passions, by which he saw that he was from time to time grievously oppressed, he should cease from caring about those things which even formerly were not his own, entangled in the chains of which he certainly could not make progress towards purifying himself of his faults: with an angry expression he did not hesitate to answer, "If you have that with which you can support others, why do you forbid me to have it as well?"

CHAPTER 13
WHAT THE ELDERS RELATE TO THE JUNIORS IN THE MATTER OF STRIPPING OFF SINS

BUT LET NOT THIS SEEM SUPERFLUOUS OR OBJECTIONABLE to any one. For unless the different kinds of sins are first explained, and the origin and causes of diseases traced out, the proper healing remedies cannot be applied to the sick, nor can the preservation of perfect health be secured by the strong. For both these matters and many others besides these are generally put forward for the instruction of the younger brethren by the elders in their conferences, as they have had experience of numberless falls and the ruin of all sorts of people. And often recognizing in ourselves many of these things, when the elders explained and showed them, as men who were themselves disquieted by the same passions, we were cured without any shame or confusion on our part, since without saying anything we learnt both the remedies and the causes of the sins which beset us, which we have passed over and said nothing about, not from fear of the brethren, but lest our book should chance to fall into the hands of some who have had no instruction in this way of life, and might disclose to inexperienced persons what ought to be known only to those who are toiling and striving to reach the heights of perfection.

CHAPTER 14

INSTANCES TO SHOW THAT THE DISEASE OF COVETOUSNESS IS THREEFOLD

AND SO THIS DISEASE AND UNHEALTHY STATE IS THREEFOLD, and is condemned with equal abhorrence by all the fathers. One feature is this, of which we described the taint above, which by deceiving wretched folk persuades them to hoard though they never had anything of their own when they lived in the world. Another, which forces men afterwards to resume and once more desire those things which in the early days of their renunciation of the world they gave up. A third, which springing from a faulty and hurtful beginning and making a bad start, does not suffer those whom it has once infected with this lukewarmness of mind to strip themselves of all their worldly goods, through fear of poverty and want of faith; and those who keep back money and property which they certainly ought to have renounced and forsaken, it never allows to arrive at the perfection of the gospel. And we find in Holy Scripture instances of these three catastrophes which were visited with no light punishment. For when Gehazi wished to acquire what he had never had before, not only did he fail to obtain the gift of prophecy which it would have been his to receive from his master by hereditary succession, but on the contrary he was covered by the curse of the holy Elisha with a perpetual leprosy: while Judas, wanting to resume the possession of the wealth which he had formerly cast away when he followed Christ, not only fell into betraying the Lord, and lost his apostolic rank, but also was not allowed to close his life with the common lot of all but ended it by a violent death. But Ananias and Sapphira, keeping back a part of that which was formerly their own, were at the Apostle's word punished with death.

CHAPTER 15

OF THE DIFFERENCE BETWEEN ONE WHO RENOUNCES THE WORLD BADLY AND ONE WHO DOES NOT RENOUNCE IT AT ALL

OF THOSE THEN WHO SAY THAT THEY HAVE RENOUNCED THIS world, and afterwards being overcome by want of faith are afraid of losing their worldly goods, a charge is given mystically in Deuteronomy. "If any man is afraid and of a fearful heart let him not go forth to war: let him go back and return home, lest he make the hearts of his brethren to fear as he himself is timid and frightened." What can one want plainer than this testimony? Does not Scripture clearly prefer that they should not take on them even the earliest stages of this profession and its name, rather than by their persuasion and bad example turn others back from the perfection of the gospel, and weaken them by their faithless terror. And so they are bidden to withdraw from the battle and return to their homes, because a man cannot fight the Lord's battle with a double heart. For "a double-minded man is unstable in all his ways." And thinking, according to that Parable in the Gospel, that he who goes forth with ten thousand men against a king who comes with twenty thousand, cannot possibly fight, they should, while he is yet a great way off, ask for peace; that is, it is better for them not even to take the first step towards renunciation, rather than afterwards following it up coldly, to involve themselves in still greater dangers. For "it is better not to vow, than to vow and not pay." But finely is the one described as coming with ten thousand and the other with twenty. For the number of sins which attack us is far larger than that of the virtues which fight for us. But "no man can serve God and Mammon." And "no man putting his hand to the plough and looking back is fit for the kingdom of God."

CHAPTER 16
OF THE AUTHORITY UNDER WHICH THOSE SHELTER THEMSELVES WHO OBJECT TO STRIPPING THEMSELVES OF THEIR GOODS

THESE THEN TRY TO MAKE OUT A CASE FOR THEIR ORIGINAL avarice, by some authority from Holy Scripture, which they interpret with base ingenuity, in their desire to wrest and pervert to their own purposes a saying of the Apostle or rather of the Lord Himself: and, not adapting their own life or understanding to the meaning of the Scripture, but making the meaning of Scripture bend to the desires of their own lust, they try to make it to correspond to their own views, and say that it is written, "It is more blessed to give than to receive." And by an entirely wrong interpretation of this they think that they can weaken the force of that saying of the Lord in which he says: "If thou wilt be perfect, go sell all that thou hast and give to the poor, and thou shalt have treasure in heaven; and come, follow me." And they think that under color of this they need not deprive themselves of their riches: declaring indeed that they are more blessed if, supported by that which originally belonged to them, they give to others also out of their superabundance. And while they are shy of embracing with the Apostle that glorious state of abnegation for Christ's sake, they will not be content either with manual labor or the sparing diet of the monastery. And the only thing is that these must either know that they are deceiving themselves, and have not really renounced the world while they are clinging to their former riches; or, if they really and truly want to make trial of the monastic life, they must give up and forsake all these things and keep back nothing of that which they have renounced, and, with the Apostle, glory "in hunger and thirst, in cold and nakedness.

CHAPTER 17
OF THE RENUNCIATION OF THE APOSTLES AND THE PRIMITIVE CHURCH

AS IF HE (WHO, BY HIS ASSERTION THAT HE WAS ENDOWED with the privileges of a Roman citizen from his birth, testifies that he was no mean person according to this world's rank) might not likewise have been supported by the property which formerly belonged to him! And as if those men who were possessors of lands and houses in Jerusalem and sold everything and kept back nothing whatever for themselves, and brought the price of them and laid it at the feet of the apostles, might not have supplied their bodily necessities from their own property, had this been considered the best plan by the apostles, or had they themselves deemed it preferable! But they gave up all their property at once, and preferred to be supported by their own labor, and by the contributions of the Gentiles, of whose collection the holy Apostle speaks in writing to the Romans, and declaring his own office in this matter to them, and urging them on likewise to make this collection: "But now I go to Jerusalem to minister to the saints. For it has pleased them of Macedonia and Achaia to make a certain contribution for the poor saints who are at Jerusalem: it has pleased them indeed, and their debtors they are. For if the Gentiles are made partakers of their spiritual things, they ought also to minister to them in carnal things." To the Corinthians also he shows the same anxiety about this, and urges them the more diligently to prepare before his arrival a collection, which he was intending to send for their needs. "But concerning the collection for the saints, as I appointed to the churches of Galatia, so also do ye. Let each one of you on the first day of the week put apart with himself, laying up what it shall well please him, that when I come the collections be not then to be made. But when I come whomsoever you shall approve by your letters, them I will send to carry your grace to Jerusalem." And that he may stimulate them to make a larger collection, he adds, "But if it be meet that I also go, they shall go with me:" meaning if your offering is of such a character as to deserve to be taken there by my ministration. To the Galatians too, he testifies that when he was settling the division of the ministry of preaching with the apostles, he had arranged this with James, Peter, and John: that he should undertake the preaching to the Gentiles, but should never repudiate care and anxious thought for the poor who were at Jerusalem, who for Christ's sake gave up all their goods, and submitted to voluntary poverty. "And when they saw," said he, "the grace of God which was given to me, James and Cephas and John, who seemed to be pillars, gave to me and to Barnabas the right hand: of fellowship, that we should preach to the: Gentiles, but they to those of the circumcision: only they would that we should be mindful of the poor." A matter which he testifies that he attended to most carefully, saying, "which also I was anxious of myself to do. Who then are the more blessed, those who but lately were gathered out of the number of the heathen, and being unable to climb to the heights of the perfection of the gospel, clung to their own property, in whose case it was considered a great thing by the Apostle if at least they were restrained from the worship of idols, and from fornication, and from things strangled, and from blood, and had embraced the faith of Christ, with their goods and all: or those who live up to the demands of the gospel, and carry the Lord's cross daily, and want nothing out of their property to remain for their own use? And if the blessed Apostle himself, bound with chains and fetters, or hampered by the difficulties of traveling, and for these reasons not being able to provide with his hands, as he generally did, for the supply of his food, declares that he received that which supplied his wants from the brethren who came from Macedonia; "For that which was lacking to me," he says, "the brethren who came from Macedonia supplied:" and to the Philippians he says: "For ye Philippians know also that in the beginning of the gospel, when I came from Macedonia, no church communicated with me in the matter of giving and receiving, except you only; because even in Thessalonica once and again you sent to supply my needs:" (if this was so) then, according to the notion of these men, which they have formed in the coldness of their heart, will those men really be more blessed than the Apostle, because it is found that they have ministered to him of their substance? But this no one will venture to assert, however big a fool he may be.

CHAPTER 18
THAT IF WE WANT TO IMITATE THE APOSTLES WE OUGHT NOT TO LIVE ACCORDING TO OUR OWN PRESCRIPTIONS, BUT TO FOLLOW THEIR EXAMPLE

WHEREFORE IF WE WANT TO OBEY THE GOSPEL PRECEPT, and to show ourselves the followers of the Apostle and the whole primitive church, or of the fathers who in our own days succeeded to their virtues and perfection, we should not acquiesce in our own prescriptions, promising ourselves perfection from this wretched and lukewarm condition of ours: but following their footsteps, we should by no means aim at looking after our own interests, but should seek out the discipline and system of a monastery, that we may in very truth renounce this world; preserving nothing of those things which we have despised through the temptation of want of faith; and should look for our daily food, not from any store of money of our own, but from our own labors.

CHAPTER 19
A SAYING OF S. BASIL, THE BISHOP, DIRECTED AGAINST SYNCLETIUS.

THERE IS CURRENT A SAYING OF S. BASIL, BISHOP OF CAESAREA, directed against a certain Syncletius, who was growing indifferent with the sort of lukewarmness of which we have spoken; who, though he professed to have renounced this world, had yet kept back for himself some of his property, not liking to be supported by the labor of his own hands, and to acquire true humility by stripping himself and by grinding toil, and the subjection of the monastery: "You have," said he, "spoilt Syncletius, and not made a monk."

CHAPTER 20
HOW CONTEMPTIBLE IT IS TO BE OVERCOME BY COVETOUSNESS

AND SO IF WE WANT TO STRIVE LAWFULLY IN OUR SPIRITUAL combat, let us expel this dangerous enemy also from our hearts. For to overcome him does not so much show great virtue, as to be beaten by him is shameful and disgraceful. For when you are overpowered by a strong man, though there is grief in being overthrown, and distress at the loss of victory, yet some consolation may be derived by the vanquished from the strength of their opponent. But if the enemy is a poor creature, and the struggle a feeble one, besides the grief for defeat there is confusion of a more disgraceful character, and a shame which is worse than loss.

CHAPTER 21
HOW COVETOUSNESS CAN BE CONQUERED

AND IN THIS CASE IT WILL BE THE GREATEST VICTORY AND a lasting triumph, if, as is said, the conscience of the monk is not defiled by the possession of the smallest coin. For it is an impossibility for him who, overcome in the matter of a small possession, has once admitted into his heart a root of evil desire, not to be inflamed presently with the heat of a still greater desire. For the soldier of Christ will be victorious and in safety, and free from all the attacks of desire, so long as this most evil spirit does not implant in his heart a seed of this desire. Wherefore, though in the matter of all kinds of sins we ought ordinarily to watch the serpent's head, yet in this above all we should be more keenly on our guard. For if it has been admitted it will grow by feeding on itself, and will kindle for itself a worse fire. And so we must not only guard against the possession of money, but also must expel from our souls the desire for it. For we should not so much avoid the results of covetousness, as cut off by the roots all disposition towards it. For it will do no good not to possess money, if there exists in us the desire for getting it

CHAPTER 22
THAT ONE WHO ACTUALLY HAS NO MONEY MAY STILL BE DEEMED COVETOUS

FOR IT IS POSSIBLE EVEN FOR ONE WHO HAS NO MONEY TO be by no means free from the malady of covetousness, and for the blessing of penury to do him no good, because he has not been able to root out the sin of cupidity: delighting in the advantages of poverty, not in the merit of the virtue, and satisfied with the burden of necessity, not without coldness of heart. For just as the word of the gospel declares of those who are not defiled in body, that they are adulterers in heart; so it is possible that those who are in no way pressed down with the weight of money may be condemned with the covetous in disposition and intent. For it was the opportunity of possessing which was wanting in their case, and not the will for it: which latter is always crowned by God, rather than compulsion. And so we must use all diligence lest the fruits of our labors should be destroyed to no purpose. For it is a wretched thing to have endured the effects of poverty and want, but to have lost their fruits, through the fault of a shattered will.

CHAPTER 23
AN EXAMPLE DRAWN FROM THE CASE OF JUDAS

WOULD YOU LIKE TO KNOW HOW DANGEROUSLY AND harmfully that incitement, unless it has been carefully eradicated, will shoot up for the destruction of its owner, and put forth all sorts of branches of different sins? Look at Judas, reckoned among the number of the apostles, and see how because he would not bruise the deadly head of this serpent it destroyed him with its poison, and how when he was caught in the snares of concupiscence, it drove him into sin and a headlong downfall, so that he was persuaded to sell the Redeemer of the world and the author of man's salvation for thirty pieces of silver. And he could never have been impelled to this heinous sin of the betrayal if he had not been contaminated by the sin of covetousness: nor would he have made himself wickedly guilty of betraying the Lord, unless he had first accustomed himself to rob the bag intrusted to him.

CHAPTER 24
THAT COVETOUSNESS CANNOT BE OVERCOME EXCEPT BY STRIPPING ONE'S SELF OF EVERYTHING

THIS IS A SUFFICIENTLY DREADFUL AND CLEAR INSTANCE OF this tyranny, which, when once the mind is taken prisoner by it, allows it to keep to no rules of honesty, nor to be satisfied with any additions to its gains. For we must seek to put an end to this madness, not by riches, but by stripping ourselves of them. Lastly, when he (viz. Judas) had received the bag set apart for the distribution to the poor, and intrusted to his care for this purpose, that he might at least satisfy himself with plenty of money, and set a limit to his avarice, yet his plentiful supply only broke out into a still greedier incitement of desire, so that he was ready no longer secretly to rob the bag, but actually to sell the Lord Himself. For the madness of this avarice is not satisfied with any amount of riches.

CHAPTER 25
OF THE DEATHS OF ANANIAS AND SAPPHIRA, AND JUDAS, WHICH THEY UNDERWENT THROUGH THE IMPULSE OF COVETOUSNESS

LASTLY, THE CHIEF OF THE APOSTLES, TAUGHT BY THESE instances, and knowing that one who has any avarice cannot bridle it, and that it cannot be put an end to by a large or small sum of money, but only by the virtue of renunciation of everything, punished with death Ananias and Sapphira, who were mentioned before, because they had kept back something out of their property, that that death which Judas had voluntarily met with for the sin of betraying the Lord, they might also undergo for their lying avarice. How closely do the sin and punishment correspond in each case! In the one case treachery, in the other falsehood, was the result of covetousness. In the one case the truth is betrayed, in the other the sin of lying is committed. For though the issues of their deeds may appear different, yet they coincide in having one and the same aim. For the one, in order to escape poverty, desired to take back what he had forsaken; the others, for fear lest they might become poor, tried to keep back something out of their property, which they should have either offered to the Apostle in good faith, or have given entirely to the brethren. And so in each case there follows the judgment of death; because each sin sprang from the root of covetousness. And so if against those who did not covet other persons' goods, but tried to be sparing of their own, and had no desire to acquire, but only the wish to retain, there went forth so severe a sentence, what should we think of those who desire to amass wealth, without ever having had any of their own, and, making a show of poverty before men, are before God convicted of being rich, through the passion of avarice?

CHAPTER 26
THAT COVETOUSNESS BRINGS UPON THE SOUL A SPIRITUAL LEPROSY

AND SUCH ARE SEEN TO BE LEPERS IN SPIRIT AND HEART, after the likeness of Gehazi, who, desiring the uncertain riches of this world, was covered with the taint of foul leprosy, through which he left us a clear example that every soul which is defiled with the stain of cupidity is covered with the spiritual leprosy of sin, and is counted as unclean before God with a perpetual curse.

CHAPTER 27
SCRIPTURE PROOFS BY WHICH ONE WHO IS AIMING AT PERFECTION IS TAUGHT NOT TO TAKE BACK AGAIN WHAT HE HAS GIVEN UP AND RENOUNCED

IF THEN THROUGH THE DESIRE OF PERFECTION YOU HAVE forsaken all things and followed Christ who says to thee, "Go sell all that thou hast, and give to the poor, and thou shalt have treasure in heaven: and come follow me," why, having put your hand to the plough, do you look back, so that you will be declared by the voice of the same Lord not to be fit for the kingdom of heaven? When secure on the top of the gospel roof, why do you descend to carry away something from the house, from those things, namely, which beforetime you despised? When you are out in the field and working at the virtues, why do you run back and try to clothe yourself again with what belongs to this world, which you stripped off when you renounced it? But if you were hindered by poverty from having anything to give up, still less ought you to amass what you never had before. For by the grace of the Lord you were for this purpose made ready that you might hasten to him the more readily, being hampered by no snares of wealth. But let no one who is wanting in this be disappointed; for there is no one who has not something to give up. He has renounced all the possessions of this world, whoever has thoroughly eradicated the desire to possess them.

CHAPTER 28
THAT THE VICTORY OVER COVETOUSNESS CAN ONLY BE GAINED BY STRIPPING ONE'S SELF BARE OF EVERYTHING

THIS THEN IS THE PERFECT VICTORY OVER COVETOUSNESS: not to allow a gleam from the very smallest scrap of it to remain in our heart, as we know that we shall have no further power of quenching it, if we cherish even the tiniest bit of a spark of it in us.

CHAPTER 29
HOW A MONK CAN RETAIN HIS POVERTY

AND WE CAN ONLY PRESERVE THIS VIRTUE UNIMPAIRED IF WE remain in a monastery, and as the Apostle says, having food and clothing, are therewith content.

CHAPTER 30
THE REMEDIES AGAINST THE DISEASE OF COVETOUSNESS.

KEEPING THEN IN MIND THE JUDGMENT OF ANANIAS AND Sapphira let us dread keeping back any of those things which we gave up and vowed utterly to forsake. Let us also fear the example of Gehazi, who for the sin of covetousness was chastised with the punishment of perpetual leprosy. From this let us beware of acquiring that wealth which we never formerly possessed. Moreover also dreading both the fault and the death of Judas, let us with all the power that we have avoid taking back any of that wealth which once we cast away from us. Above all, considering the state of our weak and shifty nature, let us beware lest the day of the Lord come upon us as a thief in the night, and find our conscience defiled even by a single penny; for this would make void all the fruits of our renunciation of the world, and cause that which was said to the rich man in the gospel to be directed towards us also by the voice of the Lord: "Thou fool, this night thy soul shall be required of thee: then whose shall those things be which thou hast prepared?" And taking no thought for the morrow, let us never allow ourselves to be enticed away from the rule of the Coenobium.

CHAPTER 31
THAT NO ONE CAN GET THE BETTER OF COVETOUSNESS UNLESS HE STAYS IN THE COENOBIUM: AND HOW ONE CAN REMAIN THERE

BUT WE SHALL CERTAINLY NOT BE SUFFERED TO DO THIS, nor even to remain under the rule of a system, unless the virtue of patience, which can only spring from humility as its source, is first securely fixed and established in us. For the one teaches us not to trouble any one else; the other, to endure with magnanimity wrongs offered to us.

BOOK 8

OF THE SPIRIT OF ANGER

CHAPTER 1
HOW OUR FOURTH CONFLICT IS AGAINST THE SIN OF ANGER, AND HOW MANY EVILS THIS PASSION PRODUCES

IN OUR FOURTH COMBAT THE DEADLY POISON OF ANGER HAS to be utterly rooted out from the inmost corners of our soul. For as long as this remains in our hearts, and blinds with its hurtful darkness the eye of the soul, we can neither acquire right judgment and discretion, nor gain the insight which springs from an honest gaze, or ripeness of counsel, nor can we be partakers of life, or retentive of righteousness, or even have the capacity for spiritual and true light: "for," says one, mine eye is disturbed by reason of anger." Nor can we become partakers of wisdom, even though we are considered wise by universal consent, for "anger rests in the bosom of fools." Nor can we even attain immortal life, although we are accounted prudent in the opinion of everybody, for "anger destroys even the prudent." Nor shall we be able with clear judgment of heart to secure the controlling power of righteousness, even though we are reckoned perfect and holy in the estimation of all men, for "the wrath of man worketh not the righteousness of God." Nor can we by any possibility acquire that esteem and honor which is so frequently seen even in worldlings, even though we are thought noble and honorable through the privileges of birth, because "an angry man is dishonored." Nor again can we secure any ripeness of counsel, even though we appear to be weighty, and endowed with the utmost knowledge; because "an angry man acts without counsel." Nor can we be free from dangerous disturbances, nor be without sin, even though no sort of disturbances be brought upon us by others; because "a passionate man engenders quarrels, but an angry man digs up sins."

CHAPTER 2
OF THOSE WHO SAY THAT ANGER IS NOT INJURIOUS, IF WE ARE ANGRY WITH THOSE WHO DO WRONG, SINCE GOD HIMSELF IS SAID TO BE ANGRY

WE HAVE HEARD SOME PEOPLE TRYING TO EXCUSE THIS most pernicious disease of the soul, in such a way as to endeavor to extenuate it by a rather shocking way of interpreting Scripture: as they say that it is not injurious if we are angry with the brethren who do wrong, since, say they, God Himself is said to rage and to be angry with those who either will not know Him, or, knowing Him, spurn Him, as here "And the anger of the Lord was kindled against His people;" or where the prophet prays and says, "O Lord, rebuke me not in thine anger, neither chasten me in thy displeasure;" not understanding that, while they want to open to men an excuse for a most pestilent sin, they are ascribing to the Divine Infinity and Fountain of all purity a taint of human passion.

CHAPTER 3
OF THOSE THINGS WHICH ARE SPOKEN OF GOD ANTHROPOMORPHICALLY

FOR IF WHEN THESE THINGS ARE SAID OF GOD THEY ARE TO be understood literally in a material gross signification, then also He sleeps, as it is said, "Arise, wherefore sleepest thou, O Lord?" though it is elsewhere said of Him: "Behold he that keepeth Israel shall neither slumber nor sleep." And He stands and sits, since He says, "Heaven is my seat, and earth the footstool for my feet:" though He "measure out the heaven with his hand, and holdeth the earth in his fist." And He is "drunken with wine" as it is said, "The Lord awoke like a sleeper, a mighty man, drunken with wine;" He "who only hath immortality and dwelleth in the light which no man can approach unto:" not to say anything of the "ignorance" and "forgetfulness," of which we often find mention in Holy Scripture: nor lastly of the outline of His limbs, which are spoken of as arranged and ordered like a man's; e.g., the hair, head, nostrils, eyes, face, hands, arms, fingers, belly, and feet: if we are willing to take all of which according to the bare literal sense, we must think of God as in fashion with the outline of limbs, and a bodily form; which indeed is shocking even to speak of, and must be far from our thoughts.

CHAPTER 4
IN WHAT SENSE WE SHOULD UNDERSTAND THE PASSIONS AND HUMAN ARTS WHICH ARE ASCRIBED TO THE UNCHANGING AND INCORPOREAL GOD

AND SO AS WITHOUT HORRIBLE PROFANITY THESE THINGS cannot be understood literally of Him who is declared by the authority of Holy Scripture to be invisible, ineffable, incomprehensible, inestimable, simple, and uncompounded, so neither can the passion of anger and wrath be attributed to that unchangeable nature without fearful blasphemy. For we ought to see that the limbs signify the divine powers and boundless operations of God, which can only be represented to us by the familiar expression of limbs: by the mouth we should understand that His utterances are meant, which are of His mercy continually poured into the secret senses of the soul, or which He spoke among our fathers and the prophets: by the eyes we can understand the boundless character of His sight with which He sees and looks through all things, and so nothing is hidden from Him of what is done or can be done by us, or even thought. By the expression "hands," we understand His providence and work, by which He is the creator and author of all things; the arms are the emblems of His might and government, with which He upholds, rules and controls all things. And not to speak of other things, what else does the hoary hair of His head signify but the eternity and perpetuity of Deity, through which He is without any beginning, and before all times, and excels all creatures? So then also when we read of the anger or fury of the Lord, we should take it not ἀνθρωποπαθῶς ; i.e., according to an unworthy meaning of human passion, but in a sense worthy of God, who is free from all passion; so that by this we should understand that He is the judge and avenger of all the unjust things which are done in this world; and by reason of these terms and their meaning we should dread Him as the terrible rewarder of our deeds, and fear to do anything against His will. For human nature is wont to fear those whom it knows to be indignant, and is afraid of offending: as in the case of some most just judges, avenging wrath is usually feared by those who are tormented by some accusation of their conscience; not indeed that this passion exists in the minds of those who are going to judge with perfect equity, but that, while they so fear, the disposition of the judge towards them is that which is the precursor of a just and impartial execution of the law. And this, with whatever kindness and gentleness it may be conducted, is deemed by those who are justly to be punished to be the most savage wrath and vehement anger. It would be tedious and outside the scope of the present work were we to explain all the things which are spoken metaphorically of God in Holy Scripture, with human figures. Let it be enough for our present purpose, which is aimed against the sin of wrath, to have said this that no one may through ignorance draw down upon himself a cause of this evil and of eternal death, out of those Scriptures in which he should seek for saintliness and immortality as the remedies to bring life and salvation.

CHAPTER 5
HOW CALM A MONK OUGHT TO BE

AND SO A MONK AIMING AT PERFECTION, AND DESIRING TO strive lawfully in his spiritual combat, should be free from all sin of anger and wrath, and should listen to the charge which the "chosen vessel" gives him. "Let all anger," says he, and wrath, and clamor, and evil speaking, be taken away from among you, with all malice." When he says, "Let all anger be taken away from you," he excepts none whatever as necessary or useful for us. And if need be, he should at once treat an erring brother in such a way that, while he manages to apply a remedy to one afflicted with perhaps a slight fever, he may not by his wrath involve himself in a more dangerous malady of blindness. For he who wants to heal another's wound ought to be in good health and free from every affection of weakness himself, lest that saying of the gospel should be used to him, "Physician, first heal thyself;" and lest, seeing a mote in his brother's eye, he see not the beam in his own eye, for how will he see to cast out the mote from his brother's eye, who has the beam of anger in his own eye?

CHAPTER 6
OF THE RIGHTEOUS AND UNRIGHTEOUS PASSION OF WRATH

FROM ALMOST EVERY CAUSE THE EMOTION OF WRATH BOILS over, and blinds the eyes of the soul, and, bringing the deadly beam of a worse disease over the keenness of our sight, prevents us from seeing the sun of righteousness. It makes no difference whether gold plates, or lead, or what metal you please, are placed over our eyelids, the value of the metal makes no difference in our blindness.

CHAPTER 7
OF THE ONLY CASE IN WHICH ANGER IS USEFUL TO US

WE HAVE, IT MUST BE ADMITTED, A USE FOR ANGER excellently implanted in us for which alone it is useful and profitable for us to admit it, viz., when we are indignant and rage against the lustful emotions of our heart, and are vexed that the things which we are ashamed to do or say before men have risen up in the lurking places of our heart, as we tremble at the presence of the angels, and of God Himself, who pervades all things everywhere, and fear with the utmost dread the eye of Him from whom the secrets of our hearts cannot possibly be hid.

CHAPTER 8
INSTANCES FROM THE LIFE OF THE BLESSED DAVID IN WHICH ANGER WAS RIGHTLY FELT

AND AT ANY RATE (THIS IS THE CASE), WHEN WE ARE agitated against this very anger, because it has stolen on us against our brother, and when in wrath we expel its deadly incitements, nor suffer it to have a dangerous lurking place in the recesses of our heart. To be angry in this fashion even that prophet teaches us who had so completely expelled it from his own feelings that he would not retaliate even on his enemies and those delivered by God into his hands: when he says "Be ye angry and sin not." For he, when he had longed for water from the well of Bethlehem, and had been given it by his mighty men, who had brought it through the midst of the hosts of the enemy, at once poured it out on the ground: and thus in his anger extinguished the delicious feeling of his desire, and poured it out to the Lord, without satisfying the longing that he had expressed, saying: "That be far from me that I should do this! Shall I drink the blood of those men who went forth on the danger of their souls?"

And when Shimei threw stones at King David and cursed him, in his hearing, before everybody, and Abishai, the son of Zeruiah, the captain of the host, wished to cut off his head and avenge the insult to the king, the blessed David moved with pious wrath against this dreadful suggestion of his, and keeping the due measure of humility and a strict patience, said with imperturbable gentleness, "What have I to do with you, ye sons of Zeruiah? Let him alone that he may curse. For the Lord hath commanded him to curse David. And who is he who shall dare to say, Why hast thou done this? Behold my son, who came forth from my loins, seeks my life, and how much more this son of Benjamin? Let him alone, that he may curse, according to the command of the Lord. It may be the Lord will look upon my affliction, and return to me good for this cursing to-day."

CHAPTER 9

OF THE ANGER WHICH SHOULD BE DIRECTED AGAINST OURSELVES

AND SOME ARE COMMANDED TO "BE ANGRY" AFTER A wholesome fashion, but with our own selves, and with evil thoughts that arise, and "not to sin," viz., by bringing them to a bad issue. Finally, the next verse explains this to be the meaning more clearly: "The things you say in your hearts, be sorry for them on your beds:" i.e., whatever you think of in your hearts when sudden and nervous excitements rush in on you, correct and amend with wholesome sorrow, lying as it were on a bed of rest, and removing by the moderating influence of counsel all noise and disturbance of wrath. Lastly, the blessed Apostle, when he made use of the testimony of this verse, and said, "Be ye angry and sin not," added, "Let not the sun go down upon your wrath, neither give place to the devil." If it is dangerous for the sun of righteousness to go down upon our wrath, and if when we are angry we straightway give place to the devil in our hearts, how is it that above he charges us to be angry, saying, "Be ye angry, and sin not"? Does he not evidently mean this: be ye angry with your faults and your tempers, lest, if you acquiesce in them, Christ, the sun of righteousness, may on account of your anger begin to go down on your darkened minds, and when He departs you may furnish a place for the devil in your hearts?

CHAPTER 10

OF THE SUN, OF WHICH IT IS SAID THAT IT SHOULD NOT GO DOWN UPON YOUR WRATH

AND OF THIS SUN GOD CLEARLY MAKES MENTION BY THE prophet, when He says, "But to those that fear my name the sun of righteousness shall arise with healing in His wings." And this again is said to "go down" at midday on sinners and false prophets, and those who are angry, when the prophet says, "Their sun is gone down at noon." And at any rate "tropically" the mind, that is the nou-v or reason, which is fairly called the sun because it looks over all the thoughts and discernings of the heart, should not be put out by the sin of anger: lest when it "goes down" the shadows of disturbance, together with the devil their author, fill all the feelings of our hearts, and, overwhelmed by the shadows of wrath, as in a murky night, we know not what we ought to do. In this sense it is that we have brought forward this passage of the Apostle, handed down to us by the teaching of the elders, because it was needful, even at the risk of a somewhat lengthy discourse, to show how they felt with regard to anger, for they do not permit it even for a moment to effect an entrance into our heart: observing with the utmost care that saying of the gospel: "Whosoever is angry with his brother is in danger of the judgment." But if it be lawful to be angry up till sunset, the surfeit of our wrath and the vengeance of our anger will be able to give full play to passion and dangerous excitement before that sun inclines towards its setting.

CHAPTER 11

OF THOSE TO WHOSE WRATH EVEN THE GOING DOWN OF THE SUN SETS NO LIMIT

BUT WHAT AM I TO SAY OF THOSE (AND I CANNOT SAY IT without shame on my own part) to whose implacability even the going down of the sun sets no bound: but prolonging it for several days, and nourishing rancorous feelings against those against whom they have been excited, they say in words that they are not angry, but in fact and deed they show that they are extremely disturbed? For they do not speak to them pleasantly, nor address them with ordinary civility, and they think that they are not doing wrong in this, because they do not seek to avenge themselves for their upset. But since they either do not dare, or at any rate are not able to show their anger openly, and give place to it, they drive in, to their own detriment, the poison of anger, and secretly cherish it in their hearts, and silently feed on it in themselves; without shaking off by an effort of mind their sulky disposition, but digesting it as the days go by, and somewhat mitigating it after a while.

CHAPTER 12
HOW THIS IS THE END OF TEMPER AND ANGER WHEN A MAN CARRIES IT INTO ACT AS FAR AS HE CAN

BUT IT LOOKS AS IF EVEN THIS WAS NOT THE END OF vengeance to every one, but some can only completely satisfy their wrath or sulkiness if they carry out the impulse of anger as far as they are able; and this we know to be the case with those who restrain their feelings, not from desire of calming them, but simply from want of opportunity of revenge. For they can do nothing more to those with whom they are angry, except speak to them without ordinary civility: or it looks as if anger was to be moderated only in action, and not to be altogether rooted out from its hiding place in our bosom: so that, overwhelmed by its shadows, we are unable not only to admit the light of wholesome counsel and of knowledge, but also to be a temple of the Holy Spirit, so long as the spirit of anger dwells in us. For wrath that is nursed in the heart, although it may not injure men who stand by, yet excludes the splendor of the radiance of the Holy Ghost, equally with wrath that is openly manifested.

CHAPTER 13
THAT WE SHOULD NOT RETAIN OUR ANGER EVEN FOR AN INSTANT

OR HOW CAN WE THINK THAT THE LORD WOULD HAVE IT retained even for an instant, since He does not permit us to offer the spiritual sacrifices of our prayers, if we are aware that another has any bitterness against us: saying, "If then thou bringest thy gift to the altar and there rememberest that thy brother hath aught against thee, leave there thy gift at the altar and go thy way; first be reconciled to thy brother, and then come and offer thy gift." How then may we retain displeasure against our brother, I will not say for several days, but even till the going down of the sun, if we are not allowed to offer our prayers to God while he has anything against us? And yet we are commanded by the Apostle: "Pray without ceasing;" and "in every place lifting up holy hands without wrath and disputing." It remains then either that we never pray at all, retaining this poison in our hearts, and become guilty in regard of this apostolic or evangelic charge, in which we are bidden to pray everywhere and without ceasing; or else if, deceiving ourselves, we venture to pour forth our prayers, contrary to His command, we must know that we are offering to God no prayer, but an obstinate temper with a rebellious spirit.

CHAPTER 14
OF RECONCILIATION WITH OUR BROTHER

AND BECAUSE WE OFTEN SPURN THE BRETHREN WHO ARE injured and saddened, and despise them, and say that they were not hurt by any fault of ours, the Healer of souls, who knows all secrets, wishing utterly to eradicate all opportunities of anger from our hearts, not only commands us to forgive if we have been wronged, and to be reconciled with our brothers, and keep no recollection of wrong or injuries against them, but He also gives a similar charge, that in case we are aware that they have anything against us, whether justly or unjustly, we should leave our gift, that is, postpone our prayers, and hasten first to offer satisfaction to them; and so when our brother's cure is first effected, we may bring the offering of our prayers without blemish. For the common Lord of all does not care so much for our homage as to lose in one what He gains in another, through displeasure being allowed to reign in us. For in any one's loss He suffers some loss, who desires and looks for the salvation of all His servants in one and the same way. And therefore our prayer will lose its effect, if our brother has anything against us, just as much as if we were cherishing feelings of bitterness against him in a swelling and wrathful spirit.

CHAPTER 15
HOW THE OLD LAW WOULD ROOT OUT ANGER NOT ONLY FROM THE ACTIONS BUT FROM THE THOUGHTS

BUT WHY SHOULD WE SPEND ANY MORE TIME OVER evangelic and apostolic precepts, when even the old law, which is thought to be somewhat slack, guards against the same thing, when it says, "Thou shall not hate thy brother in thine heart;" and again, "Be not mindful of the injury of thy citizens;" and again, "The ways of those who preserve the recollection of wrongs are towards death"? You see there too that wickedness is restrained not only in action, but also in the secret thoughts, since it is commanded that hatred be utterly rooted out from the heart, and not merely retaliation for, but the very recollection of, a wrong done.

CHAPTER 16
HOW USELESS IS THE RETIREMENT OF THOSE WHO DO NOT GIVE UP THEIR BAD MANNERS

SOMETIMES WHEN WE HAVE BEEN OVERCOME BY PRIDE OR impatience, and we want to improve our rough and bearish manners, we complain that we require solitude, as if we should find the virtue of patience there where nobody provokes us: and we apologize for our carelessness, and say that the reason of our disturbance does not spring from our own impatience, but from the fault of our brethren. And while we lay the blame of our fault on others, we shall never be able to reach the goal of patience and perfection.

CHAPTER 17

THAT THE PEACE OF OUR HEART DOES NOT DEPEND ON ANOTHER'S WILL, BUT LIES IN OUR OWN CONTROL

THE CHIEF PART THEN OF OUR IMPROVEMENT AND PEACE of mind must not be made to depend on another's will, which cannot possibly be subject to our authority, but it lies rather in our own control. And so the fact that we are not angry ought not to result from another's perfection, but from our own virtue, which is acquired, not by somebody else's patience, but by our own long-suffering.

CHAPTER 18

OF THE ZEAL WITH WHICH WE SHOULD SEEK THE DESERT, AND OF THE THINGS IN WHICH WE MAKE PROGRESS THERE

FURTHER, IT IS THOSE WHO ARE PERFECT AND PURIFIED from all faults who ought to seek the desert, and when they have thoroughly exterminated all their faults amid the assembly of the brethren, they should enter it not by way of cowardly flight, but for the purpose of divine contemplation, and with the desire of deeper insight into heavenly things, which can only be gained in solitude by those who are perfect. For whatever faults we bring with us uncured into the desert, we shall find to remain concealed in us and not to be got rid of. For just as when the character has been improved, solitude can lay open to it the purest contemplation, and reveal the knowledge of spiritual mysteries to its clear gaze, so it generally not only preserves but intensifies the faults of those who have undergone no correction. For a man appears to himself to be patient and humble, just as long as he comes across nobody in intercourse; but he will presently revert to his former nature, whenever the chance of any sort of passion occurs: I mean that those faults will at once appear on the surface which were lying hid, and, like unbridled horses diligently fed up during too long a time of idleness, dash forth from the barriers the more eagerly and fiercely, to the destruction of their charioteer. For when the opportunity for practicing them among men is removed, our faults will more and more increase in us, unless we have first been purified from them. And the mere shadow of patience, which, when we mixed with our brethren, we seemed fancifully to possess, at least out of respect for them and publicity, we lose altogether through sloth and carelessness.

CHAPTER 19

AN ILLUSTRATION TO HELP IN FORMING AN OPINION ON THOSE WHO ARE ONLY PATIENT WHEN THEY ARE NOT TRIED BY ANY ONE

BUT IT IS LIKE ALL POISONOUS KINDS OF SERPENTS OR OF wild beasts, which, while they remain in solitude and their own lairs, are still not harmless; for they cannot really be said to be harmless, because they are not actually hurting anybody. For this results in their case, not from any feeling of goodness, but from the exigencies of solitude, and when they have secured an opportunity of hurting some one, at once they produce the poison stored up in them, and show the ferocity of their nature. And so in the case of men who are aiming at perfection, it is not enough not to be angry with men. For we recollect that when we were living in solitude a feeling of irritation would creep over us against our pen because it was too large or too small; against our penknife when it cut badly and with a blunt edge what we wanted cut; and against a flint if by chance when we were rather late and hurrying to the reading, a spark of fire flashed out, so that we could not remove and get rid of our perturbation of mind except by cursing the senseless matter, or at least the devil. Wherefore for a method of perfection it will not be of any use for there to be a dearth of men against whom our anger might be roused: since, if patience has not already been acquired, the feelings of passion which still dwell in our hearts can equally well spend themselves on dumb things and paltry objects, and not allow us to gain a continuous state of peacefulness, or to be free from our remaining faults: unless perhaps we think that some advantage and a sort of cure may be gained for our passion from the fact that inanimate and speechless things cannot possibly reply to our curses and rage, nor provoke our ungovernable temper to break out into a worse madness of passion.

CHAPTER 20

OF THE WAY IN WHICH AUGER SHOULD BE BANISHED ACCORDING TO THE GOSPEL

WHEREFORE IF WE WISH TO GAIN THE SUBSTANCE OF that divine reward of which it is said, "Blessed are the pure in heart, for they shall see God," we ought not only to banish it from our actions, but entirely to root it out from our inmost soul. For it will not be of any good to have checked anger in words, and not to have shown it in deeds, if God, from whom the secrets of the heart are not hid, sees that it remains in the secret recesses of our bosom. For the word of the gospel bids us destroy the roots of our faults rather than the fruits; for these, when the incitements are all removed, will certainly not put forth shoots any more; and so the mindwill be able to continue in all patience and holiness, when this anger has been removed, not from the surface of acts and deeds, but from the very innermost thoughts. And, therefore to avoid the commission of murder, anger and hatred are cut off, without which the crime of murder cannot possibly be committed. For "whosoever is angry with his brother, is in danger of the judgment;" and "whosoever hateth his brother is a murderer;" viz., because in his heart he desires to kill him, whose blood we know that he has certainly not shed among men with his own hand or with a weapon; yet, owing to his burst of anger, he is declared to be a murderer by God, who renders to each man, not merely for the result of his actions, but for his purpose and desires and wishes, either a reward or a punishment; according to that which He Himself says through the prophet: "But I come that I may gather them together with all nations and tongues;" and again: "Their thoughts between themselves accusing or also defending one another, in the day when God shall judge the secrets of men."

CHAPTER 22

THE REMEDIES BY WHICH WE CAN ROOT OUT ANGER FROM OUR HEARTS

WHEREFORE THE ATHLETE OF CHRIST WHO STRIVES lawfully ought thoroughly to root out the feeling of wrath. And it will be a sure remedy for this disease, if in the first place we make up our mind that we ought never to be angry at all, whether for good or bad reasons: as we know that we shall at once lose the light of discernment, and the security of good counsel, and our very uprightness, and the temperate character of righteousness, if the main light of our heart has been darkened by its shadows: next, that the purity of our soul will presently be clouded, and that it cannot possibly be made a temple for the Holy Ghost while the spirit of anger resides in us; lastly, that we should consider that we ought never to pray, nor pour out our prayer to God, while we are angry. And above all, having before our eyes the uncertain condition of mankind, we should realize daily that we are soon to depart from the body, and that our continence and chastity, our renunciation of all our possessions, our contempt of wealth, our efforts in fastings and vigils will not help us at all, if solely on account of anger and hatred eternal punishments are awarded to us by the judge of the world.

BOOK 9

OF THE SPIRIT OF DEJECTION

CHAPTER 1
HOW OUR FIFTH COMBAT IS AGAINST THE SPIRIT OF DEJECTION, AND OF THE HARM WHICH IT INFLICTS UPON THE SOUL

IN OUR FIFTH COMBAT WE HAVE TO RESIST THE PANGS OF gnawing dejection: for if this, through separate attacks made at random, and by haphazard and casual changes, has secured an opportunity of gaining possession of our mind it keeps us back at all times from all insight in divine contemplation, and utterly ruins and depresses the mind that has fallen away from its complete state of purity. It does not allow it to say its prayers with its usual gladness of heart, nor permit it to rely on the comfort of reading the sacred writings, nor suffer it to be quiet and gentle with the brethren; it makes it impatient and rough in all the duties of work and devotion: and, as all wholesome counsel is lost, and steadfastness of heart destroyed, it makes the feelings almost mad and drunk, and crushes and overwhelms them with penal despair.

CHAPTER 2
OF THE CARE WITH WHICH THE MALADY OF DEJECTION MUST BE HEALED

WHEREFORE IF WE ARE ANXIOUS TO EXERT OURSELVES lawfully in the struggle of our spiritual combat we ought with no less care to set about healing this malady also. For "as the moth injures the garment, and the worm the wood, so dejection the heart of man." With sufficient clearness and appropriateness has the Divine Spirit expressed the force of this dangerous and most injurious fault.

CHAPTER 3
TO WHAT THE SOUL MAY BE COMPARED WHICH IS A PREY TO THE ATTACKS OF DEJECTION

FOR THE GARMENT THAT IS MOTH-EATEN HAS NO LONGER any commercial value or good use to which it can be put; and in the same way the wood that is worm-eaten is no longer worth anything for ornamenting even an ordinary building, but is destined to be burnt in the fire. So therefore the soul also which is a prey to the attacks of gnawing dejection will be useless for that priestly garment which, according to the prophecy of the holy David, the ointment of the Holy Spirit coming down from heaven, first on Aaron's beard, then on his skirts, is wont to assume: as it is said, "It is like the ointment upon the head which ran down upon Aaron's beard, which ran down to the skirts of his clothing. Nor can it have anything to do with the building or ornamentation of that spiritual temple of which Paul as a wise master builder laid the foundations, saying, "Ye are the temple of God, and the Spirit of God dwelleth in you:" and what the beams of this are like the bride tells us in the Song of Songs: "Our rafters are of cypress: the beams of our houses are of cedar." And therefore those sorts of wood are chosen for the temple of God which are fragrant and not liable to rot, and which are not subject to decay from age nor to be worm-eaten.

CHAPTER 4
WHENCE AND IN WHAT WAY DEJECTION ARISES

BUT SOMETIMES IT IS FOUND TO RESULT FROM THE FAULT of previous anger, or to spring from the desire of some gain which has not been realized, when a man has found that he has failed in his hope of securing those things which he had planned. But sometimes without any apparent reason for our being driven to fall into this misfortune, we are by the instigation of our crafty enemy suddenly depressed with so great a gloom that we cannot receive with ordinary civility the visits of those who are near and dear to us; and whatever subject of conversation is started by them, we regard it as ill-timed and out of place; and we can give them no civil answer, as the gall of bitterness is in possession of every corner of our heart.

CHAPTER 5

THAT DISTURBANCES ARE CAUSED IN US NOT BY THE FAULTS OF OTHER PEOPLE, BUT BY OUR OWN

WHENCE IT IS CLEARLY PROVED THAT THE PAINS OF disturbances are not always caused in us by other people's faults, but rather by our own, as we have stored up in ourselves the causes of offense, and the seeds of faults, which, as soon as a shower of temptation waters our soul, at once burst forth into shoots and fruits.

CHAPTER 6

THAT NO ONE COMES TO GRIEF BY A SUDDEN FALL, BUT IS DESTROYED BY FALLING THROUGH A LONG COURSE OF CARELESSNESS.

FOR NO ONE IS EVER DRIVEN TO SIN BY BEING PROVOKED through another's fault, unless he has the fuel of evil stored up in his own heart. Nor should we imagine that a man has been deceived suddenly when he has looked on a woman and fallen into the abyss of shameful lust: but rather that, owingto the opportunity of looking on her, the symptoms of disease which were hidden and concealed in his inmost soul have been brought to the surface.

CHAPTER 7
THAT WE OUGHT NOT TO GIVE UP INTERCOURSE WITH OUR BRETHREN IN ORDER TO SEEK AFTER PERFECTION, BUT SHOULD RATHER CONSTANTLY CULTIVATE THE VIRTUE OF PATIENCE

AND so God, the creator of all things, having regard above everything to the amendment of His own work, and because the roots and causes of our falls are found not in others, but in ourselves, commands that we should not give up intercourse with our brethren, nor avoid those who we think have been hurt by us, or by whom we have been offended, but bids us pacify them, knowing that perfection of heart is not secured by separating from men so much as by the virtue of patience. Which when it is securely held, as it can keep us at peace even with those who hate peace, so, if it has not been acquired, it makes us perpetually differ from those who are perfect and better than we are: for opportunities for disturbance, on account of which we are eager to get away from those with whom we are connected, will not be wanting so long as we are living among men; and therefore we shall not escape altogether, but only change the causes of dejection on account of which we separated from our former friends.

CHAPTER 8
THAT IF WE HAVE IMPROVED OUR CHARACTER IT IS POSSIBLE FOR US TO GET ON WITH EVERYBODY

WE must then do our best to endeavor to amend our faults and correct our manners. And if we succeed in correcting them we shall certainly be at peace, I will not say with men, but even with beasts and the brute creation, according to what is said in the book of the blessed Job: "For the beasts of the field will be at peace with thee;" for we shall not fear offenses coming from without, nor will any occasion of falling trouble us from outside, if the roots of such are not admitted and implanted within in our own selves: for "they have great peace who love thy law, O God; and they have no occasion of falling."

CHAPTER 9

OF ANOTHER SORT OF DEJECTION WHICH PRODUCES DESPAIR OF SALVATION

THERE IS, TOO, ANOTHER STILL MORE OBJECTIONABLE SORT of dejection, which produces in the guilty soul no amendment of life or correction of faults, but the most destructive despair: which did not make Cain repent after the murder of his brother, or Judas, after the betrayal, hasten to relieve himself by making amends, but drove him to hang himself in despair.

CHAPTER 10

OF THE ONLY THING IN WHICH DEJECTION IS USEFUL TO US

AND SO WE MUST SEE THAT DEJECTION IS ONLY USEFUL TO us in one case, when we yield to it either in penitence for sin, or through being inflamed with the desire of perfection, or the contemplation of future blessedness. And of this the blessed Apostle says: "The sorrow which is according to God worketh repentance steadfast unto salvation: but the sorrow of the world worketh death."

CHAPTER 11
HOW WE CAN DECIDE WHAT IS USEFUL AND THE SORROW ACCORDING TO GOD, AND WHAT IS DEVILISH AND DEADLY

BUT THAT DEJECTION AND SORROW WHICH "WORKETH repentance steadfast unto salvation" is obedient, civil, humble, kindly, gentle, and patient, as it springs from the love of God, and unweariedly extends itself from desire of perfection to every bodily grief and sorrow of spirit; and somehow or other rejoicing and feeding on hope of its own profit preserves all the gentleness of courtesy and forbearance, as it has in itself all the fruits of the Holy Spirit of which the same Apostle gives the list: "But the fruit of the Spirit is love, joy, peace, forbearance, goodness, benignity, faith, mildness, modesty." But the other kind is rough, impatient, hard, full of rancor and useless grief and penal despair, and breaks down the man on whom it has fastened, and hinders him from energy and wholesome sorrow, as it is unreasonable, and not only hampers the efficacy of his prayers, but actually destroys all those fruits of the Spirit of which we spoke, which that other sorrow knows how to produce.

CHAPTER 12
THAT EXCEPT THAT WHOLESOME SORROW, WHICH SPRINGS UP IN THREE WAYS, ALL SORROW AND DEJECTION SHOULD BE RESISTED AS HURTFUL

WHEREFORE EXCEPT THAT SORROW WHICH IS ENDURED either for the sake of saving penitence, or for the sake of aiming at perfection, or for the desire of the future, all sorrow and dejection must equally be resisted, as belonging to this world, and being that which "worketh death," and must be entirely expelled from our hearts like the spirit of fornication and covetousness and anger.

CHAPTER 13
THE MEANS BY WHICH WE CAN ROOT OUT DEJECTION FROM OUR HEARTS

WE SHOULD THEN BE ABLE TO EXPEL THIS MOST INJURIOUS passion from our hearts, so that by spiritual meditation we may keep our mind constantly occupied with hope of the future and contemplation of the promised blessedness. For in this way we shall be able to get the better of all those sorts of dejection, whether those which flow from previous anger or those which come to us from disappointment of gain, or from some loss, or those which spring from a wrong done to us, or those which arise from an unreasonable disturbance of mind, or those which bring on us a deadly despair, if, ever joyful with an insight into things eternal and future, and continuing immovable, we are not depressed by present accidents, or over-elated by prosperity, but look on each condition as uncertain and likely soon to pass away.

BOOK 10

OF THE SPIRIT OF ACCIDIE

CHAPTER 1
HOW OUR SIXTH COMBAT IS AGAINST THE SPIRIT OF ACCIDIE, AND WHAT ITS CHARACTER IS

OUR SIXTH COMBAT IS WITH WHAT THE GREEKS CALL ἀκηδία, which we may term weariness or distress of heart. This is akin to dejection, and is especially trying to solitaires, and a dangerous and frequent foe to dwellers in the desert; and especially disturbing to a monk about the sixth hour, like some fever which seizes him at stated times, bringing the burning heat of its attacks on the sick man at usual and regular hours. Lastly, there are some of the elders who declare that this is the "midday demon" spoken of in the ninetieth Psalm.

CHAPTER 2
A DESCRIPTION OF ACCIDIE, AND THE WAY IN WHICH IT CREEPS OVER THE HEART OF A MONK, AND THE INJURY IT INFLICTS ON THE SOUL

AND WHEN THIS HAS TAKEN POSSESSION OF SOME UNHAPPY soul, it produces dislike of the place, disgust with the cell, and disdain and contempt of the brethren who dwell with him or at a little distance, as if they were careless or unspiritual. It also makes the man lazy and sluggish about all manner of work which has to be done within the enclosure of his dormitory. It does not suffer him to stay in his cell, or to take any pains about reading, and he often groans because he can do no good while he stays there, and complains and sighs because he can bear no spiritual fruit so long as he is joined to that society; and he complains that he is cut off from spiritual gain, and is of no use in the place, as if he were one who, though he could govern others and be useful to a great number of people, yet was edifying none, nor profiting any one by his teaching and doctrine. He cries up distant monasteries and those which are a long way off, and describes such places as more profitable and better suited for salvation; and besides this he paints the intercourse with the brethren there as sweet and full of spiritual life. On the other hand, he says that everything about him is rough, and not only that there is nothing edifying among the brethren who are stopping there, but also that even food for the body cannot be procured without great difficulty. Lastly he fancies that he will never be well while he stays in that place, unless he leaves his cell (in which he is lure to die if he stops in it any longer) and takes himself off from thence as quickly as possible. Then the fifth or sixth hour brings him such bodily weariness and longing for food that he seems to himself worn out and wearied as if with a long journey, or some very heavy work, or as if he had put off taking food during a fast of two or three days. Then besides this he looks about anxiously this way and that, and sighs that none of the brethren come to see him, and often goes in and out of his cell, and frequently gazes up at the sun, as if it was too slow in setting, and so a kind of unreasonable confusion of mind takes possession of him like some foul darkness, and makes him idle and useless for every spiritual work, so that he imagines that no cure for so terrible an attack can be found in anything except visiting some one of the brethren, or in the solace of sleep alone. Then the disease suggests that he ought to show courteous and friendly hospitalities to the brethren, and pay visits to the sick, whether near at hand or far off. He talks too about some dutiful and religious offices; that those kinsfolk ought to be inquired after, and that he ought to go and see them oftener; that it would be a real work of piety to go more frequently to visit that religious woman, devoted to the service of God, who is deprived of all support of kindred; and that it would be a most excellent thing to get what is needful for her who is neglected and despised by her own kinsfolk; and that he ought piously to devote his time to these things instead of staying uselessly and with no profit in his cell.

CHAPTER 3
OF THE DIFFERENT WAYS IN WHICH ACCIDIE OVERCOMES A MONK

AND SO THE WRETCHED SOUL, EMBARRASSED BY SUCH contrivances of the enemy, is disturbed, until, worn out by the spirit of accidie, as by some strong battering ram, it either learns to sink into slumber, or, driven out from the confinement of its cell, accustoms itself to seek for consolation under these attacks in visiting some brother, only to be afterwards weakened the more by this remedy which it seeks for the present. For more frequently and more severely will the enemy attack one who, when the battle is joined, will as he well knows immediately turn his back, and whom he sees to look for safety neither in victory nor in fighting but in flight: until little by little he is drawn away from his cell, and begins to forget the object of his profession, which is nothing but meditation and contemplation of that divine purity which excels all things, and which can only be gained by silence and continually remaining in the cell, and by meditation, and so the soldier of Christ becomes a runaway from His service, and a deserter, and "entangles himself in secular business," without at all pleasing Him to whom he engaged himself.

CHAPTER 4
HOW ACCIDIE HINDERS THE MIND FROM ALL CONTEMPLATION OF THE VIRTUES

ALL THE INCONVENIENCES OF THIS DISEASE ARE ADMIRABLY expressed by David in a single verse, where he says, "My soul slept from weariness," that is, from accidie. Quite rightly does he say, not that his body, but that his soul slept. For in truth the soul which is wounded by the shaft of this passion does sleep, as regards all contemplation of the virtues and insight of the spiritual senses.

CHAPTER 5
HOW THE ATTACK OF ACCLDIE IS TWOFOLD

AND SO THE TRUE CHRISTIAN ATHLETE WHO DESIRES TO strive lawfully in the lists of perfection, should hasten to expel this disease also from the recesses of his soul; and should strive against this most evil spirit of accidie in both directions, so that he may neither fall stricken through by the shaft of slumber, nor be driven out from the monastic cloister, even though under some pious excuse or pretext, and depart as a runaway.

CHAPTER 6
HOW INJURIOUS ARE THE EFFECTS OF ACCIDIE

AND WHENEVER IT BEGINS IN ANY DEGREE TO OVERCOME any one, it either makes him stay in his cell idle and lazy, without making any spiritual progress, or it drives him out from thence and makes him restless and a wanderer, and indolent in the matter of all kinds of work, and it makes him continually go round, the cells of the brethren and the monasteries, with an eye to nothing but this; viz., where or with what excuse he can presently procure some refreshment. For the mind of an idler cannot think of anything but food and the belly, until the society of some man or woman, equally cold and indifferent, is secured, and it loses itself in their affairs and business, and is thus little by little ensnared by dangerous occupations, so that, just as if it were bound up in the coils of a serpent, it can never disentangle itself again and return to the perfection of its former profession.

CHAPTER 7
TESTIMONIES FROM THE APOSTLE CONCERNING THE SPIRIT OF ACCIIE

THE BLESSED APOSTLE, LIKE A TRUE AND SPIRITUAL physician, either seeing this disease, which springs from the spirit of accidie, already creeping in, or foreseeing, through the revelation of the Holy Spirit, that it would arise among monks, is quick to anticipate it by the healing medicines of his directions. For in writing to the Thessalonians, and at first, like a skillful and excellent physician, applying to the infirmity of his patients the soothing and gentle remedy of his words, and beginning with charity, and praising them in that point, that this deadly wound, having been treated with a milder remedy, might lose its angry fostering and more easily bear severer treatment, he says: "But concerning brotherly charity ye have no need that I write to you: for you yourselves are taught of God to love one another. For this ye do toward all the brethren in the whole of Macedonia." He first began with the soothing application of praise, and made their ears submissive and ready for the remedy of the healing words. Then he proceeds: "But we ask you, brethren, to abound more."

Thus far he soothes them with kind and gentle words; for fear lest he should find them not yet prepared to receive their perfect cure. Why is it that you ask, O Apostle, that they may abound more in charity, of which you had said above, "But concerning brotherly charity we have no need to write to you"? And why is it necessary that you should say to them: "But we ask you to abound more," when they did not need o be written to at all on this matter? especially as you add the reason why they do not need it, saying, "For you yourselves have been aught of God to love one another." And you add a third thing still more important: hat not only have they been taught of God, but also that they fulfill in deed that which they are taught. "For ye do this," he says, not to one or two, but "to all the brethren;" and not to your own citizens and friends only, but "in the whole of Macedonia." Tell us then, I pray, why it is that you so particularly begin with this. Again he proceeds, "But we ask you, brethren, to abound the more." And with difficulty at last he breaks out into that at which he was driving before: "and that ye take pains to be quiet." He gave the first aim. Then he adds a second, "and to do your own business;" and a third as well: "and work with your own hands, as we commanded you;" a fourth: "and to walk honestly towards those that are without; "a fifth: "and to covet no man's goods." Lo, we can see through that hesitation, which made him with these preludes put off uttering what his mind was full of: "And that ye take pains to be quiet;" i.e., that you stop in your cells, and be not disturbed by rumors, which generally spring from the wishes and gossip of idle persons, and so yourselves disturb others. And, "to do your own business," you should not want to require curiously of the world's actions, or, examining the lives of others, want to spend your strength, not on bettering yourselves and aiming at virtue, but on depreciating your brethren. "And work with your own hands, as we charged you;" to secure that which he had warned them above not to do; i.e., that they should not be restless and anxious about other people's affairs, nor walk dishonestly towards those without, nor covet another man's goods, he now adds and says, "and work with your own hands, as we charged you." For he has clearly shown that leisure the reason why those things were done which he blamed above. For no one can be restless or anxious about other people's affairs, but one who is not satisfied to apply himself to the work of his own hands. He adds also a fourth evil, which springs also from this leisure, i.e., that they should not walk dishonestly: when he says: "And that ye walk honestly towards those without." He cannot possibly walk honestly, even among those who are men of this world, who is not content to cling to the seclusion of his cell and the work of his own hands; but he is sure to be dishonest, while he seeks his needful food; and to take pains to flatter, to follow up news and gossip, to seek for opportunities for chattering and stories by means of which he may gain a footing and obtain an entrance into the houses of others. "And that you should not covet another man's goods." He is sure to look with envious eyes on another's gifts and boons, who does not care to secure sufficient for his daily food by the dutiful and peaceful labor of his hands. You see what conditions, and how serious and shameful ones, spring solely from the malady of leisure. Lastly, those very people, whom in his first Epistle he had treated with the gentle application of his words, in his second Epistle he endeavors to heal with severer and sterner remedies, as those who had not profited by more gentle treatment; and he no longer applies the treatment of gentle words, no mild and kindly expressions, as these, "But we ask you, brethren," but "We adjure you, brethren, in the name of our Lord Jesus Christ, that ye withdraw from every brother that walketh disorderly." There he asks; here he adjures. There is the kindness of one who is persuading; here the sternness of one protesting and threatening. "We adjure you, brethren:" because, when we first asked you, you scorned to listen; now at least obey our threats. And this adjuration he renders terrible, not by his bare word, but by the imprecation of the name of our Lord Jesus Christ: for fear lest they might again scorn it, as merely man's word, and think that it was not of much importance. And forthwith, like a well-skilled physician with festering limbs, to which he could not apply the remedy of a mild treatment, he tries to cure by an incision with a spiritual knife, saying, "that ye withdraw yourselves from every brother that walketh disorderly, and not according to the tradition which ye received of us." And so he bids them withdraw from those who will not make time for work, and to cut them off like limbs tainted with the festering sores of leisure: test the malady of idleness, like some deadly contagion, might infect even the healthy portion of their limbs, by the gradual advance of infection. And when he is going to speak of those who will not work with their own hands and eat their bread in quietness, from whom he urges them to withdraw, hear with what reproaches he brands them at starting. First he calls them "disorderly," and "not walking according to the tradition." In other words, he stigmatizes them as obstinate, since they will not walk according to his appointment; and "dishonest," i.e., not keeping to the right and proper times for going out, and visiting, and talking. For a disorderly person is sure to be subject to all those faults. "And not according to the tradition which they received from us." And in this he stamps them as in some sort rebellious, and despisers, who scorned to keep the tradition which they had received from him, and would not follow that which they not only remembered that the master had taught in word, but which they knew that he had performed in deed. "For you yourselves know how ye ought to be followers of us." He heaps up an immense pile of censure when he asserts that they did not observe that which was still in their memory, and which not only had they learned by verbal instruction, but also had received by the incitement of his example in working.

CHAPTER 8
THAT HE IS SURE TO BE RESTLESS WHO WILL NOT BE CONTENT WITH THE WORK OF HIS OWN HANDS

"BECAUSE WE WERE NOT RESTLESS AMONG YOU." When he wants to prove by the practice of work that he was not restless among them, he fully shows that those who will not work are always restless, owing to the fault of idleness. "Nor did we eat any man's bread for nought." By each expression the teacher of the Gentiles advances a step in the rebuke. The preacher of the gospel says that he has not eaten any man's bread for nought, as he knows that the Lord commanded that "they who preach the gospel should live of the gospel:" again, "The laborer is worthy of his meat." And so if he who preached the gospel, performing a work so lofty and spiritual, did not venture in reliance on the Lord's command to eat his bread for nought, what shall we do to whom not merely is there no preaching of the word intrusted, but no cure of souls except our own committed? with what confidence shall we dare with idle hands to eat our bread for nought, when the "chosen vessel," constrained by his anxiety for the gospel and his work of preaching, did not venture to eat without laboring with his own hands? "But in labor," he says "and weariness, working night and day lest we should be burdensome to any of you." Up to this point he amplifies and adds to his rebuke. For he did not simply say, "We did not eat bread for nought from any of and then stop short. For it might have been thought that he was supported by his own private means, and by money which he had saved, or by other people's, though not by their collections and gifts. "But in labor," he says, "and weariness, working night and day is, being specially supported by our own labor. And this, he says, we did not of our own wish, and for our own pleasure, as rest and bodily exercise suggested, but as our necessities and the want of food compelled us to do, and that not without great bodily weariness. For not only throughout the whole day, but also by night, which seems to be granted for bodily rest, I was continually plying the work of my hands, through anxiety for food.

CHAPTER 9
THAT NOT THE APOSTLE ONLY, BUT THOSE TWO WHO WERE WITH HIM LABORED WITH THEIR OWN HANDS

AND HE TESTIFIES THAT IT WAS NOT HE ALONE WHO SO lived among them, lest haply this method might not seem important or general if he depended only on his example. But he declares that all those who were appointed with him for the ministry of the gospel, i.e., Silvanus and Timothy, who wrote this with him, worked in the same fashion. For by saying, "lest we should be burdensome to any of you, he covers them with great shame. For if he who preached the gospel and commended it by signs and mighty works, did not dare to eat bread for nought, lest he should be burdensome to any, how can those men help thinking that they are burdensome who take it every day in idleness and at their leisure?

CHAPTER 10
THAT FOR THIS REASON THE APOSTLE LABORED WITH HIS OWN HANDS, THAT HE MIGHT SET US AN EXAMPLE OF WORK

"NOT AS IF WE HAD NOT POWER; BUT THAT WE MIGHT GIVE ourselves a pattern to you to imitate us." He lays bare the reason why he imposed such labor on himself: "that we might," says he, "give a pattern to you to imitate us, that if by chance you become forgetful of the teaching of our words which so often passes through your ears, you may at least keep in your recollection the example of my manner of life given to you by ocular demonstration. There is here too no slight reproof of them, where he says that he has gone through this labor and weariness by night and day, for no other reason but to set an example, and that nevertheless they would not be instructed, for whose sakes he, although not obliged to do it, yet imposed on himself such toil. "And indeed," he says "though we had the power, and opportunities were open to us of using all your goods and substance, and I knew that I had the permissionof our Lord to use them: yet I did not use this power, lest what was rightly and lawfully done on my part might set an example of dangerous idleness to others. And therefore when preaching the gospel, I preferred to be supported by my own hands and work, that I might open up the way of perfection to you who wish to walk in the path of virtue, and might set an example of good life by my work."

CHAPTER 11
THAT HE PREACHED AND TAUGHT MEN TO WORK NOT ONLY BY HIS EXAMPLE, BUT ALSO BY HIS WORDS

BUT LEST HAPLY IT MIGHT BE THOUGHT THAT, WHILE HE worked in silence and tried to teach them by example, he had not instructed them by precepts and warnings, he proceeds to say: "For when we were with you, this we declared to you, that if a man will not work neither should he eat." Still greater does he make their idleness appear, for, though they knew that he, like a good master, worked with his hands for the sake of his teaching and in order to instruct them, yet they were ashamed to imitate him; and he emphasizes our diligence and care by saying that he did not only give them this for an example when present, but that he also proclaimed it continually in words; saying that if any one would not work, neither should he eat.

CHAPTER 12
OF HIS SAYING: "IF ANY WILL NOT WORK, NEITHER SHALL HE EAT."

AND NOW HE NO LONGER ADDRESSES TO THEM THE ADVICE OF a teacher or physician, but proceeds with the severity of a judicial sentence, and, resuming his apostolic authority, pronounces sentence on his despisers as if from the judgment seat: with that power, I mean, which, when writing with threats to the Corinthians, he declared was given him of the Lord, when he charged those taken in sin, that they should make haste and amend their lives before his coming: thus charging them, "I beseech you that I may not be bold when I am present, against some, with that power which is given to me over you." And again: "For if I also should boast somewhat of the power which the Lord has given me unto edification, and not for your destruction, I shall not be ashamed." With that power, I say, he declares, "If a man will not work, neither let him eat." Not punishing them with a carnal sword, but with the power of the Holy Ghost forbidding them the goods of this life, that if by chance, thinking but little of the punishment of future death, they still should remain obstinate through love of ease, they may at last, forced by the requirements of nature and the fear of immediate death, be compelled to obey his salutary charge.

CHAPTER 13
OF HIS SAYING: "WE HAVE HEARD THAT SOME AMONG YOU WALK DISORDERLY."

THEN AFTER ALL THIS RIGOR OF GOSPEL SEVERITY, HE NOW lays bare the reason why he put forward all these matters. "For we have heard that some among you walk disorderly, working not at all, but curiously meddling." He is nowhere satisfied to speak of those who will not give themselves up to work, as if they were victims of but a single malady. For in his first Epistle he speaks of them as "disorderly," and not walking according to the traditions which they had received from him: and he also asserts that they were restless, and ate their bread for nought. Again he says here, "We have heard that there are some among you who walk disorderly." And at once he subjoins a second weakness, which is the root of this restlessness, and says, "working not at all;" a third malady as well he adds, which springs from this last like some shoot: "but curiously meddling."

CHAPTER 14
HOW MANUAL LABOR PREVENTS MANY FAULTS

AND SO HE LOSES NO TIME IN AT ONCE APPLYING A SUITABLE remedy to the incentive to so many faults, and laying aside that apostolic power of his which he had made use of a little before, he adopts once more the tender character of a good father, or of a kind physician, and, as if they were his children or his patients, applies by his healing counsel remedies to cure them, saying: "Now we charge them that are such, and beseech them by the Lord Jesus, that working with silence they would eat their own bread." The cause of all these ulcers, which spring from the root of idleness, he heals like some well-skilled physician by a single salutary charge to work; as he knows that all the other bad symptoms, which spring as it were from the same clump, will at once disappear when the cause of the chief malady has been removed.

CHAPTER 15
HOW KINDNESS SHOULD BE SHOWN EVEN TO THE IDLE AND CARELESS

NEVERTHELESS, LIKE A FAR-SIGHTED AND CAREFUL physician, he is not only anxious to heal the wounds of the sick, but gives suitable directions as well to the whole, that their health may be preserved continually, and says: "But be not ye weary in well doing:" ye who following us, i.e., our ways, copy the example given to you by imitating us in work, and do not follow their sloth and laziness: "Do not be weary in well doing;" i.e., do you likewise show kindness towards them if by chance they have failed to observe what we said. As then he was severe with those who were weak, for fear lest being enervated by laziness they might yield to restlessness and inquisitiveness, so he admonishes those who are in good health neither to restrain that kindness which the Lord's command bids us show to the good and evil, even if some bad men will not turn to sound doctrine; nor to desist from doing good and encouraging them both by words of consolation and by rebuke as well as by ordinary kindness and civility.

CHAPTER 16
HOW WE OUGHT TO ADMONISH THOSE WHO GO WRONG, NOT OUT OF HATRED, BUT OUT OF LOVE

BUT AGAIN IN CASE SOME MIGHT BE ENCOURAGED BY THIS gentleness, and scorn to obey his commands, he proceeds with the severity of an apostle: "But if any man obey not our word by this Epistle, note that man and do not keep company with him that he may be ashamed." And in warning them of what they ought to observe out of regard for him and for the good of all, and of the care with which they should keep the apostolic commands, at once he joins to the warning the kindness of a most indulgent father; and teaches them as well, as if they were his children, what a brotherly disposition they should cultivate towards those mentioned above, out of love. "Yet do not esteem him as an enemy, but admonish him as a brother." With the severity of a judge he combines the affection of a father, and tempers with kindness and gentleness the sentence delivered with apostolic sternness. For he commands them to note that man who scorns to obey his commands, and not to keep company with him; and yet he does not bid them do this from a wrong feeling of dislike, but from brotherly affection and out of consideration for their amendment. "Do not keep company," he says, "with him that he may be ashamed;" so that, even if he is not made better by my mild charges, he may at last be brought to shame by being publicly separated from all of you, and so may some day begin to be restored to the way of salvation.

CHAPTER 17
DIFFERENT PASSAGES IN WHICH THE APOSTLE DECLARES THAT WE OUGHT TO WORK, OR IN WHICH IT IS SHOWN THAT HE HIMSELF WORKED

IN THE EPISTLE TO THE EPHESIANS ALSO HE THUS GIVES A charge on this subject of work, saying: "He that stole, let him now steal no more, but rather let him labor, working with his hands the thing that is good, that he may have something to give to him that suffereth need." And in the Acts of the Apostles too we find that he not only taught this, but actually practiced it himself. For when he had come to Corinth, he did not permit himself to lodge anywhere except with Aquila and Priscilla, because they were of the same trade which he himself was accustomed to practice. For we thus read: "After this, Paul departing from Athens came to Corinth; and finding a certain Jew named Aquila, born in Pontus, and Priscilla his wife, he came to them because they were of the same trade; and abode with them, and worked: for they were tent-makers by trade."

CHAPTER 18
THAT THE APOSTLE WROUGHT WHAT HE THOUGHT WOULD BE SUFFICIENT FOR HIM AND FOR OTHERS WHO WERE WITH HIM

THEN GOING TO MILETUS, AND FROM THENCE SENDING TO Ephesus, and summoning to him the elders of the church of Ephesus, he charged them how they ought to rule the church of God in his absence, and said: "I have not coveted any man's silver and gold; you yourselves know how for such things as were needful for me and them that are with me these hands have ministered. I have showed you all things, how that so laboring you ought to support the weak, and to remember the words of the Lord Jesus, how he said: It is more blessed to give than to receive." He left us a weighty example in his manner of life, as he testifies that he not only wrought what would supply his own bodily wants alone, but also what would be sufficient for the needs of those who were with him: those, I mean, who, being taken up with necessary duties, had no chance of procuring food for themselves with their own hands. And as he tells the Thessalonians that he had worked to give them an example that they might imitate him, so here too he implies something of the same sort when he says: "I have showed you all things, how that so laboring you ought to support the weak," viz., whether in mind or body; i.e., that we should be diligent in supplying their needs, not from the store of our abundance, or money laid by, or from another's generosity and substance, but rather by securing the necessary money through their own effort.

CHAPTER 19
HOW WE SHOULD UNDERSTAND THESE WORDS: "IT IS MORE BLESSED TO GIVE THAN TO RECEIVE."

AND HE SAYS THAT THIS IS A COMMAND OF THE LORD: "For He Himself," namely the Lord Jesus, said he, "said it is more blessed to give than to receive." That is, the bounty of the giver is more blessed than the need of the receiver, where the gift is not supplied from money that has been kept back through unbelief or faithlessness, nor from the stored-up treasures of avarice, but is produced from the fruits of our own labor and honest toil. And so "it is more blessed to give than to receive," because while the giver shares the poverty of the receiver, yet still he is diligent in providing with pious care by his own toil, not merely enough for his own needs, but also what he can give to one in want; and so he is adorned with a double grace, since by giving away all his goods he secures the perfect abnegation of Christ, and yet by his labor and thought displays the generosity of the rich; thus honoring God by his honest labors, and plucking for him the ary sum by our own labor and toil fruits of his righteousness, while another, enervated by sloth and indolent laziness, proves himself by the saying of the Apostle unworthy of food, as in defiance of his command he takes it in idleness, not without the guilt of sin and of obstinacy.

CHAPTER 20
OF A LAZY BROTHER WHO TRIED TO PERSUADE OTHERS TO LEAVE THE MONASTERY

WE KNOW A BROTHER, WHOSE NAME WE WOULD GIVE IF IT would do any good, who, although he was remaining in the monastery and compelled to deliver to the steward his fixed task daily, yet for fear lest he might be led on to some larger portion of work, or put to shame by the example of one laboring more zealously, when he had seen some brother admitted into the monastery, who in the ardor of his faith wanted to make up the sale of a larger piece of work, if he found that he could not by secret persuasion check him from carrying out his purpose, he would by bad advice and whisperings persuade him to depart thence. And in order to get rid of him more easily he would pretend that he also had already been for many reasons offended, and wanted to leave, if only he could find a companion and support for the journey. And when by secretly running down the monastery he had wheedled him into consenting, and arranged with him the time at which to leave the monastery, and the place to which he should go before, and where he should wait for him, he himself, pretending that he would follow, stopped where he was. And when the other out of shame for his flight did not dare to return again to the monastery from which he had run away, the miserable author of his flight stopped behind in the monastery. It will be enough to have given this single instance of this sort of men in order to put beginners on their guard, and to show clearly what evils idleness, as Scripture says, can produce in the mind of a monk, and how "evil communications corrupt good manners."

CHAPTER 21
DIFFERENT PASSAGES FROM THE WRITINGS OF SOLOMON AGAINST ACCIDIE

AND SOLOMON, THE WISEST OF MEN, CLEARLY POINTS TO this fault of idleness in many passages, as he says: "He that followeth idleness shall be filled with poverty," either visible or invisible, in which an idle person and one entangled with different faults is sure to be involved, and he will always be a stranger to the contemplation of God, and to spiritual riches, of which the blessed Apostle says: "For in all things ye were enriched in him, in all utterance and in all knowledge." But concerning this poverty of the idler elsewhere he also writes thus: "Every sluggard shall be clothed in torn garments and rags." For certainly he will not merit to be adorned with that garment of incorruption (of which the Apostle says, "Put ye on the Lord Jesus Christ," and again: "Being clothed in the breastplate of righteousness and charity," concerning which the Lord Himself also speaks to Jerusalem by the prophet: "Arise, arise, O Jerusalem, put on the garments of thy glory)," whoever, overpowered by lazy slumber or by accidie, prefers to be clothed, not by his labor and industry, but in the rags of idleness, which he tears off from the solid piece and body of the Scriptures, and fits on to his sloth no garment of glory and honor, but an ignominious cloak and excuse.

For those, who are affected by this laziness, and do not like to support themselves by the labor of their own hands, as the Apostle continually did and charged us to do, are wont to make use of certain Scripture proofs by which they try to cloak their idleness, saying that it is written, "Labor not for the meat that perisheth, but for that which remains to life eternal;" and "My meat is to do the will of my Father." But these proofs are (as it were) rags, from the solid piece of the gospel, which are adopted for this purpose, viz., to cover the disgrace of our idleness and shame rather than to keep us warm, and adorn us with that costly and splendid garment of virtue which that wise woman in the Proverbs, who was clothed with strength and beauty, is said to have made either for herself or for her husband; of which presently it is said: "Strength and beauty are her clothing, and she rejoices in the latter days." Of this evil of idleness Solomon thus makes mention again: "The ways of the idlers are strewn with thorns;" i.e., with these and similar faults, which the Apostle above declared to spring from idleness. And again: "Every sluggard is always in want." And of these the Apostle makes mention when he says, "And that you want nothing of any man's." And finally: "For idleness has been the teacher of many evils:" which the Apostle has clearly enumerated in the passage which he expounded above: "Working not at all, but curiously meddling." To this fault also he joins another: "And that ye study to be quiet;" and then, "that ye should do your own business and walk honestly towards them that are without, and that you want nothing of any man's." Those also whom he notes as disorderly and rebellious, from these he charges those who are earnest to separate themselves: "That ye withdraw yourselves," says he, "from every brother that walketh disorderly and not according to the tradition which they received from us."

CHAPTER 22
HOW THE BRETHREN IN EGYPT WORK WITH THEIR HANDS, NOT ONLY TO SUPPLY THEIR OWN NEEDS, BUT ALSO TO MINISTER TO THOSE WHO ARE IN PRISON

AND SO TAUGHT BY THESE EXAMPLES THE FATHERS IN EGYPT never allow monks, and especially the younger ones, to be idle, estimating the purpose of their hearts and their growth in patience and humility by their diligence in work; and they not only do not allow them to receive anything from another to supply their own wants, but further, they not merely refresh pilgrims and brethren who come to visit them by means of their labors, but actually collect an enormous store of provisions and food, and distribute it in the parts of Libya which suffer from famine and barrenness, and also in the cities, to those who are pining away in the squalor of prison; as they believe that by such an offering of the fruit of their hands they offer a reasonable and true sacrifice to the Lord.

CHAPTER 23
THAT IDLENESS IS THE REASON WHY THERE ARE NOT MONASTERIES FOR MONKS IN THE WEST

HENCE IT IS THAT IN THESE COUNTRIES WE SEE NO monasteries found with such numbers of brethren: for they are not supported by the resources of their own labor in such a way that they can remain in them continually; and if in some way or other, through the liberality of another, there should be a sufficient provision to supply them, yet love of ease and restlessness of heart does not suffer them to continue long in the place. Whence this saying has been handed down from the old fathers in Egypt: that a monk who works is attacked by but one devil; but an idler is tormented by countless spirits.

CHAPTER 24
ABBOT PAUL WHO EVERY YEAR BURNT WITH FIRE ALL THE WORKS OF HIS HANDS

LASTLY, ABBOT PAUL, ONE OF THE GREATEST OF THE Fathers, while he was living in a vast desert which is called the Porphyrian desert, and being relieved from anxiety by the date palms and a small garden, had plenty to support himself, and an ample supply of food, and could not find any other work to do, which would support him, because his dwelling was separated from towns and inhabited districts by seven days' journey, or even more, through the desert, and more would be asked for the carriage of the goods than the price of the work would be worth; he collected the leaves of the palms, and regularly exacted of himself his daily task, as if he was to be supported by it. And when his cave had been filled with a whole year's work, each year he would burn with fire that at which he had so diligently labored: thus proving that without manual labor a monk cannot stop in a place nor rise to the heights of perfection: so that, though the need for food did not require this to be done, yet he performed it simply for the sake of purifying his heart, and strengthening his thoughts, and persisting in his cell, and gaining a victory over accidie and driving it away.

CHAPTER 26
THE WORDS OF ABBOT MOSES WHICH HE SAID TO ME ABOUT THE CURE OF ACCIDIE\

WHEN I WAS BEGINNING MY STAY IN THE DESERT, AND HAD said to Abbot Moses, the chief of all the saints, that I had been terribly troubled yesterday by an attack of accidie, and that I could only be freed from it by running at once to Abbot Paul, he said, "You have not freed yourself from it, but rather have given yourself up to it as its slave and subject. For the enemy will henceforth attack you more strongly as a deserter and runaway, since it has seen that you fled at once when overcome in the conflict: unless on a second occasion when you join battle with it you make up your mind not to dispel its attacks and heats for the moment by deserting your cell, or by the inactivity of sleep, but rather learn to triumph over it by endurance and conflict." Whence it is proved by experience that a fit of acedie should not be evaded by running away from it, but overcome by resisting it.

BOOK 11

OF THE SPIRIT OF VAINGLORY

CHAPTER 1
HOW OUR SEVENTH COMBAT IS AGAINST THE SPIRIT OF VAINGLORY, AND WHAT ITS NATURE

OUR SEVENTH COMBAT IS AGAINST THE SPIRIT OF κενοδοξία, which we may term vain or idle glory: a spirit that takes many shapes, and is changeable and subtle, so that it can with difficulty, I will not say be guarded against, but be seen through and discovered even by the keenest eyes.

CHAPTER 2
HOW VAINGLORY ATTACKS A MONK NOT ONLY ON HIS CARNAL, BUT ALSO ON HIS SPIRITUAL SIDE

FOR NOT ONLY DOES THIS, LIKE THE REST OF HIS FAULTS, attack a monk on his carnal side, but on his spiritual side as well, insinuating itself by craft and guile into his mind: so that those who cannot be deceived by carnal vices are more grievously wounded through their spiritual proficiency; and it is so much the worse to fight against, as it is harder to guard against. For the attack of all other vices is more open and straightforward, and in the case of each of them, when he who stirs them up is met by a determined refusal, he will go away the weaker for it, and the adversary who has been beaten will on the next occasion attack his victim with less vigor. But this malady when it has attacked the mind by means of carnal pride, and has been repulsed by the shield of reply, again, like some wickedness that takes many shapes, changes its former guise and character, and under the appearance of the virtues tries to strike down and destroy its conqueror.

CHAPTER 3
HOW MANY FORMS AND SHAPES VAINGLORY TAKES

FOR OUR OTHER FAULTS AND PASSIONS MAY BE SAID TO BE simpler and of but one form: but this takes many forms and shapes, and changes about and assails the man who stands up against it from every quarter, and assaults its conqueror on all sides. For it tries to injure the soldier of Christ in his dress, in his manner, his walk, his voice, his work, his vigils, his fasts, his prayers, when he withdraws, when he reads, in his knowledge, his silence, his obedience, his humility, his patience; and like some most dangerous rock hidden by surging waves, it causes an unforeseen and miserable shipwreck to those who are sailing with a fair breeze, while they are not on the lookout for it or guarding against it.

CHAPTER 4
HOW VAINGLORY ATTACKS A MONK ON THE RIGHT HAD AND ON THE LEFT

AND SO ONE WHO WISHES TO GO ALONG THE KING'S highway by means of the "arms of righteousness which are on the right hand and on the left," ought by the teaching of the Apostle to pass through "honor and dishonor, evil report and good report," and with such care to direct his virtuous course amid the swelling waves of temptation, with discretion at the helm, and the Spirit of the Lord breathing on us, since we know that if we deviate ever so little to the right hand or to the left, we shall presently be dashed against most dangerous crags. And so we are warned by Solomon, the wisest of men: "Turn not aside to the right hand or to the left;" i.e., do not flatter yourself on your virtues and be puffed up by your spiritual achievements on the right hand; nor, swerving to the path of vices on the left hand, seek from them for yourself (to use the words of the Apostle) "glory in your shame." For where the devil cannot create vainglory in a man by means of his well-fitting and neat dress, he tries to introduce it by means of a dirty, cheap, and uncared-for style. If he cannot drag a man down by honor, he overthrows him by humility. If he cannot make him puffed up by the grace of knowledge and eloquence, he pulls him down by the weight of silence. If a man fasts openly, he is attacked by the pride of vanity. If he conceals it for the sake of despising the glory of it, he is assailed by the same sin of pride. In order that he may not be defiled by the stains of vainglory he avoids making long prayers in the sight of the brethren; and yet because he offers them secretly and has no one who is conscious of it, he does not escape the pride of vanity.

CHAPTER 5

A COMPARISON WHICH SHOWS THE NATURE OF VAINGLORY

OUR ELDERS ADMIRABLY DESCRIBE THE NATURE OF THIS malady as like that of an onion, and of those bulbs which When stripped of one covering you find to be sheathed in another; and as often as you strip them, you find them still protected.

CHAPTER 6

THAT VAINGLORY IS NOT ALTOGETHER GOT RID OF BY THE ADVANTAGES OF SOLITUDE

IN SOLITUDE ALSO IT DOES NOT CEASE FROM PURSUING HIM who has for the sake of glory fled from intercourse with all men. And the more thoroughly a man has shunned the whole world, so much the more keenly does it pursue him. It tries to lift up with pride one man because of his great endurance of work and labor, another because of his extreme readiness to obey, another because he outstrips other men in humility. One man is tempted through the extent of his knowledge, another through the extent of his reading, another through the length of his vigils. Nor does this malady endeavor to wound a man except through his virtues; introducing hindrances which lead to death by means of those very things through which the supplies of life are sought. For when men are anxious to walk in the path of holiness and perfection, the enemies do not lay their snares to deceive them anywhere except in the way along which they walk, in accordance with that saying of the blessed David: "In the way wherein I walked have they laid a snare for me;" that in this very way of virtue along which we are walking, when pressing on to "the prize of our high calling," we may be elated by our successes, and so sink down, and fall with the

feet of our soul entangled and caught in the snares of vainglory. And so it results that those of us who could not be vanquished in the conflict with the foe are overcome by the very greatness of our triumph, or else (which is another kind of deception) that, overstraining the limits of that self-restraint which is possible to us, we fail of perseverance in our course on account of bodily weakness.

CHAPTER 7

HOW VAINGLORY, WHEN IT HAS BEEN OVERCOME, RISES AGAIN KEENER THAN EVER FOR THE FIGHT

ALL, VICES WHEN OVERCOME GROW FEEBLE, AND WHEN beaten are day by day rendered weaker, and both in regard to place and time grow less and subside, or at any rate, as they are unlike the opposite virtues, are more easily shunned and avoided: but this one when it is beaten rises again keener than ever for the struggle; and when we think that it is destroyed, it revives again, the stronger for its death. The other kinds of vices usually only attack those whom they have overcome in the conflict; but this one pursues its victors only the more keenly; and the more thoroughly it has been resisted, so much the more vigorously does it attack the man who is elated by his victory over it. And herein lies the crafty cunning of our adversary, namely, in the fact that, where he cannot overcome the soldier of Christ by the weapons of the foe, he lays him low by his own spear.

CHAPTER 8

HOW VAINGLORY IS NOT ALLAYED EITHER IN THE DESERT OR THROUGH ADVANCING YEARS

OTHER VICES, AS WE SAID, ARE SOMETIMES ALLAYED BY THE advantages of position, and when the matter of the sin and the occasion and opportunity for it are removed, grow slack, and are diminished: but this one penetrates the deserts with the man who is flying from it, nor can it be shut out from any place, nor When outward material for it is removed does it fail. For it is simply encouraged by the achievements of the virtues of the man whom it attacks. For all other vices, as we said above, are sometimes diminished by the lapse of time, and disappear: to this one length of life, unless it is supported by skillful diligence and prudent discretion, is no hindrance, but actually supplies it with new fuel for vanity.

CHAPTER 9
THAT VAINGLORY IS THE MORE DANGEROUS THROUGH BEING MIXED UP WITH VIRTUES

LASTLY, OTHER PASSIONS WHICH ARE ENTIRELY DIFFERENT from the virtues which are their opposites, and which attack us openly and as it were in broad daylight, are more easily overcome and guarded against: but this being interwoven with our virtues and entangled in the battle, fighting as it were under cover of the darkness of night, deceives the more dangerously those who are off their guard and not on the lookout.

CHAPTER 10
AN INSTANCE SHOWING HOW KIN HEZEKIAH WAS OVERTHROWN BY THE DART OF VAINGLORY

FOR SO WE READ THAT HEZEKIAH, KING OF JUDAH, A MAN of most perfect righteousness in all things, and one approved by the witness of Holy Scripture, after unnumbered commendations for his virtues, was overthrown by a single dart of vainglory. And he who by a single prayer of his was able to procure the death of a hundred and eighty-five thousand of the army of the Assyrians, whom the angel destroyed in one night, is overcome by boasting and vanity. Of whom — to pass over the long list of his virtues, which it would take a long time to unfold — I will say but this one thing. He was a man who, after the close of his life had been decreed and the day of his death determined by the Lord's sentence, prevailed by a single prayer to extend the limits set to his life by fifteen years, the sun returning by ten steps, on which it had already shone in its course towards its setting, and by its return dispersing those lines which the shadow that followed its course had already marked, and by this giving two days in one to the whole world, by a stupendous miracle contrary to the fixed laws of nature. Yet after signs so great and so incredible, after such immense proofs of his goodness, hear the Scripture tell how he was destroyed by his very successes. "In those days," we are told, "Hezekiah was sick unto death: and he prayed to the Lord, and He heard him and gave him a sign," that, namely of which we read in the fourth book of the kingdoms, which was given by Isaiah the prophet through the going back of the sun. "But," it says, "he did not render again according to the benefits which he had received, for his heart was lifted up; and wrath was kindled against him and against Judah and Jerusalem: and he humbled himself afterwards because his heart had been lifted up, both he and the inhabitants of Jerusalem, and therefore the wrath of the Lord came not upon them in the days of Hezekiah." How dangerous, how terrible is the malady of vanity! So much goodness, so many virtues, faith and devotion, great enough to prevail to change nature itself and the laws of the whole world, perish by a single act of pride! So that all his good deeds would have been forgotten as if they had never been, and he would at once have been subject to the wrath of the Lord unless he had appeased Him by recovering his humility: so that he who, at the suggestion of pride, had fallen from so great a height of excellence, could only mount again to the height he had lost by the same steps of humility. Do you want to see another instance of a similar downfall?

CHAPTER 11

THE INSTANCE OF KING UZZIAH WHO WAS OVERCOME BY THE TAINT OF THE SAME MALADY

OF UZZIAH, THE ANCESTOR OF THIS KING OF WHOM WE have been speaking, himself also praised in all things by the witness of the Scripture, after great commendation for his virtue, after countless triumphs which he achieved by the merit of his devotion and faith, learn how he was cast down by the pride of vainglory. "And," we are told, "the name of Uzziah went forth, for the Lord helped him and had strengthened him. But when he was made strong, his heart was lifted up to his destruction, and he neglected the Lord his God." You behold another instance of a most terrible downfall, and see how two men so upright and excellent were undone by their very triumphs and victories. Whence you see how dangerous the successes of prosperity generally are, so that those who could not be injured by adversity are ruined, unless they are careful, by prosperity; and those who in the conflict of battle have escaped the danger of death fall before their own trophies and triumphs.

CHAPTER 12
SEVERAL TESTIMONIES AGAINST VAINGLORY

AND SO THE APOSTLE WARNS US: "BE NOT DESIROUS OF vainglory." And the Lord, rebuking the Pharisees, says, "How can ye believe, who receive glory from one another, and seek not the glory which comes from God alone?" Of these too the blessed David speaks with a threat: "For God hath scattered the bones of them that please men."

CHAPTER 13
OF THE WAYS IN WHICH VAINGLORY ATTACKS A MONK

IS THE CASE ALSO OF BEGINNERS AND OF THOSE WHO HAVE as yet made but little progress either in powers of mind or in knowledge it usually puffs up their minds, either because of the quality of their voice because they can sing well, or because their bodies are emaciated, or because they are of a good figure, or because they have rich and noble kinsfolk, or because they have despised a military life and honors. Sometimes too it persuades a man that if he had remained in the world he would easily have obtained honors and riches, which perhaps could not possibly have been secured, and inflates him with a vain hope of uncertain things; and in the case of those things which he never possessed, puffs him up with pride and vanity, as if he were one who had despised them.

CHAPTER 14
HOW IT SUGGESTS THAT A MAN MAY SEEK TO TAKE HOLY ORDERS

BUT SOMETIMES IT CREATES A WISH TO TAKE HOLY ORDERS, and a desire for the priesthood or diaconate. And it represents that if a man has even against his will received this office, he will fulfill it with such sanctity and strictness that he will be able to set an example of saintliness even to other priests; and that he will win over many people, not only by his manner of life, but also by his teaching and preaching. It makes a man, even when alone and sitting in his cell, to go round in mind and imagination to the dwellings and monasteries of others, and to make many conversions under the inducements of imaginary exultatio

CHAPTER 15
HOW VAINGLORY INTOXICATES THE MIND

AND SO THE MISERABLE SOUL IS AFFECTED BY SUCH VANITY — as if it were deluded by a profound slumber — that it is often led away by the pleasure of such thoughts, and filled with such imaginations, so that it cannot even look at things present, or the brethren, while it enjoys dwelling upon these things, of which with its wandering thoughts it has waking dreams, as if they were true.

CHAPTER 16
OF HIM WHOM THE SUPERIOR CAME UPON AND FOUND IN HIS CELL, DELUDED BY IDLE VAINGLORY

I REMEMBER AN ELDER, WHEN I WAS STAYING IN THE desert of Scete, who went to the cell of a certain brother to pay him a visit, and when he had reached the door heard him muttering inside, and stood still for a little while, wanting to know what it was that he was reading from the Bible or repeating by heart (as is customary) while he was at work. And when this most excellent eavesdropper diligently applied his ear and listened with some curiosity, he found that the man was induced by an attack of this spirit to fancy that he was delivering a stirring sermon to the people. And when the elder, as he stood still, heard him finish his discourse and return again to his office, and give out the dismissal of the catechumens, as the deacon does, then at last he knocked at the door, and the man came out, and met the elder with the customary reverence, and brought him in and (for his knowledge of what had been his thoughts made him uneasy) asked him when he had arrived, for fear lest he might have taken some harm from standing too long at the door: and the old man joking pleasantly replied, "I only got here while you were giving out the dismissal of the catechumens."

CHAPTER 17
HOW FAULTS CANNOT BE CURED UNLESS THEIR ROOTS AND CAUSES HAVE BEEN DISCOVERED

I THOUGHT IT WELL TO INSERT THESE THINGS IN THIS little work of mine, that we might learn, not only by reason, but also by examples, about the force of temptations and the order of the sins which hurt an unfortunate soul, and so might be more careful in avoiding the snares and manifold deceits of the enemy. For these things are indiscriminately brought forward by the Egyptian fathers, that by telling them, as those who are still enduring them, they may disclose and lay bare the combats with all the vices, which they actually do suffer, and those which the younger ones are sure to suffer; so that, when they explain the illusions arising from all the passions, those who are but beginners and fervent in spirit may know the secret of their struggles, and seeing them as in a glass, may learn both the causes of the sins by which they are troubled, and the remedies for them, and instructed beforehand concerning the approach of future struggles, may be taught how they ought to guard against them, or to meet them and to fight with them. As clever physicians are accustomed not only to heal already existing diseases, but also by a wise skill to seek to obviate future ones, and to prevent them by their prescriptions and healing draughts, so these true physicians of the soul, by means of spiritual conferences, like some celestial antidote, destroy beforehand those maladies of the soul which would arise, and do not allow them to gain a footing in the minds of the juniors, as they unfold to them the causes of the passions which threaten them, and the remedies which will heal them.

CHAPTER 18

HOW A MONK OUGHT TO AVOID WOMEN AND BISHOPS

WHEREFORE THIS IS AN OLD MAXIM OF THE FATHERS that is still current, — though I cannot produce it without shame on my own part, since I could not avoid my own sister, nor escape the hands of the bishop, — viz., that a monk ought by all means to fly from women and bishops. For neither of them will allow him who has once been joined in close intercourse any longer to care for the quiet of his cell, or to continue with pure eyes in divine contemplation through his insight into holy things.

CHAPTER 19
REMEDIES BY WHICH WE CAN OVERCOME VAINGLORY

AND SO THE ATHLETE OF CHRIST WHO DESIRES TO STRIVE lawfully in this true and spiritual combat, should strive by all means to overcome this changeable monster of many shapes, which, as it attacks us on every side like some manifold wickedness, we can escape by such a remedy as this; viz., thinking on that saying of David: "The Lord hath scattered the bones of those who please men. To begin with we should not allow ourselves to do anything at the suggestion of vanity, and for the sake of obtaining vainglory. Next, when we have begun a thing well, we should endeavor to maintain it with just the same care, for fear lest afterwards the malady of vainglory should creep in and make void all the fruits of our labors. And anything which is of very little use or value in the common life of the brethren, we should avoid as leading to boasting; and whatever would render us remarkable amongst the others, and for which credit would be gained among men, as if we were the only people who could do it, this should be shunned by us. For by these signs the deadly taint of vainglory will be shown to cling to us: which we shall most easily escape if we consider that we shall not merely lose the fruits of those labors of ours which we have performed at the suggestion of vainglory, but that we shall also be guilty of a great sin, and as impious persons undergo eternal punishments, inasmuch as we have wronged God by doing for the favor of men what we ought to have done for His sake, and are convicted by Him who knows all secrets of having preferred men to God, and the praise of the world to the praise of the Lord.

BOOK 12

THE SPIRIT OF PRIDE

CHAPTER 1
HOW OUR EIGHTH COMBAT IS AGAINST THE SPIRIT OF PRIDE, AND OF ITS CHARACTER

OUR EIGHTH AND LAST COMBAT IS AGAINST THE SPIRIT OF pride, which evil, although it is the latest in our conflict with our faults and stands last on the list, yet in beginning and in the order of time is the first: an evil beast that is most savage and more dreadful than all the former ones, chiefly trying those who are perfect, and devouring with its dreadful bite those who have almost attained the consummation of virtue.

CHAPTER 2
HOW THERE ARE TWO KINDS OF PRIDE

AND OF THIS PRIDE THERE ARE TWO KINDS: THE ONE, THAT by which we said that the best of men and spiritually minded ones were troubled; the other, that which assaults even beginners and carnal persons. And though each kind of pride is excited with regard to both God and man by a dangerous elation, yet that first kind more particularly has to do with God; the second refers especially to men. Of the origin of this last and the remedies for it we will by God's help treat as far as possible in the latter part of this book. We now propose to say a few things about that former kind, by which, as I mentioned before, those who are perfect are especially tried.

CHAPTER 3
HOW PRIDE IS EQUALLY DESTRUCTIVE OF ALL VIRTUES

THERE IS THEN NO OTHER FAULT WHICH IS SO DESTRUCTIVE of all virtues, and robs and despoils a man of all righteousness and holiness, as this evil of pride, which like some pestilential disease attacks the whole man, and, not content to damage one part or one limb only, injures the entire body by its deadly influence, and endeavors to cast down by a most fatal fall, and destroy those who were already at the top of the tree of the virtues. For every other fault is satisfied within its own bounds and limits, and though it clouds other virtues as well, yet it is in the main directed against one only, and specially attacks and assaults that. And so (to make my meaning clearer) gluttony, i.e., the appetites of the belly and the pleasures of the palate, is destructive of strict temperance: lust stains purity, anger destroys patience: so that sometimes a man who is in bondage to some one sin is not altogether wanting in other virtues: but being simply deprived of that one virtue which in the struggle yields to the vice which is its rival and opposed to it, can to some extent preserve his other virtues: but this one when once it has taken possession of some unfortunate soul, like some most brutal tyrant, when the lofty citadel of the virtues has been taken, utterly destroys and lays waste the whole city; and leveling with the ground of vices the once high walls of saintliness, and confusing them together, it allows no shadow of freedom henceforth to survive in the soul subject to it. And in proportion as it was originally the richer, so now will the yoke of servitude be the severer, through which by its cruel ravages it will strip the soul it has subdued of all its powers of virtue.

CHAPTER 4

HOW BY REASON OF PRIDE LUCIFER WAS TURNED FROM AN ARCHANGEL INTO A DEVIL

AND THAT WE MAY UNDERSTAND THE POWER OF ITS AWFUL tyranny we see that that angel who, for the greatness of his splendor and beauty was termed Lucifer, was cast out of heaven for no other sin but this, and, pierced with the dart of pride, was hurled down from his grand and exalted position as an angel into hell. If then pride of heart alone was enough to cast down from heaven to earth a power that was so great and adorned with the attributes of such might, the very greatness of his fall shows us with what care we who are surrounded by the weakness of the flesh ought to be on our guard. But we can learn how to avoid the most deadly poison of this evil if we trace out the origin and causes of his fall. For weakness can never be cured, nor the remedies for bad states of health be disclosed unless first their origin and causes are investigated by a wise scrutiny. For as he (viz., Lucifer) was endowed with divine splendor, and shone forth among the other higher powers by the bounty of his Maker, he believed that he had acquired the splendor of that wisdom and the beauty of those powers, with which he was graced by the gift of the Creator, by the might of his own nature, and not by the beneficence of His generosity. And on this account he was puffed up as if he stood in no need of divine assistance in order to continue in this state of purity, and esteemed himself to be like God, as if, like God, he had no need of any one, and trusting in the power of his own will, fancied that through it he could richly supply himself with everything which was necessary for the consummation of virtue or for the perpetuation of perfect bliss.

This thought alone was the cause of his first fall. On account of which being forsaken by God, whom he fancied he no longer needed, he suddenly became unstable and tottering, and discovered the weakness of his own nature, and lost the blessedness which he had enjoyed by God's gift. And because he "loved the words of ruin," with which he had said, will ascend into heaven," and the "deceitful tongue," with which he had said of himself, "I will be like the Most High," and of Adam and Eve, "Ye shall be as gods," therefore "shall God destroy him forever and pluck him out and remove him from his dwelling place and his root out of the land of the living." Then the just, when they see his ruin, shall fear, and shall laugh at him and say" (what may also be most justly aimed at those who trust that they can obtain the highest good without the protection and assistance of God): "Behold the man that made not God his helper, but trusted in the abundance of his riches, and prevailed in his vanity."

CHAPTER 5
THAT INCENTIVES TO ALL SINS SPRING FROM PRIDE

THIS IS THE REASON OF THE FIRST FALL, AND THE STARING point of the original malady, which again insinuating itself into the first man, through him who had already been destroyed by it, produced the weaknesses and materials, of all faults. For while he believed that by the freedom of his will and by his own efforts he could obtain the glory of Deity, he actually lost that glory which he already possessed through the free gift of the Creator.

CHAPTER 6
THAT THE SIN OF PRIDE IS LAST IN THE ACTUAL ORDER OF THE COMBAT, BUT FIRST IN TIME AND ORIGIN

AND SO IT IS MOST CLEARLY ESTABLISHED BY INSTANCES and testimonies from Scripture that the mischief of pride, although it comes later in the order of the combat, is yet earlier in origin, and is the beginning of all sins and faults: nor is it (like the other vices) simply fatal to the virtue opposite to it (in this case, humility), but it is also at the same time destructive of all virtues: nor does it only tempt ordinary folk and small people, but chiefly those who already stand on the heights of valor. For thus the prophet speaks of this spirit, "His meat is choice." And so the blessed David, although he guarded the recesses of his heart with the utmost care, so that he dared to say to Him from whom the secrets of his conscience were not hid, "Lord, my heart is not exalted, nor are my eyes lofty: neither have I walked in great matters, nor in wonderful things above me. If I was not humbly minded;" and again, "He that worketh pride shall not dwell in the midst of my house;" yet, as he knew how hard is that watchfulness even for those that are perfect, he did not so presume on his own efforts, but prayed to God and implored His help, that he might escape unwounded by the darts of this foe, saying, "Let not the foot of pride come to me, " for he feared and dreaded falling into that which is said of the proud, viz., "God resisteth the proud;" and again: "Every one that exalteth his heart is unclean before the Lord."

CHAPTER 7
THAT THE EVIL OF PRIDE IS SO GREAT THAT IT RIGHTLY HAS EVEN GOD HIMSELF AS ITS ADVERSARY

HOW GREAT IS THE EVIL OF PRIDE, THAT IT RIGHTLY HAS NO angel, nor other virtues opposed to it, but God Himself as its adversary! Since it should be noted that it is never said of those who are entangled in other sins that they have God resisting them; I mean it is not said that God is opposed "to the gluttonous, fornicators, passionate, or covetous," but only "to the proud." For those sins react only on those who commit them, or seem to be committed against those who share in them, i.e., against other men; but this one has more properly to do with God, land therefore it is especially right that it should have Him opposed to it.

CHAPTER 8
HOW GOD HAS DESTROYED THE PRIDE OF THE DEVIL BY THE VIRTUE OF HUMILITY, AND VARIOUS PASSAGES IN PROOF OF THIS

AND so God, the Creator and Healer of all, knowing that pride is the cause and fountain head of evils, has been careful to heal opposites with opposites, that those things which were ruined by pride might be restored by humility. For the one says, "I will ascend into heaven;" the other, "My soul was brought low even to the ground." The one says, "And I will be like the most High;" the other, "Though He was in the form of God, yet

He emptied Himself and took the form of a servant, and humbled Himself and became obedient unto death." The one says, "I will exalt my throne above the stars of God;" the other, "Learn of me, for I am meek and lowly of heart." The one says, "I know not the Lord and will not let Israel go;" the other, "If I say that I know Him not, I shall be a liar like unto you: but I know Him, and keep His commandments." The one says, "My rivers are mine and I made them:" the other: "I can do nothing of myself, but my Father who abideth in me, He doeth the works." The one says, "All the kingdoms of the world and the glory of them are mine, and to whomsoever I will, I give them;" the other, "Though He were rich yet He became poor, that we through His poverty might be made rich." The one says, "As eggs are gathered together which are left, so have I gathered all the earth: and there was none that moved the wing or opened the mouth, or made the least noise;" the other, "I am become like a solitary pelican; I watched and became as a sparrow alone upon the roof." The one says, "I have dried up with the sole of my foot all the rivers shut up in banks;" the other, "Cannot I ask my Father, and He shall presently give me more than twelve legions of angels?" If we look at the reason of our original fall, and the foundations of our salvation, and consider by whom and in what way the latter were laid and the former originated, we may learn, either through the fall of the devil, or through the example of Christ, how to avoid so terrible a death from pride.

CHAPTER 9
HOW WE TOO MAY OVERCOME PRIDE

AND SO WE CAN ESCAPE THE SNARE OF THIS MOST EVIL spirit, if in the case of every virtue in which we feel that we make progress, we say these words of the Apostle: "Not I, but the grace of God with me," and "by the grace of God I am what I am;" and "it is God that worketh in us both to will and to do of His good pleasure." As the author of our salvation Himself also says: "If a man abide in me and I in him, the same beareth much fruit; for without me ye can do nothing." And "Except the Lord build the house, they labor in vain that build it. Except the Lord keep the city, the watchman waketh but in vain." And "Vain is it for you to rise up before light." For "it is not of him that willeth, nor of him that runneth, but of God that hath mercy."

CHAPTER 10
HOW NO ONE CAN OBTAIN PERFECT VIRTUE AND THE PROMISED BLISS BY HIS OWN STRENGTH ALONE

FOR THE WILL AND COURSE OF NO ONE, HOWEVER EAGER AND anxious, is sufficiently ready for him, while still enclosed in the flesh which warreth against the spirit, to reach so great a prize of perfection, and the palm of uprightness and purity, unless he is protected by the divine compassion, so that he is privileged to attain to that which he greatly desires and to which he runs. For "every good gift and every perfect gift is from above, and cometh down from the Father of lights." "For what hast thou which thou didst not receive? But if thou hast received it, why dost thou glory as if thou hadst not received it?"

CHAPTER 11

THE CASE OF THE THIEF AND OF DAVID, AND OF OUR CALL IN ORDER TO ILLUSTRATE THE GRACE OF GOD

FOR IF WE RECALL THAT THIEF WHO WAS BY REASON OF A single confession admitted into paradise, we shall feel that he did not acquire such bliss by the merits of his life, but obtained it by the gift of a merciful God. Or if we bear in mind those two grievous and heinous sins of King David, blotted out by one word of penitence, we shall see that neither here were the merits of his works sufficient to obtain pardon for so great a sin, but that the grace of God superabounded, as, when the opportunity for true penitence was taken, He removed the whole weight of sins through the full confession of but one word. If we consider also the beginning of the call and salvation of mankind, in which, as the Apostle says, we are saved not of ourselves, nor of our works, but by the gift and grace of God, we can clearly see how the whole of perfection is "not of him that willeth nor of him that runneth, but of God that hath mercy," who makes us victorious over our faults, without any merits of works and life on our part to outweigh them, or any effort of our will availing to scale the difficult heights of perfection, or to subdue the flesh which we have to use: since no tortures of this body, and no contrition of heart, can be sufficient for the acquisition of that true chastity of the inner man so as to be able to gain that great virtue of purity (which is innate in the angels alone and indigenous as it were to heaven) merely by human efforts, i.e., without the aid of God: for the performance of everything good flows from His grace, who by multiplying His bounty has granted such lasting bliss, and vast glory to our feeble will and short and

CHAPTER 12
THAT NO TOIL IS WORTHY TO BE COMPARED WITH THE PROMISED BLISS

FOR ALL THE LONG YEARS OF THIS PRESENT LIFE DISAPPEAR when you have regard to the eternity of the future glory: and all our sorrows vanish away in the contemplation of that vast bliss, and like smoke melt away, and come to nothing, and like ashes are no more seen.

CHAPTER 13
THE TEACHING OF THE ELDERS ON THE METHOD OF ACQUIRING PURITY

WHEREFORE IT IS NOW TIME TO PRODUCE, IN THE VERY words in which they hand it down, the opinion of the Fathers; viz., of those who have not painted the way of perfection and its character in high-sounding words, but rather, possessing it in deed and truth, and in the virtue of their spirit, have passed it on by their own experience and sure example. And so they say that no one can be altogether cleansed from carnal sins, unless he has realized that all his labors and efforts are insufficient for so great and perfect an end; and unless, taught, not by the system handed down to him, but by his feelings and virtues and his own experience, he recognizes that it can only be gained by the mercy and assistance of God. For in order to acquire such splendid and lofty prizes of purity and perfection, however great may be the efforts of fastings and vigils and readings and solitude and retirement applied to it, they will not be sufficient to secure it by the merits of the actual efforts and toil For a man's own efforts and human exertions will never make up for the lack of the divine gift, unless it is granted by divine compassion in answer to his prayer.

CHAPTER 14
THAT THE HELP OF GOD IS GIVEN TO THOSE WHO LABOR.

NOR DO I SAY THIS TO CAST A SLIGHT ON HUMAN EFFORTS, or in the endeavor to discourage any one from his purpose of working and doing his best. But clearly and most earnestly do I lay down, not giving my own opinion, but that of the elders, that perfection cannot possibly be gained without these, but that by these only without the grace of God nobody can ever attain it. For when we say that human efforts cannot of themselves secure it without the aid of God, we thus insist that God's mercy and grace are bestowed only upon those who labor and exert themselves, and are granted (to use the Apostle's expression) to them that "will" and "run," according to that which is sung in the person of God in the eighty-eighth Psalm: "I have laid help upon one that is mighty, and have exalted one chosen out of my people." For we say, in accordance with our Savior's words, that it is given to them that ask, and opened to them that knocks and found by them that seek; but that the asking, the seeking, and the knocking on our part are insufficient unless the mercy of God gives what we ask, and opens that at which we knock, and enables us to find that which we seek. For He is at hand to bestow all these things, if only the opportunity is given to Him by our good will. For He desires and looks for our perfection and salvation far more than we do ourselves. And the blessed David knew so well that by his own efforts he could not secure the increase of his work and labor, that he entreated with renewed prayers that he might obtain the "direction" of his work from the Lord, saying, "Direct thou the work of our hands over us; yea, the work of our hands do thou direct;" and again: "Confirm, O God, what thou hast wrought in us."

CHAPTER 15
FROM WHOM WE CAN LEARN THE WAY OF PERFECTION

AND SO, IF WE WISH IN VERY DEED AND TRUTH TO ATTAIN TO the crown of virtues, we ought to listen to those teachers and guides who, not dreaming with pompous declamations, but learning by act and experience, are able to teach us as well, and direct us likewise, and show us the road by which we may arrive at it by a most sure pathway; and who also testify that they have themselves reached it by faith rather than by any merits of their efforts. And further, the purity of heart that they have acquired has taught them this above all; viz., to recognize more and more that they are burdened with sin (for their compunction for their faults increases day by day in proportion as their purity of soul advances), and to sigh continually from the bottom of their heart because they see that they cannot possibly avoid the spots and blemishes of those faults which are ingrained in them through the countless triflings of the thoughts. And therefore they declared that they looked for the reward of the future life, not from the merits of their works, but from the mercy of the Lord, taking no credit to themselves for their great circumspection of hear in comparison with others, since they ascribed this not to their own exertions, but to divine grace; and without flattering themselves on account of the carelessness of those who are cold, and worse than they themselves are, they rather aimed at a lasting humility by fixing their gaze on those whom they knew to be really free from sin and already in the enjoyment of eternal bliss in the kingdom of heaven, and so by this consideration they avoided the downfall of pride, and at the same time always saw both what they were aiming at and what they had to grieve over: as they knew that they could not attain that purity of heart for which they yearned while weighed down by the burden of the flesh.

CHAPTER 16
THAT WE CANNOT EVEN MAKE THE EFFORT TO OBTAIN PERFECTION WITHOUT THE MERCY AND INSPIRATION OF GOD

WE OUGHT THEREFORE, IN ACCORDANCE WITH THEIR TEACHING and instruction, so to press towards it, and to be diligent in fastings, vigils, prayers, and contrition of heart and body, for fear lest all these things should be rendered useless by an attack of this malady. For we ought to believe not merely that we cannot secure this actual perfection by our own efforts and exertions, but also that we cannot perform those things which we practice for its sake, viz., our efforts and exertions and desires, without the assistance of the divine protection, and the grace of His inspiration, chastisement, and exhortation, which He ordinarily sheds abroad in our hearts either through the instrumentality of another, or in His own person coming to visit us.

CHAPTER 17

VARIOUS PASSAGES WHICH CLEARLY SHOW THAT WE CANNOT DO ANYTHING WHICH BELONGS TO OUR SALVATION WITHOUT THE AID OF GOD

LASTLY, THE AUTHOR OF OUR SALVATION TEACHES US WHAT we ought not merely to think, but also to acknowledge in everything that we do. "I can," He says, "of mine own self do nothing, but the Father which abideth in me, He doeth the works." He says, speaking in the human nature which He had taken, that He could do nothing of Himself; and shall we, who are dust and ashes, think that we have no need of God's help in what pertains to our salvation? And so let us learn in everything, as we feel our own weakness, and at the same time His help, to declare with the saints, "I was overturned that I might fall, but the Lord supported me. The Lord is my strength and my praise: and He is become my salvation." And "Unless the Lord had helped me, my soul had almost dwelt in hell. If I said, My foot is moved: Thy mercy, O Lord, assisted me. According to the multitude of my sorrows in my heart, Thy comforts have given Joy to my soul" Seeing also that our heart is strengthened in the fear of the Lord, and in patience, let us say: "And the Lord became my protector; and He brought me forth into a large place." And knowing that knowledge is increased by progress in work, let us say: "For thou lightest my lamp, O Lord: O my God, enlighten my darkness, for by Thee I shall be delivered from temptation, and through my God I shall go over a wall." Then, feeling that we have ourselves sought for courage and endurance, and are being directed with greater ease and without labor in the path of the virtues, let us say, "It is God who girded me with strength, and made my way perfect; who mad my feet like hart's feet, and setteth me up on high: who teacheth my hands to war." And having also secured discretion, strengthened with which we can dash down our enemies, let us cry aloud to God: "Thy discipline hath set me up unto the end, and Thy discipline the same shall teach me. Thou hast enlarged my steps under me, and my feet are not weakened." And because I am thus strengthened with Thy knowledge and power, I will boldly take up the words which follow, and will say, "I will pursue after my enemies and overtake them: and I will not turn again till they are consumed. I will break them, and they shall not be able to stand: they shall fall under my feet." Again, mindful of our own infirmity, and of the fact that while still burdened with the weak flesh we cannot without His assistance overcome such bitter foes as our sins are, let us say, "Through Thee we will scatter our enemies: and through Thy name we will despise them that rise up against us. For I will not trust in my bow: neither shall my sword save me. For Thou hast saved us from them that afflict us: and hast put them to shame that hate us." But further: "Thou hast guided me with strength unto the battle, and hast subdued under me them that rose up against me. And Thou hast made mine enemies turn their backs upon me, and hast destroyed them that hated me." And reflecting that with our own arms alone we cannot conquer, let us say, "Take hold of arms and shield: and rise up to help me. Bring out the sword and stop the way against them that persecute me: say to my soul, I am thy salvation." And Thou hast made my arms like a brazen bow. And Thou hast given me the protection of Thy salvation: and Thy right hand hath held me up." "For our fathers got not the possession of the land through their own sword; neither did their own arm save them: but Thy right hand and Thine arm and the light of Thy countenance because Thou wast pleased with them." Lastly, as with anxious mind we regard all His benefits with thankfulness, let us cry to Him with the inmost feelings of our heart, for all these things, because we have fought, and have obtained from Him the light of knowledge, and self-control and discretion, and because He has furnished us with His own arms, and strengthened us with a girdle of virtue, and because He has made our enemies turn their backs upon us, and has given us the power of scattering them like the dust before the wind: "I will love Thee, O Lord my Strength; the Lord is my stronghold, my refuge and my deliverer. My God is my helper, and in Him will I put my trust. My protector and the horn of my salvation, and my support. Praising I will call upon the name of the Lord; and I shall be saved from mine enemies."

CHAPTER 18
HOW WE ARE PROTECTED BY THE GRACE OF GOD NOT ONLY IN OUR NATURAL CONDITION, BUT ALSO BY HIS DAILY PROVIDENCE

NOT ALONE GIVING THANKS TO HIM FOR THAT HE HAS created us as reasonable beings, and endowed us with the power of free will, and blessed us with the grace of baptism, and granted to us the knowledge and aid of the law, but for these things as well, which are bestowed upon us by His daily providence; viz., that He delivers us from the craft of our enemies; that He works with us so that we can overcome the sins of the flesh, that, even without our knowing it, He shields us from dangers; that He protects us from falling into sin; that He helps us and enlightens us, so that we can understand and recognize the actual help which He gives us, (which some will have it is what is meant by the law); that, when we are through His influence secretly struck with compunction for our sins and negligences, He visits us with His regard and chastens us to our soul's health; that even against our will we are sometimes drawn by Him to salvation; lastly that this very free will of ours, which is more readily inclined to sin, is turned by Him to a better purpose, and by His prompting and suggestion, bent towards the way of virtue.

CHAPTER 19
HOW THIS FAITH CONCERNING THE GRACE OF GOD WAS DELIVERED TO US BY THE ANCIENT FATHERS

THIS THEN IS THAT HUMILITY TOWARDS GOD, THIS IS THAT genuine faith of the ancient fathers which still remains intact among their successors, And to this faith, the apostolic virtues, which they so often showed, bear an undoubted witness, not only among us but also among infidels and unbelievers: for keeping in simplicity of heart the simple faith of the fishermen they did not receive it in a worldly spirit through dialectical syllogisms or the eloquence of a Cicero, but learnt by the experience of a pure life, and stainless actions, and by correcting their faults, and (to speak more truly) by visible proofs, that the character of perfection is to be found in that faith without which neither piety towards God, nor purification from sin, nor amendment of life, nor perfection of virtue can be secured.

CHAPTER 20
OF ONE WHO FOR HIS BLASPHEMY WAS GIVEN OVER TO A MOST UNCLEAN SPIRIT

I KNEW ONE OF THE NUMBER OF THE BRETHREN, WHOM I heartily wish I had never known; since afterwards he allowed himself to be saddled with the responsibilities of my order: who confessed to a most admirable elder that he was attacked by a terrible sin of the flesh: for he was inflamed with an intolerable lust, with the unnatural desire of suffering rather than: of committing a shameful act: then the other like a true spiritual physician, at once saw through the inward cause and origin of this evil. And, sighing deeply, said: "Never would the Lord have suffered you to be given over to so foul a spirit unless you had blasphemed against Him." And he, when this was discovered, at once fell at his feet on the ground, and, struck with the utmost astonishment, as if he saw the secrets of his heart laid bare by God, confessed that he had blasphemed with evil thoughts against the Son of God. Whence it is clear that one who is possessed by the spirit of pride, or who has been guilty of blasphemy against God, — as one who offers a wrong to Him from whom the gift of purity must be looked for — is deprived of his uprightness and perfection, and does not deserve the sanctifying grace of chastity.

CHAPTER 21

THE INSTANCE OF JOASH, KING OF JUDAH, SHOWING WHAT WAS THE CONSEQUENCE OF HIS PRIDE

SOME SUCH THING WE READ OF IN THE BOOK OF CHRONICLES. For Joash the king of Judah at the age of seven was summoned by Jehoiada the priest to the kingdom and by the witness of Scripture is commended for all his actions as long as the aforesaid priest lived. But hear what Scripture relates of him after Jehoiada's death, and how he was puffed up with pride and given over to a most disgraceful state. "But after the death of Jehoiada the princes went in and worshipped the king: and he was soothed by their services and hearkened unto them. And they forsook the temple of the Lord, the God of their fathers, and served groves and idols, and great wrath came upon Judah and Jerusalem because of this sin." And after a little: "When a year was come about, the army of Syria came up against him: and they came to Judah and Jerusalem, and killed all the princes of the people, and they sent all the spoils to the king to Damascus. And whereas there came a very small number of the Syrians, the Lord delivered into their hands an infinite multitude, because they had forsaken the Lord the God of their fathers: and on Joash they executed shameful judgments. And departing they left him in great diseases." You see how the consequence of pride was that he was given over to shocking and filthy passions. For he who is puffed up with pride and has permitted himself to be worshipped as God, is (as the Apostle says) "given over to shameful passions and a reprobate mind to do those things which are not convenient." And because, as Scripture says, "every on, who exalts his heart is unclean before God," he who is puffed up with swelling pride of heart is given over to most shameful confusion to be deluded by it, that when thus humbled he may know that he is unclean through impurity of the flesh and knowledge of impure desires, — a thing which he had refused to recognize in the pride of his heart; and also that the shameful infection of the flesh may disclose the hidden impurity of the heart, which he contracted through the sin of pride, and that through the patent pollution of his body he may be proved to be impure, who did not formerly see that he had become unclean through the pride of his spirit.

CHAPTER 22
THAT EVERY PROUD SOUL IS SUBJECT TO SPIRITUAL WICKEDNESS TO BE DECEIVED BY IT

AND THIS CLEARLY SHOWS THAT EVERY SOUL OF WHICH THE swellings of pride have taken possession, is given over to the Syrians of the soul, i.e., to spiritual wickedness, and that it is entangled in the lusts of the flesh, that the soul being at last humbled by earthly faults, and carnally polluted, may recognize its uncleanness, though while it stood erect in the coldness of its heart, it could not understand that through pride of heart it was rendered unclean in the sight of God; and by this means being humbled, a man may get rid of his former coldness, and being cast down and confused with the shame of his fleshly lusts, may thenceforward hasten to betake himself the more eagerly towards fervor and warmth of spirit.

CHAPTER 23
HOW PERFECTION CAN ONLY BE ATTAINED THROUGH THE VIRTUE OF HUMILITY

ANY SO IT IS CLEARLY SHOWN THAT NONE CAN ATTAIN THE end of perfection and purity, except through true humility, which he displays in the first instance to the brethren, and shows also to God in his inmost heart, believing that without His protection and aid extended to him at every instant, he cannot possibly obtain the perfection which he desires and to which he hastens so eagerly.

CHAPTER 24
WHO ARE ATTACKED BY SPIRITUAL AND WHO BY CARNAL PRIDE

THUS MUCH LET IT SUFFICE TO HAVE SPOKEN, AS FAR AS, BY God's help, our slender ability was able, concerning spiritual pride of which we have said that it attacks advanced Christians. And this kind of pride is not familiar to or experienced by most men, because the majority do not aim at attaining perfect purity of heart, so as to arrive at the stage of these conflicts; nor have they secured any purification from the preceding faults of which we have here explained both the character and the remedies in separate books. But it generally attacks those only who have conquered the former faults and have already almost arrived at the top of the tree in respect of the virtues. And because our most crafty enemy has not been able to destroy them through a carnal fall, he endeavors to cast them down and overthrow them by a spiritual catastrophe, trying by this to rob them of the prizes of their ancient rewards secured as they were with great labor. But as for us, who are still entangled in earthly passions, he never deigns to tempt us in this fashion, but overthrows us by a courser and what I called a carnal pride. And therefore I think it well, as I promised, to say a few things about this kind of pride by which we and men of our stamp are usually affected, and the minds especially of younger men and beginners are endangered.

CHAPTER 25
A DESCRIPTION OF CARNAL PRIDE, AND OF THE EVILS WHICH IT PRODUCES IN THE SOUL OF A MONK

THIS CARNAL PRIDE THEREFORE, OF WHICH WE SPOKE, WHEN it has gained an entrance into the heart of a monk, which is but lukewarm, and has made a bad start in renouncing the world, does not suffer him to stoop from his former state of worldly haughtiness to the true humility of Christ, but first of all makes him disobedient and rough; then it does not let him be gentle and kindly; nor allows him to be on a level with and like his brethren: nor does it permit him to be stripped and deprived of his worldly goods, as God and our Savior commands: and, though renunciation of the world is nothing but the mark of mortification and the cross, and cannot begin or rise from any other foundations, but these; viz., that a man should recognize that he is not merely spiritually dead to the deeds of this world, but also should realize daily that he must die in the body — it makes him on the contrary hope for a long life, and sets before him many lengthy infirmities, and covers him with shame and confusion. If when stripped of everything he has begun to be supported by the property of others and not his own, it persuades him that it is much better for food and clothing to be provided for him by his own rather than by another's means according to that text (which, as was before said, those who are rendered dense through such dullness and coldness of heart, cannot possibly understand.) "It is more blessed to give than to receive."

CHAPTER 26
THAT A MAN WHOSE FOUNDATION IS BAD, SINKS DAILY FROM BAD TO WORSE

THOSE THEN WHO ARE POSSESSED BY SUCH DISTRUST OF mind, and who through the devil's own want of faith fall away from that spark of faith, by which they seemed in the early days of their conversion to be enkindled, begin more anxiously to watch over the money which before they had begun to give away, and treasure it up with greater avarice, as men who cannot recover again what they have once wasted: or — what is still worse — take back what they had formerly cast away: or else (which is a third and most disgusting kind of sin), collect what they never before possessed, and thus are convicted of having gone no further in forsaking the world than merely to take the name and style of monk. With this beginning therefore, and on this bad and rotten foundation, it is a matter of course that the whole superstructure of faults must rise, nor can anything be built on such villainous foundations, except what will bring the wretched soul to the ground with a hopeless collapse.

CHAPTER 27

A DESCRIPTION OF THE FAULTS WHICH SPRING FROM THE EVIL OF PRIDE

THE MIND THEN THAT IS HARDENED BY SUCH FEELINGS, AND which begins with this miserable coldness is sure to go daily from bad to worse and to conclude its life with a more hideous end: and while it takes delight in its former desires, and is overcome, as the apostle says, by impious avarice (as he says of it "and covetousness, which is idolatry, or the worship of idols," and again "the love of money," says he, "is the root of all evils") can never admit into the heart the true and unfeigned humility of Christ, while the man boasts himself of his high birth, or is puffed up by his position in the world (which he has forsaken in body but not in mind) or is proud of his wealth which he retains to his own destruction; and because of this he is no longer content to endure the yoke of the monastery, or to be instructed by the teaching of any of the elders, and not only objects to observe any rule of subjection or obedience, but will not even listen to teaching about perfection; and such dislike of spiritual talk grows up in his heart that if such a conversation should happen to arise, he cannot keep his eyes fixed on one spot, but his gaze wanders blankly about here and there, and his eyes shift hither and thither, as the custom is. Instead of wholesome coughs, he spits from a dry throat: he coughs on purpose without any need, he drums with his fingers, and twiddles them and scribbles like a man writing: and all his limbs fidget so that while the spiritual conversation is proceeding, you would think that he was sitting on thorns, and those very sharp ones, or in the midst of a mass of worms: and if the conversation turns in all simplicity on something which is for the good of the hearers, he thinks that it is brought forward for his especial benefit. And all the time that the examination of the spiritual life is proceeding, he is taken up with his own suspicious thoughts, and is not on the watch for something to take home for his good, but is anxiously seeking the reason why anything is said, or is quietly turning over in his mind, how he can raise objections to it, so that he cannot at all take in any of those things which are so admirably brought forward, or be done any good to by them. And so the result is that the spiritual conference is not merely of no use to him, but is positively injurious, and becomes to him an occasion of greater sin. For while he is conscience stricken and fancies that everything is being aimed at him he hardens himself more stubbornly in the obstinacy of his heart, and is more keenly affected by the stings of his wrath: then afterwards his voice is loud, his talk harsh, his answers bitter and noisy, his gait lordly and capricious; his tongue too ready, he is forward in conversation and no friend to silence except when he is nursing in his heart some bitterness against a brother, and his silence denotes not compunction or humility, but pride and wrath: so that one can hardly say which is the more objectionable in him, that unrestrained and boisterous merriment, or this dreadful and deadly solemnity.

For in the former we see inopportune chattering, light and frivolous laughter, unrestrained and undisciplined mirth. In the latter a silence that is full of wrath and deadly; and which simply arises from the desire to prolong as long as possible the rancorous feelings which are nourished in silence against some brother, and not from the wish to obtain from it the virtues of humility and patience. And as the man who is a victim to passion readily makes everybody else miserable and is ashamed to apologize to the brother whom he has wronged, so when the brother offers to do so to him, he rejects it with scorn. And not only is he not touched or softened by the advances of his brother; but is the rather made more angry because his brother anticipates him in humility. And that wholesome humiliation and apology, which generally puts an end to the devil's temptation, becomes to him an occasion of a worse outbreak.

CHAPTER 28
ON THE PRIDE OF A CERTAIN BROTHER

I HAVE HEARD WHILE I HAVE BEEN IN THIS DISTRICT A thing which I shudder and am ashamed to recall; viz., that one of the juniors — when he was reproved by his Abbot because he had shown signs of throwing off the humility, of which he had made trial for a short time at his renunciation of the world, and of being puffed up with diabolical pride — most impertinently answered "Did I humiliate myself for a time on purpose to be always in subjection?" And at this wanton and wicked reply of his the elder was utterly aghast, and could say nothing, as if he had received this answer from old Lucifer himself and not from a man; so that he could not possibly utter a word against such impudence, but only let fall sighs and groans from his heart; turning over in silence in his mind that which is said of our Savior: "Who being in the form of God humbled Himself and became obedient" — not, as the man said who was seized with a diabolical spirit of pride, "for a time," but "even to death."

CHAPTER 29
THE SIGNS BY WHICH YOU CAN RECOGNIZE THE PRESENCE OF CARNAL PRIDE IN A SOUL

AND TO DRAW TOGETHER BRIEFLY WHAT HAS BEEN SAID OF this kind of pride, by collecting, as well as we can, some of its signs that we may somehow convey to those who are thirsting for instruction in perfection, an idea of its characteristics from the movements of the outward man: I think it well to unfold them in a few words that we may conveniently recognize the signs by which we can discern and detect it, that when the roots of this passion are laid bare and brought to the surface, and seen and traced out with ocular demonstration, they may be the more easily plucked up and avoided. For only then will this most pestilent evil be altogether escaped, and if we do not begin too late in the day, when it has already got the mastery over us, to be on our guard against its dangerous heat and noxious influence, but if, recognizing its symptoms (so to speak) beforehand, we take precautions against it with wise and careful forethought. For, as we said before, you can tell a man's inward condition from his outward gait. By these signs, then, that carnal pride, of which [we spoke earlier, is shown. To begin with, in conversation the man's voice is loud: in his silence there is bitterness: in his mirth his laughter is noisy and excessive: when he is serious he is unreasonably gloomy: in his answers there is rancor: he is too free with his tongue, his words tumbling out at random without being weighed. He is utterly lacking in patience, and without charity: impudent in offering insults to others, faint-hearted in bearing them himself: troublesome in the matter of obedience except where his own wishes and likings correspond with his duty: unforgiving in receiving admonition: weak in giving up his own wishes: very stubborn about yielding to those of others: always trying to compass his own ends, and never ready to give them up for others: and thus the result is that though he is incapable of giving sound advice, yet in everything he prefers his own opinion to that of the elders.

CHAPTER 30
HOW WHEN A MAN HAS GROWN COLD THROUGH PRIDE HE WANTS TO BE PUT TO RULE OTHER PEOPLE

AND WHEN A MAN WHOM PRIDE HAS MASTERED HAS FALLEN through these stages of descent, he shudders at the discipline of the ceonobium, and — as if the companionship of the brethren hindered his perfection, and the sins of others impeded and interfered with his advance in patience and humility — he longs to take up is abode in a solitary cell; else is eager to build a monastery and gather together some others to teach and instruct, as if he would do good to many more people, and make himself from being a bad disciple a still worse master. For when through this pride of heart a man has fallen into this most dangerous and injurious coldness, he can neither be a real monk nor a man of the world, and what is worse, promises to himself to gain perfection by means of this wretched state and manner of life of his.

CHAPTER 31
HOW WE CAN OVERCOME PRIDE AND ATTAIN PERFECTION

WHEREFORE IF WE WISH THE SUMMIT OF OUR BUILDING to be perfect and to rise well-pleasing to God, we should endeavor to lay its foundations not in accordance with the desires of our own lust, but according to the rules of evangelical strictness: which can only be the fear of God and humility, proceeding from kindness and simplicity of heart. But humility cannot possibly be acquired without giving up everything: and as long as a man is a stranger to this, he cannot possibly attain the virtue of obedience, or the strength of patience, or the serenity of kindness, or the perfection of love; without which things our hearts cannot possibly be a habitation for the Holy Spirit: as the Lord says through the prophet: "Upon whom shall My spirit rest, but on him that is humble and quiet and ears My words," or according to those copies which express the Hebrew accurately: "To whom shall I have respect, but to him that is poor and little and of a contrite spirit and that trembleth at My words?"

CHAPTER 32

HOW PRIDE WHICH IS SO DESTRUCTIVE OF ALL VIRTUES CAN ITSELF BE DESTROYED BY TRUE HUMILITY

WHEREFORE THE CHRISTIAN ATHLETE WHO STRIVES lawfully in the spiritual combat and desires to be crowned by the Lord, should endeavor by every means to destroy this most fierce beast, which is destructive of all virtues, knowing that as long as this remains in his breast he not only will never be free from all kinds of evils, but even if he seems to have any good qualities, will lose them by its malign influence. For no structure (so to speak) of virtue can possibly be raised in our soul unless first the foundations of true humility are laid in our heart, which being securely laid may be able to bear the weight of perfection and love upon them in such a way that, as we have said, we may first show to our brethren true humility from the very bottom of our heart, in nothing acquiescing in making them sad or in injuring them: and this we cannot possibly manage unless true self-denial, which consists in stripping and depriving ourselves of all our possessions, is implanted in us by the love of Christ. Next the yoke of obedience and subjection must be taken up in simplicity of heart without any pretense, so that, except for the commands of the Abbot, no will of our own is alive in us. But this can only be ensured in the case of one who considers himself not only dead to this world, but also unwise and a fool;

and performs without any discussion whatever is enjoined him by his seniors, believing it to be divine and enjoined from heaven.

CHAPTER 33
REMEDIES AGAINST THE EVIL OF PRIDE

AND WHEN MEN REMAIN IN THIS CONDITION, THERE IS NO doubt that this quiet and secure state of humility will follow, so that considering ourselves inferior to every one else we shall bear everything offered to us, even if it is hurtful, and saddening, and damaging — with the utmost patience, as if it came from those who are our superiors. And these things we shall not only bear with the greatest ease, but we shall consider them trifling and mere nothings, if we constantly bear in mind the passion of our Lord and of all His Saints: considering that the injuries by which we are tried are so much less than theirs, as we are so far behind their merits and their lives: remembering also that we shall shortly depart out of this world, and soon by a speedy end to our life here become sharers of their lot. For considerations such as these are a sure end not only to pride but to all kinds of sins. Then, next after this we must keep a firm grasp of this same humility towards God: which we must so secure as not only to acknowledge that we cannot possibly perform anything connected with the attainment of perfect virtue without His assistance and grace, but also truly to believe that this very fact that we can understand this, is His own gift.

www.ingramcontent.com/pod-product-compliance
Lightning Source LLC
LaVergne TN
LVHW051039080426
835508LV00019B/1607